Second Consul

Second Consul

The Vice Presidency: Our Greatest
Political Problem

Edgar Wiggins Waugh

THE BOBBS-MERRILL COMPANY, INC.
Indianapolis   New York

First Edition

To my loving wife, Josephine, without whose active encouragement and diligent assistance this book would not have been possible.

Contents

In Case of the Removal of the President from Office, or of his Death, Resignation, or Inability to discharge the Powers and Duties of the said Office, the same shall devolve on the Vice President, and the Congress may by Law provide for the Case of Removal, Death, Resignation or Inability, both of the President and Vice President, declaring what Officer shall then act as President, and such Officer shall act accordingly, until the Disability be removed, or a President shall be elected.

—Constitution of the United States of America, Article II, Section 1, clause 6.

Second Consul

"Gentlemen, I do not know whether the framers of the Constitution had in view the two kings of Sparta or the two consuls of Rome when they formed it; one to have all the power while he held it, and the other to be nothing. . . .

I feel great difficulty how to act. I am possessed of two separate powers; the one in esse and the other in posse. I am Vice President. In this I am nothing, but I may be everything. But I am president also of the Senate. When the President comes into the Senate, what shall I be?"

—John Adams on the Vice Presidency

I

In the Great Convention

September 24, 1955, will long linger in the minds of Americans of this generation as one of the darkest days of our era. Early that morning something serious happened to the thirty-fourth President of the United States. President Dwight David Eisenhower, vacationing in Colorado, had suffered an attack of coronary thrombosis. Shortly thereafter the nation learned that he had been taken to Fitzsimmons Army Hospital and was in an oxygen tent. The shocking news, the anxious months of convalescence and the deep concern of all loyal Americans of whatever political inclination over the progress of the President's recovery all served to put the national spotlight on the most serious structural weakness of our government.

Mr. Eisenhower's illness put in sharp relief the fact that the Constitution makes no clear-cut provision for effecting a succession to the President's office should he be unable to perform its duties. The article creating and defining the executive branch provides that "In Case of the Removal of the President from Office, or of his Death, Resignation, or Inability to discharge the Powers and Duties of the said Office, the Same shall devolve on the Vice President. . . . " How do we execute this provision in case the President is incapacitated? The Constitution provides no answer.

It very often happens in our time that a national political convention wears itself out completely on knotty problems of

11

seating contested delegations, on debates over controversial platform provisions, and on cheers and speeches and bargains and ballots to settle on a nominee for President. Then, with many delegates more interested in making hasty preparations for their trips home than in further party proceedings, the convention may nominate a candidate for Vice President by one anticlimactic and unenthusiastic ballot.

Within an hour after his first-ballot nomination for President Adlai Stevenson made a surprise appearance at the 1956 Democratic convention for the specific purpose of freeing the delegates to use their own best judgment in choosing a nominee for Vice President. His action dramatized a new national understanding of the importance of the office. It adds force to the proposal that the Vice President's role be reappraised.

Our national party conventions have been accustomed, in choosing the Vice Presidential nominee, to tread, in a sense, the same path followed by the Fathers of the Constitution. The delegates at the great Constitutional Convention spent many weary hours, days and weeks in determining the nature of the office of the President and the method of choosing its occupant. Time grew short and their energies were just about exhausted when they finally got around to serious business about the Vice President. They made very short shrift of the matter. On the whole the Fathers at Philadelphia performed with magnificent wisdom and earned our everlasting gratitude. But they were human, and we cannot say that everything they did was brilliant. Among the weakest of their products was their provision for a Vice President. Their solution to the problem of providing a successor to the President did not commend itself very highly to the framers, and it has remained weak over the years.

One of the primary flaws in the Constitutional solution is that it gives no means for deciding when the President is unable to serve. When President Eisenhower was stricken millions of Americans wondered anxiously whether anyone was empowered immediately to assume his role. The Constitution provides no clear mandate for Congress, or for any other body, to decide when the President should be relieved of his duties. No longer can we be oblivious to the chances we have taken in going merrily along for all these years without providing a method to determine the status of inability on the part of a President in order to make way for the Vice President to take over.

Both houses of Congress have reflected deep concern. The reorganization subcommittee of the Senate Committee on Government Operations has indulged in intensive study of the President's work load. Chairman Emanuel Celler of the House Judiciary Committee has requested and secured, by questionnaire, the opinions of a great many scholars in the fields of Constitutional law and political science, as well as other qualified individuals, with regard to the problem of defining inability. A special subcommittee of the House Judiciary Committee conducted hearings on the question, with Representative Celler in the chair. The problem is, of course, extremely complicated. Despite renewed interest aroused by President Eisenhower's attack of ileitis in June 1956 and his consequent hospitalization and surgery, the Eighty-fourth Congress could not, with all its efforts, complete the enormous work of review, planning and consideration that must precede any statutory solution.

Congressional study must take account not only of the "inability" defect but also of a second major weakness in the Constitutional provision for succession. This arises from the very nature of the Vice Presidency. It is an axiom of government that first-class offices with great responsibility tend to attract men and women of ability much more readily than offices of second-class responsibility. Certainly the replacement for a deceased or disabled President ought to be a first-class man, a man as capable as the President. Obviously the office of Vice President should carry responsibility worthy of the best statesmanship. In this respect the 1787 Convention failed signally.

The Constitution attaches only two duties to the office of

Vice President. First it makes him a mere benchwarmer, so to speak, to take over Presidential duties in specified situations —the removal of the President from office, or, as we've seen, his death, resignation or inability to discharge his powers and duties. A detailed discussion of the succession clause belongs to a later chapter. But it should again be pointed out here that the Fathers gave us neither norms nor methods for determining the existence of Presidential inability. Don't be too hard on them for this: they could not do everything for us. They had a whole constitution to make in a period of less than four months. We have had nearly a century and three quarters to fill in the gaps.

Yet in all this time we have not settled on a procedure for determining the increasingly important matter of Presidential inability. Our inertia in this respect has perhaps already hurt the nation and the entire world (the reference here is not to President Eisenhower's two serious illnesses), and we are taking a frightful chance in prolonging the uncertainty. Fortunately Congress and the public are showing some signs of awakening to the need for action.

Getting back to the Vice President's job, his second duty is stated in Article I, Section 3 of the Constitution: "The Vice President of the United States shall be President of the Senate, but shall have no vote, unless they be equally divided."

This feature caused a brief but fairly spirited debate toward the closing hours of the Constitutional Convention. On September 7 several members expressed decided views on the proposition to make the Vice President ex officio president of the Senate. Elbridge Gerry of Massachusetts opposed it. He argued, "We might as well put the President himself at the head of the legislature. The close intimacy that must subsist between the President and Vice President makes it absolutely improper." Gerry was against having any Vice President.

Pennsylvania's Gouverneur Morris retorted, "The Vice President then will be the first heir apparent that ever loved his father. If there should be no Vice President, the President of the Senate would be temporary successor, which would amount to the same thing."

Roger Sherman of Connecticut really rang the bell. He recognized a problem that has haunted us throughout the years: what can we find for the Vice President to do? He observed, "If the Vice President were not to be President of the Senate, he would be without employment; and some member, by being made President, must be deprived of his vote, unless when an equal division of votes might happen in the Senate, which would be but seldom."

Hugh Williamson, North Carolina delegate, declared that "such an officer as Vice President was not wanted. He was introduced merely for the sake of a valuable mode of election, which required two to be chosen at the same time." Virginia's Edmund Randolph registered his objection to the provision. George Mason, from the same state, thought the office of Vice President was "an encroachment on the rights of the Senate." Not really an enthusiastic approach to the Vice Presidency. The office of Vice President was almost stillborn.

The duties of the Vice President are the object of widespread interest for another reason, quite apart from President Eisenhower's illness. Since its creation, the duties of the executive office have so greatly multiplied that they may be too much for any one man to perform, even with a dangerous expenditure of energy. It is a far cry from the early days. James Madison, for instance, was able personally to handle not only all the correspondence of his own office but also much of that of the office of the Secretary of State—and in longhand!

Even though he now has a large staff a modern President can find time to write few letters indeed in his own hand. Nor can he begin to dictate all the correspondence that must go out from his office. The executive branch has not proved ineffective or irresponsible. In fact it has been, in all probability, the most dynamic of our political institutions. But it has become top-heavy, and the burdens of the chief executive have

become awesome. Clearly something must be done to relieve
the situation. Many people have thought that the delegation
of more executive responsibility to the Vice President might
be the answer, and President Eisenhower has moved further
in this direction than any other chief executive. Such an
answer, however, poses serious problems, which come in for
later consideration.

The return of the executive-department structure to the
center of public attention repeats our history. Again we return
to 1787 and the great Constitutional Convention. As the delegates from twelve states—all except Rhode Island—labored
through the summer months in Philadelphia's Independence
Hall to make our Constitution an almost miraculous instrument of democratic government, the executive branch posed
what were clearly the most vexing of all the many baffling
problems they faced. A discussion of these deliberations is a
necessary preface to understanding the Vice Presidency.

James Wilson of Pennsylvania, one of the ablest and most
farsighted of all the delegates, pronounced the manner of
choosing the executive to be an extremely divisive issue.
Speaking on September 4, some two weeks before the Convention adjourned, Wilson said, "This subject has greatly
divided the House, and will also divide the people out of doors.
It is in truth the most difficult of all on which we have had to
decide." Nor was the method of choice the only divisive issue
with regard to the executive. The whole structure of the department was much debated.

The delegates were debating over the executive in June.
They were debating the same issue in July. They debated it in
August, and they were still at it in September—in fact, almost
to the very last day of the Convention. When we consider that
the Convention officially opened on May 25 and closed on
September 17, we readily see that these debates, at one time
or another, over the executive covered just about the entire
span of the Convention. Nor is it surprising that they should
have. The Fathers had fairly satisfactory national patterns,
with changes here and there, for the legislative and judicial

branches. The British Parliament and British jurisprudence offered much rich experience for them to consider, not to overlook the colonial and state legislative bodies and courts. But the British executive, with a monarch at its head, could be no substantial pattern for the majority of the delegates, who contemplated a republic. The state governor was about the best thing they could find for a model, and such an office lacked national proportions.

Fortunately there was one area of general agreement. There would have to be an executive department. The old and short-lived Articles of Confederation, the constitution under which the fledgling United States had operated since 1781, had provided for little or no executive power, and absence of this element had proved so deadly that no sensible person in America imagined that the country could keep going without some kind of national executive.

But agreement stopped right there. The fervid radicalism of Revolutionary days had cooled off somewhat. The Founding Fathers at Philadelphia were, on the whole, a more conservative body than the Congress that had declared independence some eleven years before. The firebrands of the Revolution were not there. Among those conspicuously absent for a variety of reasons were Patrick Henry, Tom Paine, Richard Henry Lee, Samuel Adams, John Hancock and Thomas Jefferson. Perhaps none of the delegates desired, at least with an appreciable hope of achievement, to establish a monarchy, but some would surely go as far as possible in that direction without going all the way.

Alexander Hamilton, youthful and brilliant delegate from New York, represented the extremity of the near-monarchist group. Addressing the Convention at some length on June 18, he expressed grave distrust of government by the many, for fear they would oppress the few. He seriously doubted that a "republican government could be established over so great an extent." He spoke of the British House of Lords as "a most noble institution." With respect to the executive Hamilton declared, ". . . the English model was the only good one on this subject." He found great merit in the hereditary status of the king and proposed as chief executive a national "Governor," to be chosen by indirect election for life (or good behavior) and a Senate to be chosen in the same way and for the same term. But the great majority of the delegates were, for the time being at least, opposed to the creation either of a monarchy or of anything too closely akin to it. A few were afflicted with such excessive temerity on the subject that they favored providing a divided and weak executive.

James Wilson was a tower of strength in favor of a middle course. On June 1 he spoke out vigorously and effectively for a single magistrate, "as giving most energy, dispatch and responsibility to the office." Others, like Edmund Randolph of Virginia, preferred more than one executive. On June 1 Randolph opposed unity in the executive magistracy, calling it "the foetus of monarcy." On June 2 he returned to the subject, arguing that the people would not have the "necessary confidence" in a single magistrate. He declared himself ". . . in favor of three members of the Executive, to be drawn from different portions of the country."

Wilson countered, on June 4, that a single executive would not be a move toward monarchy and that it would not be so construed by the people. He observed, "All thirteen States, though agreeing in scarce any other instance, agree in placing a single magistrate at the head of the government. The idea of three heads had taken place in none." On June 16 Wilson was still battling for a single chief executive, declaring, "One man will be more responsible than three. Three will contend among themselves, till one becomes the master of his colleagues."

The Convention was still worse divided on the manner of choosing the executive. Some wanted the national legislature (Congress) to select him, while others were very much opposed to this. Opponents feared that this method of choice would seriously weaken the independence of the executive, making him a mere parrot of the legislature—particularly if the executive should be eligible for a second term. This plan was several times approved, then finally voted down. Gerry on June 9 moved that the national executive be appointed by the state executives, arguing that "the Executives would be most likely to select the fittest men." Randolph spoke forcefully against this on the same day, insisting that an executive thus chosen "will not be likely to defend with becoming vigilance and firmness the national rights against State encroachments." On July 25 Virginia's James Madison also opposed this manner of appointment, fearing that the state executives, being standing bodies, "could and would be courted, and intrigued with by the candidates, by their partizans, and by the ministers of foreign powers."

Election by the people was opposed, though James Wilson valiantly supported this idea on June 1. He wished to "derive not only both branches of the Legislature from the people without the intervention of the State Legislatures, but the Executive also, in order to make them as independent as possible of each other, as well as of the States." But popular election met stern opposition. Some delegates thought it would give too great an advantage to the more populous states. Others didn't think the people were capable of rendering proper judgment. On July 19 Elbridge Gerry expressed a widely held view when he asserted, "The people are uninformed and would be misled by a few designing men." Mason on July 17 expressed the thought that "it would be as unnatural to refer the choice of a proper character for Chief Magistrate to the people, as it would, to refer a trial of colors to a blind man. The extent of the country renders it impossible, that the people can have the requisite capacity to judge of the respective pretensions of the candidates."

There seemed to be one other possibility upon which the Convention might agree—the election of the chief executive by electors in the various states. Alexander Hamilton in his proposal for a life-tenure executive and life-tenure Senate had suggested in both cases election by electors chosen by the people. But this system posed provocative issues: how the electors would be chosen, and how they would be apportioned among the several states.

Elbridge Gerry thought the electors should be chosen by the state executives—that would be pretty close to his plan for having the national executive chosen directly by the state governors. Luther Martin of Maryland on July 17 moved that "the Executive be chosen by electors appointed by the several legislatures of the individual states."

Morris on August 24 spoke out vigorously in favor of popular election of the electors. But this does not mean that Morris was for mass voting by the people. He was no advocate of manhood suffrage. He believed in a pretty narrowly restricted electorate. In his opinion only the freeholders should be privileged to vote. In discussing the qualifications for voting for members of the House of Representatives he had, on August 7, declared, "Give the votes to the people who have no property and they will sell them to the rich, who will be able to buy them. We should not confine our attention to the present moment. The time is not distant when this country will abound with mechanics and manufacturers, who will receive their bread from their employers. Will such men be the secure and faithful guardians of liberty? . . . Children do not vote. Why? Because they want prudence; because they have no will of their own. The ignorant and the dependent can be as little trusted with the public interest." Nor was this view of Gouverneur Morris an isolated one. A very large element of the Convention, perhaps a majority, though this is questioned by some scholars, were devotees of this ancient precept of Aristotle and were decidedly opposed to anything so radical as universal manhood suffrage.

All the above ideas with respect to the executive—and other proposals as well—were bandied about the Convention hall. It is amazing that agreement was ever reached. The Fathers were not creampuffs. They had very strong convictions, from which they would not readily retreat, but fortunately most of them were not dogmatic and inflexible. The final result, largely the work of a committee of one member from each state present, was a masterpiece of compromise. It was the super-compromise of the entire Convention. Students have used barrels of ink in writing about the provisions commonly termed the "three great compromises"—the "Connecticut Compromise," the "Three-Fifths Compromise" and the "Commerce–Slave Trade Compromise"—while many (but surely not all) have had little to say about the greatest of the compromises, the provision for the executive. Actually the arrangement for the executive, without needing to mention the above three compromises, incorporated two of them in substance and, by implication, also enveloped the third.

Perhaps the elements of the compromise will be clearer if we first examine the original plan the Fathers gave us in Article II of the Constitution. The executive power was vested in a single magistrate, the President, who would serve for a four-year term with no bar to re-eligibilty. He was to be chosen by electors. Each state was to have as many electors as its total membership in Congress. In other words a state having four members in the House would have four plus two, or six, electors, since each state, large or small, would have two Senators. The electors in each state were to be chosen in such manner as the legislature of that state directed—the legislature could designate itself the instrument to choose them or could designate the people or some other instrumentality.

The above provisions remain unchanged today, except that the Twenty-second Amendment limits all persons except Harry S. Truman, who was President at the time the amendment was proposed, to two elective terms and a total of ten years of occupancy of the White House. According to the Constitution each state legislature still has the authority to determine how the electors in the state shall be chosen. In our day all state legislatures have by law designated the people as the ones to make the choice.

Getting back to the original plan, when the electors met in their respective states to cast their ballots, there would be no votes for Vice President. All votes would be for President. Each elector would vote by ballot for two persons, one of whom, at least, could not be an inhabitant of the elector's state, for the office of President. It is important to note that this system gave each elector two votes. Since the Fathers did not anticipate organized political parties, each elector was expected to use his own judgment about which men seemed best qualified for the office of President. The electoral votes from all the states were counted in the presence of the Senate and the House of Representatives, with the president of the Senate presiding and opening the certificates from the states. If any person had more electoral votes than any of the others, and if the number of his electoral votes was a majority of the whole number of electors, then he was elected President. If two or more people had majorities and the same number of votes the House of Representatives was to choose between them. If no one had the required majority the House would choose the President from the highest five. In choosing the President the House was to vote by states, the representation from each state having one vote. A majority of all the states would be necessary to a choice. In every case after the President had been chosen the runner-up would be Vice President. In case of a tie for the runner-up position the Senate would choose the Vice President from those involved in the tie.

It will be observed that advocates of delegating executive power to several men lost their cause, since the ultimate executive power is vested in the President alone. But they did have the satisfaction that there was to be no king. If the President was originally to be something of a king, he would be a monarch with a pretty elusive crown, for his term was only four years. He could be dethroned by legal means in pretty short order. Nor was he to be an untouchable prince, since he was subject to impeachment proceedings in Congress if he stooped to acts of treason, bribery or other high crimes or misdemeanors. Also, while the President was to exercise a great deal of power he was to be guarded well by Congressional checks. His veto could be overridden by a two-thirds vote of both Houses. He could spend no public funds without a Congressional appropriation. Most of his appointments would have to be confirmed by the Senate. He could not engage this country in a treaty without approval of two-thirds of the

Senate. This is by no means an exhaustive list of the checks on the President.

So the President would be chosen by electors. How many would each state have? Had this question not been handled adroitly, it could have revived all the old antagonisms in the small-state *versus* large-state controversy over representation.

But in the provision that each state have as many electors as it had senators and representatives the essence of both the Connecticut Compromise and the Three-Fifths Compromise was taken over bodily into the electoral college plan. This arrangement standing alone was not so favorable to the small states as was the compromise on Congressional representation.

In Congress the two houses were to be co-ordinate. A bill would have to receive favorable action from both before it could become a law. Thus if the House, dominated by the larger states, should seek to enact legislation unfriendly to the interests or wishes of the smaller states, then the Senate, based on absolute equality, with two members from each state, could erect a positive barrier against the scheme.

The electoral college, on the other hand, was to be no two-house affair. Even with the formula approved the larger states would still have the advantage. But the smaller states got a concession here that, it appeared then, would far more than counterbalance the large-state advantage in the electoral college.

It will be recalled that, under Article II, if the electoral college failed to give one person a vote large enough to constitute both a plurality over all other candidates and a majority of the total number of electors, then the House of Representatives would choose the President from among the highest five candidates (except where there was a tie with majorities, in which case the choice would be from among those who tied).

But the Fathers did not anticipate the rise of strongly functioning political parties with both divisive and unifying effects—but clearly more unifying than divisive in a two-party system. Since they knew that state pride and local feeling were high, they expected so many local and state favorites to receive votes from the electors that one person would seldom have a majority. This belief prevailed in spite of the fact that they planned some modification of the scattering of votes by providing that one of the people for whom an elector voted must not be from his own state. Many believed that in most cases the final selection would fall to the House of Representatives. While the electoral college in the beginning would certainly choose George Washington for President because of his extraordinary national reputation, it would afterward tend, by and large, to be what we would refer to as a nominating agency. The House would pick from among those it nominated. This expectation eased the pains of both the small-state champions and the supporters of legislative election. When the House was to choose the President, as already noted, it would vote by states, and each state, large or small, would have one vote. This meant absolute equality among the states in naming the chief executive. Likewise, those who espoused legislative election of the President were consoled by a logical expectation that in most cases one house of Congress would have the final say. We can thank political parties for the disruption of those plans.

How would the electors in each state be chosen? The sharpest cleavage in the Convention on this point was between those who wanted each state legislature to choose them and those who wished the people to elect them. Neither side won a complete victory. The electors in each state were to be appointed, "in such manner as the legislature thereof may direct." On the surface it appeared that the advocates of legislative election of electors got the better of it. After all, there was nothing to restrain a legislature from naming itself the proper authority to select the electors. In fact in the early days it became the most common, though never an exclusive, practice. But the supporters of popular choice knew that the door was not closed. Some of them no doubt expected that a rising spirit of democracy would eventually bring all state legislatures to decree popular election of the electors. That is certainly the case today, and it has been for many years.

In the arrangements for the executive department no delegate got just exactly what he had originally desired, yet virtually every one got something of what he wanted. When it was all over the Convention members appeared quite well satisfied with the method of election. But in the campaign for ratification of the Constitution critics found much to condemn in the nature of the Presidential office itself.

In *The Federalist, Number 67,* Alexander Hamilton, describing the misrepresentations by opponents of the Constitution, declared with reference to the President:

He has been decorated with attributes, superior in dignity and splendour to those of a king of Great Britain. He has been shown to us with a diadem sparkling on his brow, and the imperial purple flowing in his train. He has been seated on a throne surrounded with minions and mistresses; giving audience to the envoys of foreign potentates, in all the supercilious pomp of majesty. The images of Asiatic despotism and voluptuousness, have not been wanting to crown the exaggerated scene.

But when it came to the method of choosing the chief executive even the voices of the most severe critics of the Constitution were pretty much stilled. Hamilton attested this in *The Federalist, Number 68,* when he said, "The mode of appointment of the chief magistrate of the United States, is almost the only part of the system, of any consequence, which has escaped without severe censure, or which has received the slightest mark of approbation from its opponents."

So we see that, so far as the executive department was concerned, the Convention concentrated all its thought and energy on the Presidency. Its action on the Vice President was a hasty postscript. His office, when he is not presiding over the Senate, merely places him in the wings, ready to step on stage only if the President is unable to go on.

There was only one redeeming feature of the frightfully weak office of Vice President. That was the method of choice. That was strong—strong if political parties had not come along and upset the whole hypothesis. For the undramatic position of Vice President the delegates thought they had given us a way to get an extraordinary man. Recall that the electors were to vote only for the office of President. The runner-up was to be Vice President. Thus the Vice President was to be a person who almost gained election to the highest office in the land. Furthermore, many people in the early days expected that a Vice President, if well behaved and successful in his office, would be rewarded with subsequent election to the Presidency. This happened, as we shall see, quite regularly until the development of strong political parties made the Twelfth Amendment necessary. .

II

Until the Twelfth

The delegates to the Philadelphia convention intended for the two-vote electoral plan to serve two important purposes. First, because all the votes were cast for President—the Vice Presidency going to the candidate second in the voting—the electoral vote would select both President and Vice President, directly in most elections and at least indirectly if Constitutional provisions threw the choice into the House or (as it might be) the Senate.

But more important, the two-vote plan made feasible a national choice rather than a wide scattering of nominations prompted by strictly local considerations. If each elector had been confined to one vote, he might have been strongly tempted to cast it for someone from his own state. Since localism was then very strong, the sum total of the electoral vote might have turned out a little like the fragmented parts of a broken mirror, with the vote split among the favorite sons of the several states. But by giving each elector two votes and specifying that one must be cast for a person from outside the elector's own state the framers hoped virtually to guarantee the choice as President of one man of national stature and reputation.

The first Presidential election, often spoken of as the election of 1788, though it took place early in 1789, bore out completely the reasoning of the Founding Fathers. Since this election launched the government under the new Constitution, a few

27

observations on it are in order before we proceed further with our study of the Vice Presidency. This was the first test of the practical operation of the bold and unique new blueprint of government.

Of the thirteen original states joined in loose "league of friendship" under the Articles of Confederation, only ten participated in the choice of the first President and Vice President. The Fathers had agreed, in Article Seven, that "The Ratification of the Conventions of nine States, shall be sufficient for the Establishment of this Constitution between the States so ratifying the Same." In June 1788 New Hampshire, the ninth state, ratified.

On September 13, 1788, eleven states having by this time accepted the Constitution, the expiring Congress of the Confederation passed a resolution directing the states to choose their Presidential electors on the first Wednesday of January 1789. North Carolina and Rhode Island had not yet ratified and therefore were not members of the new Union. The two houses of the New York legislature got into a political hassle and failed to choose electors, so New York had no part in choosing the first President and Vice President.

The Confederation Congress's resolution instructed that the electors chosen in each state were to cast their votes for President on the first Wednesday of February 1789. On the first Wednesday in March (March 4) of the same year the new Congress was to convene in New York City.

The states had to act quickly to make their arrangements for choosing electors in the three months allowed. The lack of time gave an advantage to those who favored legislative election of electors. In one way or another, on the designated first Wednesday in January all the ratifying states except New York named their electors.

In five states—Connecticut, Delaware, Georgia, New Jersey and South Carolina—the state legislatures made the choices. Two, Massachusetts and New Hampshire, used a combination of popular and legislative election. In three states—Maryland, Pennsylvania and Virginia—the people elected the electors.

It is interesting to note here that the germs of political parties, scarcely anticipated by the framers of the Constitution, were responsible for New York's stalemate and gave a fore-taste of the difficulty they were later to cause. The Federalists, composed of those elements that had supported adoption of the Constitution, and the Antifederalists, made up for the most part of those who had opposed it, were competing for power. The New York legislature had designated itself to pick the electors. But the New York Assembly was Antifederalist, while the state Senate was Federalist. The two houses jockeyed so for advantage that they could reach no agreement on whether the electors should be chosen by joint or by concurrent ballot of the two houses. Failing to decide, New York went without a vote.

Curiously, the public interest in this first election centered more in the choice of a Vice President than in that of a President. This situation has but rarely occurred in our history. In the minds of the best-informed people the election of George Washington as President was a foregone conclusion. Nearly everyone surmised that Washington would receive one vote from every, or almost every, elector. This, then, the framers knew would be an exceptional election; things would not usually take such a turn. The feeling aroused in 1956 by President Eisenhower's heart attack created a situation that, though it did not exactly parallel, very nearly repeated that of 1789.

The public was quite correct in its anticipation that George Washington would be President. There were sixty-nine electors, and all sixty-nine voted for him. But though the electors were united on George Washington they were badly divided on the second vote.

On April 6, 1789, the arrival of Senator Richard Henry Lee of Virginia established a quorum of the first Senate, which proceeded to elect Senator John Langdon of New Hampshire as its president, " . . . for the sole purpose of opening and counting the vote for President of the United States." The Senate immediately notified the House that it was ready to proceed.

The two houses met together, and in their presence Langdon opened the certificates from the several states. He and the tellers named by the respective houses made the official count. Washington, as we have seen, had received sixty-nine of the 138 votes cast. The other sixty-nine votes were split among eleven people.

John Adams was in second place with thirty-four. John Jay had nine, Robert H. Harrison six, John Rutledge six, John Hancock four, George Clinton three, Samuel Huntington two, John Milton two, James Armstrong one, Edward Telfair one and Benjamin Lincoln one.

The wide distribution of the electors' second votes resulted, in small part, from the fear that John Adams might beat Washington out of first place and become President. Alexander Hamilton, whether from an unjustified suspicion that this would happen or from dislike for Adams, had sent out messages to a few states urging that they shouldn't all vote for Adams. But Adams was clearly runner-up for President. Since the Constitution did not require at that time that a person receive the votes of a majority of the electors in order to become Vice President, Adams won that office.

The design of the Founding Fathers, that the electors would make deliberate and independent judgments arising from their own knowledge and consciences, was already getting pretty shaky. True, there were no formal nominations of candidates as we have them today, no concerted campaigns and little or no actual pledging of electors in advance of the election.

But the activities of Federalists and Antifederalists in the struggle toward ratification had planted the seed of political party activity. It presaged the time when independent judgment by an elector would be a mere fiction. The Antifederalists were ready to concede the election of George Washington, the clear choice of the Federalists though he did not regard himself a partisan figure. But some Antifederalist elements bestirred themselves somewhat in a futile effort to defeat Adams for Vice President. Also, though nobody forced the electors to vote for Washington, it cannot be denied that the country so confidently expected them to that it almost amounted to a mandate.

Both for political expediency and to bring the new Union into closer harmony the Federalists had planned that the President and the Vice President should come from different sections of the country. That plan worked out perfectly. George Washington was a Virginian and John Adams, from Massachusetts, was a New Englander. This was a fairly good preview of the contemporary practice of our major political parties to get their Presidential and Vice Presidential nominees from different regions of the nation.

Perhaps the most important point to make about the 1789 election is that the original plan that both the President and the Vice President be outstanding men had functioned excellently. George Washington clearly held the first rank in the nation's esteem, and John Adams had a wide reputation as a man of large ability, even though there were many people who did not particularly fancy his personality.

As the 1956 campaign began there was much to remind one of 1789. President Eisenhower, an outstanding general and military hero in World War II, announced that he was willing to become a candidate for a second term. In all probability, had public matters been entirely out of the picture and had the President been free to consult only his personal desires and those of his family, he would have elected to retire at the end of his term to the pleasures of private life on his Pennsylvania farm. Though he no doubt longed, after his many years of public service, for the relaxation of private life, public and political considerations dictated otherwise.

So it was with George Washington. An outstanding general and military hero of the Revolution, he had performed many public services and deserved a chance to take life easy. No doubt his personal desire was to relax in peace at Mount Vernon.

But the country had called on him to serve as the first President under the new Constitution—experimental, uncharted and untried theory that it was. And it was not in Washington's nature to shirk a call of duty.

It is not strange that George Washington was not eager to become President. His fame was already so great that a term as President could do little to add to it, yet could do much to subtract. There was no particular prestige to the office. If it acquired any, General Washington himself would have to generate it. That would require persistent and constant effort.

Washington remained at Mount Vernon until the new Congress sent him official notice that he had been chosen President. He did not arrive in New York City until April 23 and did not take the oath of office until April 30.

John Adams arrived in New York before Washington and took over his duties on April 21. The Vice President is so seldom first in anything that it is well to note this.

April 30, 1789, was a momentous day in our history. In New York City Robert R. Livingston, chancellor of New York State, administered the oath of office to the first President of the United States, then shouted, "Long live George Washington, President of the United States."

Washington was assuming an awesome responsibility as he solemnly took oath that he would " . . . faithfully execute the office of President of the United Sates . . . " and that he would, to the best of his ability, " . . . preserve, protect, and defend the Constitution of the United States." So much depended on him. He would have to set precedents, with none behind him to guide the way. If this Union was to succeed, then he would have to give character, prestige and dignity to his office.

It was up to him to establish the Presidency as the highest office in the land. By no means had every person yet conceded that the new office of the President of the United States outranked the more time-honored one of state governor. Washington would have to lead the new government as it took the Constitution, then a mere document, infused life into it and translated it into an instrument of power, progress and freedom for the nation. A Herculean job.

The formal Constitution, however fine it was, could of itself alone be no more than a bare skeleton of the new governmental system. The flesh and blood would have to be acquired by careful but bold action by the Congress, by the President and by the courts. Nor would the Union be complete until North Carolina and Rhode Island ratified the Constitution.

Fortunately George Washington was the man for his job. He was not an extraordinarily brilliant man, it is true, but he was extremely able, and he had an abundance of fine common sense. When it came to courage, judgment, integrity and the confidence of the people, no one in the land could excel him. He was in every sense the First Citizen of the Republic.

One of the major precedents to be established by the first chief executive was what pattern the etiquette and system of protocol surrounding his office should follow. To both the public and the First Congress the problem was perplexing. Many people felt that the President's official life should resemble the brilliant European courts. Others rejected this notion, insisting that the administration of a republic should be free from pompous formality and elaborate ceremony.

The status of national officials was debated at length in the First Congress. What, for instance, would be a proper title for the chief executive? The Senate became deeply interested in this question. All sorts of possible titles were bandied about, among them "His Elective Majesty," "His Excellency," "His Highness," "His Elective Highness" and "His Highness, the President of the United States of America and Protector of the Rights of the Same."

The Senate appeared, though not with unanimity, to be quite favorable to some pompous appellation. Senator William Maclay of Pennsylvania, however, argued emphatically that special titles were forbidden by the provision of the Constitution that no title of nobility should be granted by the United States.

The House had no enthusiasm for a title. Representative Thomas Tucker of South Carolina, after pointing out that talk of titles would alarm the citizens of the country and cause them to doubt the good faith of those who framed the Constitution, continued, "To give dignity to our Government, we must give a lofty title to our chief magistrate. Does the dignity of a nation consist in the exaltation of one man, and the humiliation of the rest?"

Representative Jackson of Georgia wondered what title could possibly add dignity or luster to the person who filled the Presidency. For his part, he could conceive none. No House-Senate agreement was ever reached, and the whole matter simply dropped out of debate.

Nowadays a governor of a state is often addressed as "His Excellency." A member of Congress is referred to as "Honorable." The judge on the bench is called "His Honor." But the highest officer in all the land is just "Mr. President." When he is presented to an audience it is regarded improper to indulge in a lengthy introduction. Normally a master of ceremonies presenting the President merely says, "Ladies and gentlemen, the President of the United States." The simplicity of the President's title gives it dignity and sets it aside from the more pompous titles that go with offices inferior to his.

The capital's social life in the first administration was more formal and less democratic than in the later administrations of, say, Jefferson and Jackson. The personalities of the Washingtons, however, kept the atmosphere from becoming excessively aristocratic or luxurious. George and Martha Washington were country people of comparatively simple tastes. Martha, by this time a grandmother through her first husband's children, joined the President in New York in the latter part of May 1789. Though she performed her duties as First Lady well, she often found them oppressive. Writing to a friend, she once said, "I think I am more like a prisoner of the state than anything else."

In contrast to the intense public debate over the Presidency stands the obvious lack of official enthusiasm for the office of Vice President, which is placed in bold relief by the debate in the House of Representatives, First Congress, first session, over his salary.

After the House had voted a salary of $25,000 for the President, it considered a committee report recommending an annual salary of $5000 for the Vice President. The idea of paying the Vice President an annual salary brought a sharp debate on the floor—so sharp that it looked as though John Adams might experience the humiliation of a late-eighteenth-century facsimile of time-clock punching.

Representative Alexander White of Virginia argued vigorously that the Vice President should be paid by the day and only for the actual time he put in presiding over the Senate. He argued that the Constitution fixed no duty on him that required a constant attendance, that while it required that the President be paid a salary ascertained by law, " . . . it has not one syllable with respect to the pay of the Vice President" and that, after all, the Vice President gets personal advantages from his office. If the Vice President should prove to be " . . . a deserving person, there will be but little doubt of his succeeding to the presidential chair; not that I would make this an argument to diminish his compensation."

Another objection to annual pay was brought up on the floor: the Vice President might stay away from the Senate, pursue an occupation of his own and draw a government salary though a perpetual absentee. Representative Joshua Seney of Maryland declared that there was no way to compel the Vice President to perform a duty and that he "may absent himself the whole time." So went the argument for *per diem* pay. The plan was to pay Congressmen *per diem*. Why was the Vice President any better than they were?

Others took a different view, and their position prevailed in an unenthusiastic decision. Virginia Representative John Page thought the Vice President should get an annual salary but that it should be a larger sum than $5000, in view of his position as second magistrate. Page had no compliments for the office and nothing to say about its utility. He had had no part in forming the Constitution. If he had, Page stated, perhaps he should never have thought of such an officer, " . . . but as we have got him, we must maintain him."

James Madison approved the idea of an annual salary. Answering White's argument that the Vice President is in line to become President, Madison observed, "If he is to be considered as the apparent successor of the President, to qualify himself the better for that office, he must withdraw from his other avocations, and direct his attention to the obtaining of a perfect knowledge of his intended business."

In the end the House voted for the $5000 salary.

John Adams, the first man to hold this office regarded so lightly even by the Federal lawmakers, was a Harvard graduate, a very able and vigorous man, though vain and sensitive. Never in the habit of underestimating himself, Adams had now come to occupy a position that, to say the least, was not particularly suited to his great talents.

The framers of the Constitution desired a man of outstanding ability for the Vice Presidency. But, as we have noted, they did not give the office enough power and responsibility to make it very attractive to such a man. The Vice President was not to be an executive officer at all. He was to be merely an inactive stand-by to take over executive duties in case of the death, resignation, removal or inability of the President.

So long as the President was performing, the Vice President was to have only one duty—to serve as president of the Senate. And as presiding officer he was to have a vote only in case of a tie. A depressing job it was for a man of mental and physical energy.

While John Adams doubtless did not foresee what a genuinely futile position the Vice Presidency was to become over the years, he was certainly not without his suspicions. He had now left his New England soil, where he was recognized as the outstanding member of one of the region's most respected families, since the political fortunes of Samuel Adams, the great revolutionist, had undergone reverses. But on the national scene he was about to play a role distinctly second to that of George Washington, a man whose reputation clearly surpassed all others.

When he took over the Senate chair on April 21, he could

not yet take the oath of office. The Constitution prescribed the Presidential oath but did not set forth one for the Vice President. This awaited an act of Congress. The President signed the act on June 1, and John Adams took his oath on the third.

When introduced to the Senate, Adams said that he had been invited to "this respectable situation" and that, considering the times, it would be amiss for him to refuse, unaccustomed as he was " . . . to refuse any public service, however dangerous to my reputation, or disproportioned to my talents."

John Adams tried his best to make something of importance of his office. Since the Senate sat behind closed doors in those early days and kept no verbatim record of its transactions, Senator William Maclay's journal has become an invaluable source of information. We now turn to that journal for an account of Mr. Adams as Vice President in the first weeks of the new government. But as we do so we must exercise some caution. There is probably good basis for all or most of what Maclay tells us, but he was a partisan politician, an Antifederalist from Pennsylvania, who did not fancy John Adams too much. Maclay is not noted for the objectivity of his judgment.

Maclay's journal has this item for April 25, 1789—some four days after Adams had assumed the chair as the Senate's presiding officer:

The Vice-President, as usual, made us two or three speeches from the Chair. I will endeavor to recollect one of them. It was on the reading of a report which mentioned that the President should be received in the Senate chamber and proceed thence to the House of Representatives to be sworn: "Gentlemen, I do not know whether the framers of the Constitution had in view the two kings of Sparta or the two consuls of Rome when they formed it; one to have all the power while he held it, and the other to be nothing. Nor do I know whether the architect that formed our room and the wide chair in it (to hold two, I suppose) had the Constitution before him.

Gentlemen, I feel great difficulty how to act. I am possessed of two separate powers; the one in esse and the other in posse. I am Vice President. In this I am nothing, but I may be everything. But I am president also of the Senate. When the President comes into the Senate, what shall I be?

In the Roman Republic the highest executive power rotated between the two consuls to whom Adams alluded. Adams was quite correct in assuming that as Vice President he was, by comparison to the President, to be nothing. But in comparing his office to that of a Roman consul minor he was stretching the proportions of his position. For even during the months when he was second in rank a consul had extensive powers.

Adams must have been torn between two grim realities: that the Vice Presidency was a weak office and that it really should be one of distinction and prestige. The title of this book refers to the stature the office should have rather than to its actual standing.

His position was extremely annoying to Adams. He wrote his wife, Abigail, "My country has in its wisdom contrived for me the most insignificant office that ever the invention of man contrived or his imagination conceived."

Adams wanted high-sounding titles for the President and for himself. In this he was destined for disappointment. Thomas R. Marshall, humorous and talented Vice President under President Woodrow Wilson, in discussing the occasion when the Senate had temporarily concluded that a proper title for the President would be "His Excellency," had this to say:

> While unrecorded, there is a legendary story that when this finally had been determined on, one of the senators from Virginia, who did not like Vice President Adams, suggested, sotto voce, that the official title of the Vice President of the United States should be His Superfluous Excellency.

Then Mr. Marshall went on to express his personal opinion, based on eight years' experience in the office: "So far as any actual power in the affairs of government is concerned, this epithet hurled at the first vice-president expressed the truth."

Had anyone been able to give to the Vice Presidency any degree of vigor and energy, that man would have been John Adams. But try as he might, he very quickly learned that the nature of his job prevented it.

By 1792 the temporary seat of the government had been moved to Philadelphia pending occupancy of the permanent capitol. Again it was time to prepare for a national election. Though Washington clearly desired to retire from office he yielded when Hamilton, Jefferson, Madison and others urged him to remain for the good of the new country. His re-election was assured. Federalists and Antifederalists united behind him.

Full-fledged political parties were not yet here, but partisanship was lively enough. Antifederalists, perhaps from both desire and a sense of the hopelessness of any other course, decided to go along with Washington and concentrate their artillery on Adams. Perhaps they could beat Adams with George Clinton of New York as their candidate.

By this time there were fifteen states to participate in the election. North Carolina and Rhode Island had ratified the Constitution and two new states, Vermont and Kentucky, had been admitted to the growing Union. In most of the states the legislatures still chose the presidential electors, but a few had popular elections. The fifteen states had a total of 132 electors. Though there was still no legal distinction between a vote for President and a vote for Vice President, every one of the 132 voted for Washington, and they were all conscious that they were choosing him for President. The second vote was divided among four people: John Adams seventy-seven, George Clinton fifty, Thomas Jefferson four and Aaron Burr one.

So George Washington was, as expected, unanimously re-elected, and John Adams again became Vice President. Once more the prestige of George Washington had made a sham of the legal unity of the vote for President and Vice President. Everybody knew that an electoral vote for Washington meant Washington for President and that an electoral vote for Adams for President meant Adams for Vice President.

Partisanship grew more intense during George Washington's second administration. Washington himself was opposed to partisanship, but he inclined more to the views of Hamilton, his Federalist Secretary of the Treasury, than to those of

Thomas Jefferson, his Secretary of State. Jefferson left his post in late December 1793. He was bitterly opposed to Hamilton's fiscal and centralizing policies and to his views on the French Revolution. In retirement Jefferson became the recognized leader of the Democratic-Republican (or Republican) Party, the new faction organized in opposition to the Federalists.

As the time for the election of 1796 approached a genuine contest for the Presidency was for the first time in prospect. President Washington had announced that he did not care to serve for a third term. A rather informal caucus of the more influential Federalist members of the Congress agreed that their Presidential ticket would be headed by John Adams, with Thomas Pinckney of South Carolina. Adams was clearly intended to be President and Pinckney Vice President.

The Republicans still lacked organization, but their candidate for President was clearly Thomas Jefferson. They named Aaron Burr of New York for Vice President. There were now sixteen states, Tennessee having been admitted into the Union, and 138 electors. Ten states still had legislative election of electors, but the others used popular vote.

Thirteen men received electoral votes for President in 1796. John Adams got seventy-one, Thomas Jefferson sixty-eight, Thomas Pinckney fifty-nine, Aaron Burr thirty, Samuel Adams fifteen, Oliver Ellsworth eleven, George Clinton seven, John Jay five, James Iredell three, George Washington two, Samuel Johnston two, John Henry two, and Charles Cotesworth Pinckney one.

John Adams had a majority with one vote to spare. Thereafter he was often referred to as "President by one vote." The official count of the electoral vote took place on Wednesday, February 8, 1797. John Adams then had an experience very rare for any American. As Vice President, in the presence of both houses, he performed his official Constitutional duty of opening the certificates from the several states and reading them as the tellers counted. It then became Adams' duty to announce his own close victory. We find this entry for the day in the Annals of Congress:

Whereupon, the Vice President addressed the two Houses of Congress, as follows:

In obedience to the Constitution and Law of the United States, and to the commands of both Houses of Congress, expressed in their resolution passed in the present session, I now declare that

John Adams is elected President of the United States, for four years, to commence with the fourth day of March next; and that

Thomas Jefferson is elected Vice President of the United States, for four years, to commence with the fourth day of March next. And may the Sovereign of the Universe, the ordainer of civil government on earth, for the preservation of liberty, justice, and peace, among men, enable both to discharge the duties of these offices comfortably to the Constitution of the United States, with conscientious diligence, punctuality, and perseverance.

The electoral scheme had worked well again. It gave us very able men for the offices of both President and Vice President. But the impact of political parties had brought a strange anomaly. John Adams, Federalist, happily promoted from Vice President to President, was to have as his Vice President Thomas Jefferson, a member of the opposition Republican Party and his chief political antagonist. The Vice Presidency was still a weak office, but it was again to be occupied by an extraordinary man—a man who would be a political thorn in the side of the President.

The major parties, Federalist and Republican, were now assuming the proportions and the tactics of modern political parties. Before the Presidential election of 1800 both parties presented definite tickets. Federalist members of Congress met in a secret and perhaps irregular caucus and decided on President John Adams and Charles Cotesworth Pinckney of South Carolina as their candidates, employing a good geographic strategy in choosing one man from New England and the other from the South.

Later, Republican members of Congress, after criticizing the Federalists for doing the same thing, also met in secret caucus and again decided on Jefferson and Burr. This was both good geographic strategy and a masterful political tactic.

If the Republican ticket was to succeed it would have to win in Virginia and New York. With Jefferson on the ticket Virginia would be no great problem, but swinging New York would be very doubtful. But if Aaron Burr, an astute New York political organizer and a powerful Tammany figure, were paired with him it would be less difficult. This is why Jefferson and Burr, two men without excessive love for each other, were running mates. Everyone understood that Adams and Jefferson were the two opponents for President, while Pinckney and Burr were the contestants for Vice President. But because of the wording of the Constitution all four were, on the face of it, candidates for President.

Most of the electors were still chosen by their state legislatures. Only a few states allowed popular choice. The total number of states (sixteen) and of the electoral college (138) had not changed since the last election. Seventy-three of the electors were Republicans and sixty-five Federalists.

Under the Constitutional system, as we have seen, the only way a Republican elector could designate Burr for Vice President was to cast one of his two votes for him as President. So all seventy-three voted for Jefferson for President and for Burr for President. All the Federalist electors voted for Adams, giving him sixty-five, but one Rhode Island elector, fearing a mix-up, cast his second vote for John Jay instead of Pinckney. So the vote stood: Thomas Jefferson seventy-three, Aaron Burr, seventy-three, John Adams sixty-five, Charles Cotesworth Pinckney sixty-four and John Jay once.

Adams and Pinckney were definitely defeated. Jefferson and Burr each had the required majority of all the electors, and they had an equal number of votes. So it was up to the House of Representatives to decide between them.

People often ask how two could have received a majority when a majority is more than one half. It is important to remember that each elector voted for two people and that the majority referred to was not of the total electoral vote but of the total number of electors. The total electoral vote was 276 (twice the number of electors). Of 276 votes two people could easily get more than half of 138 (the total number of electors). What it amounted to in fact was that a winning candidate had to have one more than one quarter of the total vote.

There has been so much confusion over this point that, even at the expense of begging the point, we might try another explanation. Of the 138 electors seventy-three, a clear majority thereof, voted for Jefferson. But as the same electors also had another vote for President seventy-three, a clear majority thereof, likewise voted for Burr. Therefore each candidate had a majority and both had the same number of votes.

Strange things lead to stranger ones. The House of Representatives would have to choose between Jefferson and Burr. And the House, which had been elected back in 1798, had a Federalist majority. What is more, the Federalists had majority control of the delegations of more than half of the states. This is important because the Constitution provides that when the House has to decide a Presidential election it votes by states, each state having one vote. So if all the Federalists pulled together they could absolutely control the decision.

The Federalist House was to have the consolation privilege of deciding which of the leaders of the successful enemy ticket would be President. A great many Federalists regarded Thomas Jefferson as their archenemy and the epitome of all political evil. Though themselves defeated in the Presidential campaign, they could have the Machiavellian privilege of upsetting enemy intentions. The Federalists held a caucus and decided to throw the election to Burr. But for the fact that some Federalists from the South failed to comply with the caucus decision and but for the fact that Alexander Hamilton, a leading Federalist, exerted his influence against it, it appears that we would have had Burr for President.

The House resolved that the delegation from each state was to be seated together. Elaborate provision was made for checking the honesty of the way in which each state's vote was reported. The House further resolved that it would ballot behind closed doors and that it should not adjourn until a choice had been made. The vote of each state was to go as the majority of the state delegation went. For instance, if there were five Representatives from a state and three voted for Jefferson and two for Burr, then that state would be recorded for Jefferson. If the vote within a state delegation was even, then it would be reported as "divided."

The balloting should have been a mere formality. Aaron Burr, Jefferson's running mate, knew full well that he was intended to be Vice President. Had he done the proper thing and renounced with vigor and directness the Federalist attempt to elevate him over Jefferson to the Presidency, it is probable that the Federalist efforts would have collapsed in a hurry. But Burr was willing to be the beneficiary of the Federalist scheme.

It should, however, be said that there was a limit to the degree of dishonor Burr would embrace. There is good evidence that Burr was unwilling to sell out entirely to the Federalists on policy. It must also be noted that Thomas Jefferson, who clearly played the more honorable part, may perhaps have found it necessary to let it be known to people who approached him from the Federalists that he had no intention of reversing a few principles on which Federalists were most solidly united. Apparently there was no bargain but some clarification of intentions.

The balloting started on Wednesday, February 11, 1801. There were but two absentees. Representative Jones of Georgia had died. Representative Sumter of South Carolina was ill. Representative Nicholson of Maryland was also ill, but a bed was prepared for him, which he occupied in an ante-chamber next to the House chamber. Tellers took his vote there and it was quite important, for his vote for Jefferson divided the Maryland vote, which otherwise would have gone for Burr, by a vote of four to three.

On the first ballot the vote was eight states for Jefferson, six for Burr and two divided. Jefferson led Burr, but he was not yet elected. When the House is voting for President the Constitution requires a majority of all the states for a decision. Since there were sixteen states, a candidate would have to get the votes of nine of them in order to be elected. In ballot after ballot the result was the same, eight-six-two. At midnight they took the nineteenth ballot, with the same result.

On Thursday, February 12 the twentieth ballot was taken at one A.M., the twenty-first ballot at two A.M., the twenty-second ballot at two thirty A.M., the twenty-third ballot at four A.M., the twenty-fourth ballot at five A.M., the twenty-fifth ballot at six A.M., the twenty-sixth ballot at seven A.M., and the twenty-seventh ballot at eight A.M. All had the same results: eight states for Jefferson, six states for Burr and two divided. At this point, after an all-night session, the House gave up for awhile and the members dispersed for breakfast. At noon they took the twenty-eighth ballot, but with the same result.

The twenty-ninth ballot on Friday, February 13, and the thirtieth, thirty-first, thirty-second and thirty-third ballots on Saturday, February 14, still gave Jefferson eight and Burr six, with two states divided. The House had a day of rest on Sunday, February 15. The thirty-fourth ballot on Monday, February 16, produced no change. Then came Tuesday, February 17. The thirty-fifth ballot at noon showed the same result. Finally, at one P.M., on the thirty-sixth ballot, the Burr factions in four states voted blank, bringing a final tally of ten states for Jefferson, four states for Burr and two states voting blank. Thus Thomas Jefferson was elected third President of the United States. Aaron Burr, as runner-up, automatically became Vice President-elect.

Aaron Burr was an extraordinary man. It is a pity that he did not have strength of character and principles to match his magnificent talents. There is no doubt that he had a first-class mind as well as a most engaging personality. As a political organizer he was among the very best. When placed on the ticket with Jefferson in 1800 he was, as we have noted, expected to pull New York state into the Republican column. He did just that, and it was no easy task. He got busy and arranged a strong array of Republican candidates for the New York legislature in New York City, and the complete success of the city campaign put the Republicans in the majority in the New York Assembly. Thereupon the Assembly elected a solid block of twelve Republican Presidential electors. Had the Federalists retained their old majority in the Assembly, Adams would have been re-elected.

As President of the Senate Burr presided gracefully and easily. But presiding over the Senate was a task of too much routine and too little adventure for a man of Burr's energy and ambition. Yet President Jefferson could scarcely afford to rely on him or to trust him to any appreciable degree in the administration of his policies. In 1804, though retaining his position as Vice President, Burr became a candidate for Governor of New York in a campaign somewhat tainted by a projected scheme to form a Northern confederacy. Alexander Hamilton came out vigorously in opposition to Burr's candidacy and used words about Burr's character which, though doubtless true, were undule harsh. As a result of Hamilton's efforts Burr was defeated. Burr had never forgiven Hamilton for his part in securing Jefferson's victory over him for the Presidency; now the same foe had thwarted his ambitions again. He challenged Hamilton to a duel, and on July 11, 1804, at Weehawken, New Jersey, he shot and mortally wounded the great Federalist leader. By this desperate act he earned the hatred not only of the Federalists but of all save the most bitterly partisan of his Republican associates.

When Burr returned to duties as president of the Senate he served with two indictments for murder hanging over his head, one in New York for sending the challenge to Hamilton and one in New Jersey for the actual homicide. Early in 1805 the Senate considered a bill to grant Aaron Burr, soon to become ex-Vice President, the franking privilege for life. Those who doubt that partisanship was as bitter in those days as in ours should note well the following entry in the diary of John Quincy Adams, then a member of the Senate:

Feb 28—The Vice President being absent, Mr. Anderson was chosen President pro tem. The bill to allow Mr. Burr the

privilege of franking during life passed, after a long and extraordinary debate, in which Mr. Wright said he could justify
duelling by the example of David and Goliath in the Scrip-
tures, and that this bill was now opposed only because our
David had slain the Goliath of Federalism.

When his term as Vice President was over Burr was so
thoroughly discredited that he had no political future in prospect. Naturally he had not been nominated for re-election as
Vice President on the Jefferson ticket. But if he was to be by-
passed, he was not to be forgotten. Scarcely two years after the
expiration of his Vice Presidential term he was on trial for
treason before a United States Circuit Court at Richmond,
Virginia, Supreme Court Chief Justice John Marshall presiding. This was in connection with his conspiracy for un-
authorized military action in the Mississippi Valley—the exact
purposes of which are not entirely clear today, except that
whatever they were, they would be gratifying to the personal
ambition and adventuresome soul of Aaron Burr. President
Thomas Jefferson urged vigorous prosecution. Burr was
acquitted on strictly technical grounds, but the shadow of his
amazingly irresponsible conduct haunted him for the rest of his
days.

Among the Vice Presidents Aaron Burr stands and will remain a unique figure. First, though among the ablest of the
Vice Presidents, he was undoubtedly the most untrustworthy
and dangerous in character. Second, he served as Vice President while under two indictments for murder—a record no
Vice President before or since has been able to approximate.
Third, after the expiration of his term he was prosecuted for
treason, and the prosecution was spurred on by the same President under whom Burr had once served as Vice President—
another record rather difficult to match.

The tie between Jefferson and Burr and the crisis it produced was no accident. It was the result of a straight-ticket
vote on the part of the Republican electors. They had gone
right down the line for both of their party candidates. Their
behavior was a proclamation by deeds that Presidential

electors were not to be purveyors of individual judgment. Rather, they were to be mere automatons to register party will. Without adding a word to the official Constitution they had virtually amended it to read, "The electors shall cast their votes for the nominees of their political party."

The framers of the Constitution had not planned for organized political parties, and George Washington had warned against them in his Farewell Address as President. But now parties were here and in fairly full bloom. They had upset the applecart on the two-votes-for-President system. Tie votes for President between the same party's candidates for President and Vice President would be a regular occurrence unless in each election some elector of the victorious party by pre-arranged plan would throw away one of his two votes. It seemed more propitious to amend the Constitution.

The Twelfth Amendment was proposed by Congress on December 9, 1803, and declared ratified on September 25, 1804, in time to govern the election of 1804.

This amendment leaves undisturbed the original provisions concerning both the numbers of electors each state will have and the manner in which they shall be chosen. It provides, however, that each elector shall cast one distinct vote for President and another one for Vice President. It leaves intact the stipulation that one of the people he votes for shall not be an inhabitant of his own state.

No longer is there any danger that more than one candidate for either office will get the votes of a majority of the whole number of electors, since each elector has only one vote for each office. The real hazard is that it may happen that no one receives the required majority vote. Under the amendment if any candidate for President receives the votes of a majority of the electors he is elected President. Likewise, anyone receiving the votes of a majority of the electors for Vice President is elected to that office. If no one receives a majority of the electoral vote for President, then the House of Representatives is to choose the President from the persons ". . . having the highest numbers not exceeding three on the list of those voted for as President." The House is, as of old, to vote by states, the representation from each state having one vote and a majority of all the states being necessary to a choice. If no one receives the votes of a majority of the electors for Vice President, then the Senate is to choose the Vice President from the two standing highest in electoral vote, a majority of the whole number of Senators being necessary to a choice.

III

The Decline
of the Vice Presidency

The adoption of the Twelfth Amendment in 1804 marks a great turning point in the history of the Vice Presidency, and the turn was definitely for the worse. This is not to say that the Twelfth Amendment is in itself a Constitutional culprit. The Amendment was wise, and indeed necessary, if electoral votes were to be cast according to political party mandate rather than individual judgment and conscience.

Political parties had arrived with all their evils and benefits—the latter, of course, being the greater. Even without the Twelfth Amendment political party practice was pointing the Vice Presidency toward a decline. But by specifying that each elector would cast one ballot for President and a separate ballot for Vice President the amendment made the descent of the Vice Presidency clearer and more understandable. The amendment was, in a sense, no more than a legal adjustment to a political party development—the practice of nominating one person for the office of President and another for the office of Vice President. Being a posterior ratification of a *fait accompli,* the amendment merely added pavement to a road already chartered for Vice Presidential decline.

Senator Pierce Butler of South Carolina was much opposed to the amendment. He was the author of a series of letters

50

to the governor of South Carolina as part of an effort to prevent that state from ratifying it. In these letters he prophesied that if the Twelfth Amendment were adopted the Vice President, who should be a man of irreproachable character, would instead become an "offspring of intrigue." Many historians believe that events have borne out Senator Butler's forecast.

The new tenor was not long in asserting itself. In the campaign of 1804 Aaron Burr was quite naturally dropped from the Republican ticket. His replacement was another New Yorker, George Clinton, who had served many times as governor of that state. With Jefferson for President and Clinton for Vice President the Republican ticket won handily. Jefferson and Clinton each got 162 electoral votes as against fourteen for Charles C. Pinckney and Rufus King, the Federalist candidates for President and Vice President, respectfully. So Jefferson entered upon his second administration with Clinton as his Vice President.

Before the campaign of 1808 Jefferson, fearing that Presidential tenure by the same person for more than two terms would threaten the security of republican institutions, announced that he would decline to serve for a third term. This left the door wide open for a new Republican candidate for President. Vice President Clinton, as heir apparent, was now eligible for a promotion. The opening was there, though he was sixty-nine years old. And Clinton apparently wanted to step up to the Presidency. But President Jefferson preferred Madison as his successor.

In the end the Republican Congressional caucus nominated James Madison of Virginia for President and George Clinton for a second term as Vice President. The Republican ticket was victorious, and Clinton continued as Vice President until he died in office on April 20, 1812. His was the first death of a Vice President or a President during term of office.

Prior to the Twelfth Amendment, as we have noted, we had three Vice Presidents—John Adams, Thomas Jefferson and Aaron Burr. Even though the original design was already on something of a political-action detour, all three were men of extraordinary ability. In intelligence they would measure well in comparison with any trio of Presidents or British prime ministers that we might wish to match against them. Burr lacked character, true, but he was not wanting in either intellect or political skill.

And the expectation that Vice Presidents who proved worthy would be rewarded by subsequent elevation to the Presidency had also worked perfectly. Two of the three Vice Presidents, John Adams and Thomas Jefferson, had been elected to the Presidency in their own right. The third, Aaron Burr, had demonstrated that he was unworthy. Had he been elected President it would have been a miscarriage of the original design rather than a testimonial to its proper functioning. There is even some question whether Burr should be brought into the equation at all, since the Twelfth Amendment was in effect before the first Presidential election after he took office as Vice President. But resolving all in favor of moderation, we may say that of three who served as Vice President before the Twelfth Amendment, two were promoted by election to the Presidency. The early Vice Presidents were batting at the rate of .667 in the effort to complete the circuit to the Presidency—a very good average: good enough to induce able and vigorous men to aspire to the Vice Presidency as a step toward a higher goal.

But how have the ambitions of Vice Presidents fared since the adoption of the Twelfth Amendment? Thirty-six men have served as Vice President of the United States, Richard M. Nixon being the thirty-sixth. Of these, three served prior to the said amendment and thirty-three since its adoption. Of the thirty-three who have served since the Twelfth Amendment, seven died while in office. It is therefore not fair to count them in determining the ratio of Vice Presidential promotion. It is possible, though doubtful, that but for the intervention of death there might have been some advancement to the Presidency from among them.

Subtracting the seven from thirty-three, we have left

twenty-six Vice Presidents for our comparisons. But of these remaining twenty-six, seven have advanced to the Presidency when the incumbent President died. (Three of these were elected President to succeed themselves, but their initial installation as President was not by election.)

So subtracting again, we have nineteen. Again following the course of moderation, we should substract one more, Mr. Nixon. It would be presumptuous and erroneous to count him yet as one who failed to move up. That leaves eighteen fair cases from which to determine our ratio.

No living ex-Vice President, with the exception of former President Harry S. Truman, who reached the Presidency on the death of President Franklin D. Roosevelt, should be excluded from the count. John Nance Garner, thirty-second Vice President, is in retirement from political life. It would appear that the lack of party regularity of Henry A. Wallace, thirty-third Vice President, has placed him entirely outside the realm of Presidential availability.

So we have eighteen Vice Presidents who have had the fair chance to move by election from the Vice Presidency to the Presidency. Of these only one, Martin Van Buren, succeeded. One out of eighteen gives a record of advancement of .0555. A little simple mathematics will show that the chances of advancement in the earlier period were twelve times as great as they have been since. Of course the earlier era was so short that it may afford a tricky comparison. This statistical fault is freely admitted. But the period since the ratification of the Twelfth Amendment has covered one hundred fifty-two years. So it would certainly appear nevertheless that the Vice Presidency has definitely lost its appeal as a path to election to the Presidency.

The party practice that necessitated the Twelfth Amendment has also succeeded in reducing the office of Vice President to the status of a curious fifth wheel in American political life. We inescapably take our Vice President from those whom the major parties nominate. Nor do we have a free choice between the Democratic and Republican nominees for the office. If we want as our President the Democratic nominee for that office, then we have to go along with that party's nominee for Vice President. The same is true if we want the Republican nominee, since we cannot split our ticket between the two offices.

If either party nominates a Presidential candidate and drafts a platform popular enough to carry the nation, then almost anybody can ride it through to the Vice Presidency. All too often between the Republican and the Democratic candidates for Vice President we have little to argue about. The parties use the office as a second prize—distinctly second—with which to achieve party harmony in the campaign or to pull in votes that might otherwise go to the candidates of the opposite party.

The nomination for President may be made with a great many considerations in mind, but one of these is certain to be the idea among many of the delegates that they can sell him to the voters as a man well qualified for the office he seeks. The nomination for Vice President is likewise made with many considerations in mind, but the qualifications of the man to assume the office of President, should he be called to it, are seldom a major factor.

We seem to be confirmed optimists. A President will not die—there is some magic charm about the office that will keep him alive. Hence we have often nominated for Vice President men actually or potentially afflicted with the infirmities of old age. Political expediency clearly governs the nomination of a Vice Presidential candidate.

The ticket must be balanced to draw in the votes. Is the Presidential candidate from the East? Then spread the net for votes. Get somebody from the West for Vice President. Whether or not he has earned any great distinction will not matter too much. Western voters will find out that he is from the West. As the South gets into greater political ferment and then becomes less certain how to vote, it is line for a little salve to its feelings. Second place on the ticket is a soothing unguent. Has a large following in the party lost out in the battle for the Presidential nomination? Placate hurt feelings by giving their man the Vice Presidential nomination. Has a big state become exceedingly doubtful? It is what the partisans refer to as a "pivotal state." Giving the Vice Presidential nomination to its governor or some other local favorite may be just the thing to tip the scales. Is the Presidential candidate from the liberal wing of the party? If so it is often winning politics to give the consolation prize to the conservative faction.

And so it goes. Oh yes, the Presidential candidate is often consulted about a proper running mate. It is too much, however, to say that he makes the choice. He may make a limited choice. He cannot choose from the whole rank and file of the party. Leaders at the convention come to him with a list a half-dozen availables, let us say. If the Presidential candidate gives the nod to one of these that often settles it. The word is passed on and the convention readily nominates his choice. But the Presidential candidate is not likely to turn down the whole list. He doesn't want to give a half-dozen vetoes before he ever gets into office. All in all, the Vice Presidential nominee is likely to be an instrument of compromise—compromise between factions, between sections, between interests and even perhaps between the back-room political bargainers. It is often very difficult to use a vigorous and outspoken man as the tool of such a compromise.

It is often said that we get mediocrities for Vice President. That is saying entirely too much and is a very loose use of the term mediocrity. Really we have had no Alexander Throttlebottoms for Vice President. Our Vice Presidents have usually been men who have previously been governors or United States Senators or occupants of other offices of similar distinction—offices so high that the vast majority of us, never accepting for ourselves the classification of mediocrities, will never be able to reach them, try as we may.

Thomas R. Marshall, whose eloquence on the Vice Presidency we have noted before, came nearer to the point in his observation. It is said that he was once asked why so many Vice Presidents came from Indiana. His prompt reply was that he supposed it was because Indiana produced so many "first-rate second-rate men." Undoubtedly had he explained his humorous retort he would have qualified the word second-rate.

Our Vice Presidents have never been second-rate men compared with the general run of society. They are often second rate, though, when in the company of the very best. Compared with the 160,000,000 of us common people our Vice Presidents have just about always been above average. But frequently they have been average above-average men and not distinctly and conspicuously above-average men. Average above-average is not good enough for our day. Any day, human life being as uncertain as it is, a Vice President may be called suddenly to take over the helm of this great republic. He may find himself immediately and without warning occupying the position that has more responsibility for the preservation and furtherance of the free way of life than any other position in the world. For such an eventuality we need to have in readiness a man who typifies the very best that we have in both mind and character.

We can do much better than we have done with the Vice Presidency. This is not to deprecate the qualities of those who have served in that capacity. In fact, considering the undramatic nature of the office, it is surprising that we have done as well as we have. Many men of superior and some of outstanding ability have filled the post. But looking over the situation as a whole, we must admit that while our Vice Presidents have, as a rule, been men of respectable ability, few of them have been men of extraordinary distinction among the nation's leaders.

The framers of the Constitution were none too enthusiastic about having a Vice President. Their principal reason for creating the office was to insure that we would never be without a chief executive. The Vice President would be ready immediately to take over in case the President died, resigned, was removed or became disabled. Of course the Vice President must have reached the age of thirty-five, for otherwise he would not be eligible for the Presidency. But it is not necessary that he be an old man. It would seem advisable that the Vice President be young enough to have aspirations for the Presidency and that in the course of fulfilling such aspirations he could outlast a party reverse here and there on his way.

In the early years the Vice President was younger than the President. George Washington was fifty-seven when he took the oath of office. His Vice President, John Adams, was fifty-three. Of course each was four years older at the beginning of Washington's second administration. John Adams was sixty-one when he began his term as President. Thomas Jefferson, his Vice President, was nearing fifty-four and began his first administration as President at fifty-eight (lacking a few weeks). His Vice President, Aaron Burr, was forty-five.

Then came the Twelfth Amendment, bringing an immediate change in the age factor, though the trend did not last. Thomas Jefferson was approximately sixty-two when he began his second administration, but his Vice President, George Clinton, was older. He was sixty-five. The fourth President, James Madison, was approaching his fifty-eighth birthday. George Clinton, beginning his second term as Vice President, was then sixty-nine. He died before his second term was completed.

When the Presidential campaign of 1812 approached, the dominant Republicans (still speaking of the Democratic-Republicans or Jeffersonian Republicans) had to get a new Vice Presidential running mate for Madison. They seemed determined to get a very old man. The party's Congressional caucus first nominated John Langdon, a retired New Hampshire political leader, who was seventy-one years old and no longer very vigorous. Langdon declined, so the Republicans held another caucus and nominated Elbridge Gerry of Massachusetts. Gerry was elected Vice President on the Madison ticket. Madison was sixty-two at the start of his second administration, but Vice President Gerry was sixty-eight. He died in the midst of his term. So with the ink hardly dry on the Twelfth Amendment we got two aged Vice Presidents in a row, and both died in office.

But in spite of this beginning getting old men for the

office has not become a regular practice. The truth seems rather to be that age is not a factor. We have had Vice Presidents younger than Presidents and older than Presidents. Mr. Nixon, for example, is appreciably younger than Mr. Eisenhower, while Mr. Stevenson and Mr. Kefauver are nearly the same age. Since the Vice Presidency has become a terminal position if the President survives, and since it is not an office of great significance per se, the parties have not worried too much about either the age or the physical vigor of the nominee.

Admittedly the President has a heavy job, hazardous to life and health, while the Vice President has never been overburdened. Yet the mortality score is running exactly even. Seven Presidents have met death in office, and so have seven Vice Presidents. Only four Presidents, however, have died natural deaths. Three were victims of assassins. Yet all of the Vice Presidential deaths have been from natural causes. So it would appear, on the face of it, that we have been less concerned about vigor and energy when selecting our Vice Presidents than when choosing Presidents.

IV

Succession By Election

Long before the advent of woman suffrage and the Nineteenth Amendment a great many of the wiser members of the male world began to suspect that masculine domination was more apparent than real. Maybe it was much more than the old adage, "The hand that rocks the cradle is the hand that rules the world." Women were profoundly influencing politics long before they were admitted to the voting booth.

If you doubt this, then go back to the reign of "King Andrew" Jackson, seventh President of the United States, and take a few notes on the history made by a vivacious and dashing female, one Peggy O'Neal, who had a generous assist from other influential females, the Cabinet wives.

It was not the cradle that Peggy rocked. She rocked the whole of official Washington, and she gave it such a shake as it has seldom or perhaps never experienced before or since. When the tremors had subsided South Carolina's John C. Calhoun, Vice President and Presidential hopeful, had been inundated and Martin Van Buren, astute New York politician, had been groomed well for a journey to the White House through the all but abandoned route of the Vice Presidency.

Van Buren possessed considerable ability, but certainly not nearly so much as some of the Vice Presidents who have remained entombed in the nation's second office. But he had an enormous amount of political sagacity, and he knew how to

59

take advantage of all the breaks. He got some very big ones by making skillful use of the excitement the lively Peggy afforded Washington society.

To understand the strange phenomenon that enabled Van Buren first to become Vice President and then to become the only post-Twelfth Amendment Vice President to break the jinx and advance to the Presidency by elective succession, it is necessary that we pry into the past personal affairs of President Andrew Jackson.

Old Andrew was nearly sixty-two when he took the oath of office as chief executive on March 4, 1829. It was his greatest hour of triumph, but his heart was bursting with grief and anger—grief over his wife Rachel, to whom he was devoted beyond words (for Rachel had died in the preceding December) and anger at all whom he suspected, and they were many, of questioning Rachel's good name. Her name was sacred to him. He had seen her suffer humiliation and chagrin from an innocent mistake in which he was equally involved.

Jackson had become acquainted with Rachel when, as a young attorney, he boarded in the home of her mother, the widow Donelson. Rachel was a charming young woman, a "black-eyed, black-haired brunette, as gay, bold and handsome a lass as ever danced on the deck of a flat boat." She was married to one Lewis Robards, an insanely jealous man who apparently couldn't stand to see any gentleman cast an admiring glance at Rachel.

From all accounts Rachel Robards was a young woman of fine character, but she had already found her husband's jealousy a most serious threat to their domestic tranquility. Rachel and Lewis had been separated for a while but were now undertaking a reconciliation. Suddenly Robards, apparently without reason, became suspicious of his wife and Jackson, left his wife and began proceedings for a divorce. He had married Rachel under Virginia law, so in order to secure a divorce he would have to get it under the laws of that State although he had now gone to Kentucky.

There was no general law in Virginia under which Robards could obtain the divorce. Under that state's procedures it was necessary that the state legislature pass an act authorizing a jury investigation of his allegations. The marriage would be declared dissolved only if the jury found his charges true. Robards charged before the Virginia legislature that his wife was living in adultery with Andrew Jackson. So the Virginia legislature obliged him by passing an act through which he could secure a dissolution of the marriage bond in a Kentucky court provided he could prove his charges to the satisfaction of a jury. The act was not a divorce decree or anything approximating one. It was merely the establishment of a procedure through which Robards could discharge himself from all marital obligations to Rachel.

News traveled slowly and often somewhat inaccurately in those days. When Andrew Jackson and Rachel Robards got the news they thought that it was a divorce decree. The fact that Robards had wrongfully suspected them both quite naturally brought Andrew and Rachel closer together. By the time they heard about the action of the Virginia legislature they were deeply in love. Now, thinking Rachel was free, the two were married. Then came the shock.

After they had been living together as man and wife for two years, news came that Robards had just secured his dissolution or divorce in a Kentucky court. Technically, Rachel Jackson had been guilty of bigamy for two years. Mr. and Mrs. Jackson were, of course, mortified when they heard the news. They remarried, but they both knew that gossipy tongues would wag about it for the rest of their days.

Andrew Jackson had deep anger in his heart. He was angry that his beloved Rachel, having been hurt by the blind jealousy of Lewis Robards, would have to be hurt again by the venomous addiction to scandal that always catches on with a large element of human society. It was a very dangerous thing for any man to cast reflections on Rachel in Jackson's presence. He shot and killed one man, Charles Dickinson, in a duel that was the result of an accumulation of matters, not the least of which was the fact that Dickinson had questioned the honor of Mrs. Jackson.

The most significant political result, however, was that the whole affair left Jackson reluctant to believe attacks on the honor of any woman. Now that Rachel was dead Jackson's disposition to defend the honor of maligned women, or those whom he thought maligned, was even more firmly fixed. The stage was perfectly set for the great drama of Peggy.

Just as Andrew Jackson was taking office as President the most sensational wave of gossip in the city's history hit the national capital. It all had to do with Peggy O'Neal and Andrew Jackson's incoming Secretary of War, Senator John H. Eaton of Tennessee. Peggy was the daughter of a Washington tavernkeeper. She was lively and attractive and certainly not overburdened with feminine modesty. Men were charmed by her and she enjoyed their attentions. She was "the sort of woman that men turn around to stare at and other women condemn on sight."

Peggy had been married to a Navy purser named Timberlake. Senator Eaton had lodged at the O'Neal tavern while Timberlake was there and undoubtedly was somewhat smitten by Peggy's charms. Eaton was a close friend of Jackson, in fact almost an adopted son. At a time when both were United States Senators Jackson had lodged with Eaton at the O'Neal tavern and had met Peggy. While Peggy was the wife of Timberlake the O'Neal tavern was sold for debt and Eaton purchased it. Some time later Timberlake committed suicide at sea, and gossip had it that he was depressed over the bad behavior of his wife and particularly over her relations with Senator Eaton.

Timberlake's death probably cannot be explained in such simple terms. He had got into some trouble over his accounts as purser, and it had been necessary for Eaton to contact the Secretary of the Navy in order that Timberlake could be sent out again. At any rate, shortly after Timberlake's death Senator Eaton married the notorious Peggy.

When John Eaton became Secretary of War in Jackson's Cabinet, the storm broke. Speaking of Mrs. Eaton, John Quincy Adams records in his famous diary that "her reputation was not in good odor." Well, whatever the odor, the Cabinet wives smelled a plenty and turned their noses up in contempt. Since Mrs. Jackson was dead and Andrew was having to depend on Mrs. Andrew Jackson Donelson, the wife of his nephew and private secretary, as hostess at the White House, Floride Calhoun, the wife of the Vice President, was regarded as leading lady in Washington society.

If Mrs. Calhoun had embraced Peggy Eaton it would doubtless have done much to place her in good standing. But Mrs. Calhoun did not accept her. Here accounts differ somewhat, but the majority have it that Mrs. Calhoun was the ring leader in ostracizing Mrs. Margaret Eaton. Calhoun's explanation was that his wife thought that those who knew Mrs. Eaton better should first make the decision to accept her. But whatever the case, Mrs. Calhoun did not accept her, and the Cabinet wives followed suit in the social blackballing.

Andrew Jackson was determined that official Washington was going to accept Mrs. Eaton. He loved John Eaton and had given him the green light to marry Peggy. And he was in no mood to see Mrs. Eaton snubbed by the wives of his official family. The memory of the injustices to his own dead wife was all too fresh in his mind. There was a striking parallel between his own situation and that of Eaton. He had known Mrs. Jackson while she was the wife of Robards, and Robards had suspected him. And Rachel Jackson as a young woman had had some of the same vivacious character as Peggy, though her morals were really above reproach and, in all probability, far superior to those of Mrs. Eaton.

At any rate Jackson wasn't going to have Peggy crucified by

people in his administration. The more Peggy was snubbed, the more determined he was. Recognition became a high and inexorable administration policy. Jackson blamed Calhoun and he blamed his Cabinet. He pressured them to set their wives straight on the matter. He threatened to send the Dutch minister back home because his wife would not sit by Mrs. Eaton. He even hailed two ministers of the gospel before his Cabinet and put on a ridiculous exhibition of arguing and haranguing them in an effort to convince his official family that Mrs. Eaton was being shamefully mistreated.

Old Andy was accustomed to winning. He had beaten the British at New Orleans, and he had beaten the Indians. He had beaten his opponents for the Presidency. But now he was matched against the most difficult foe he had ever faced. He was trying to bring women to terms, and they wouldn't budge an inch. Even his hostess, Mrs. Donelson, left the White House rather than give in and accept Mrs. Eaton. "King Andrew" was no more successful against the Cabinet dames than King Edward VIII or Princess Margaret Rose was when pitted against the royal family and the churchmen of England.

All this served to break the political fortunes of one man and to make those of another. The Democratic Party, which had superseded the old Democratic-Republican, was something of a divided kingdom. Andrew Jackson was President, and he had a multitudinous following. But Vice President John C. Calhoun, the tremendously able statesman from South Carolina, had a large following of his own—in fact such a following that it had been necessary for President Jackson to bring some Calhoun men into his Cabinet.

Jackson had let it be understood that he would not stand for re-election. Hence the raiment would fall on Calhoun.

Calhoun very much wanted to be President, but needed the magic word of President Jackson's recommendation. But Calhoun had a wife, and she would have nothing to do with Mrs. Eaton. This alone was enough to make the Vice President *persona non grata* to President Jackson. And other complications arose as well. Other Calhoun beans were spilled. The information came out that back in 1818, while Secretary of War in Monroe's Cabinet, Calhoun had favored disciplinary action against Jackson for his impetuous conduct in the Seminole War. This made Jackson furious, especially since he had thought up to now that Calhoun had defended him.

There was no hope left for Calhoun. Even if there had been, South Carolina's nullification movement would have erased it. But it should be observed that when Calhoun assumed the lead for nullification he knew that his hopes for the Presidency were about done for. Whether he would have taken a different stand with the Presidency within his grasp we cannot know.

While the Peggy Eaton affair was sealing the doom of Calhoun's ambitions, it was sewing up success for Martin Van Buren. Van Buren had supported Crawford over Jackson for President in 1824, but he had later joined the Jackson camp and had been the big wheel for Jackson in New York politics. He became Secretary of State in Jackson's first Cabinet. When the capital began to rock Van Buren was in a most advantageous spot, and he knew it gleefully. He had the draw on his chief rival, Calhoun. Van Buren was a widower and had no woman to give him his orders about Mrs. Eaton. He took pains to neglect no opportunity to pay his good respects to his colleague's wife and to arrange, in so far as possible, that other people would do so.

"Calhoun heads the moral party, Van Buren that of the frail sisterhood; and he is notoriously engaged in canvassing for the Presidency by paying court to Mrs. Eaton," wrote John Quincy Adams in his diary on February 6, 1830. All the while Van Buren, the only Cabinet member save Eaton himself to support Mrs. Eaton, was getting deeper and deeper into the affections of the President.

Van Buren played more cards with skill. The Cabinet had become hopelessly split over the Eaton affair and also over Jackson's break with Calhoun. Van Buren decided that it would be better if he resigned as Secretary of State in order to lead off in a general Cabinet reorganization. At first Jackson was unwilling to have him go, but the clever politician finally persuaded him that it was best for all concerned. So Van Buren resigned a few days after Eaton had. This made it easy for Jackson to ask for other resignations, which he did. Coming out with a new Cabinet, Jackson now made Eaton governor of Florida and nominated Van Buren as minister to England. Van Buren had already gone to England to take up his post there when the Senate acted on his nomination. The Senate vote was equally divided on the Van Buran confirmation, so the Vice President, as President of the Senate, had the deciding vote.

Calhoun, delighted at this opportunity to strike his adversary, voted against the confirmation, and the nomination failed. This defeat for Van Buren was really victory.

Van Buren's rejection by Calhoun and the Senate made Jackson more determined than ever to advance his favorite. On February 12, 1832, he wrote Van Buren a letter in which he significantly and prophetically said, "The people will properly resent the insult offered to the Executive, and the wound inflicted in our national character, and the injury intended to our foreign relations, in your rejection, by placing you in the chair of the very man whose casting vote rejected you." Jackson would probably have indicated the Presidency at this time for Van Buren, but he had now decided that he must remain for another term.

Jackson made good his word. He saw to it that Van Buren was nominated by the Democratic national convention as his running mate. The Jackson-Van Buren ticket won easily. Meanwhile Vice President Calhoun had resigned to take the lead in South Carolina's stand against the protective tariff. Jackson intended the Vice Presidency as only a temporary stand for Van Buren. The next stop would be the White House itself. And he saw to it that the Democrats nominated Van Buren, his faithful favorite, for President in their national convention at Baltimore in 1835. Van Buren won the election in 1836 and served one term as President. He was defeated for re-election in 1840 by William Henry Harrison, the Whig candidate.

Thus ends the story of the only Vice President since the Twelfth Amendment to rise from the political sepulcher of the Vice Presidency and advance by his own election to the Presidency. He was able to do it only because his clever strategy made President Andrew Jackson plan it that way. And for President Jackson's plans Van Buren owed a great debt of gratitude to Mrs. Margaret O'Neal Eaton. We cannot but conclude that the one case of succession by election from the Vice Presidency to the Presidency since the Twelfth Amendment was little less than accidental.

Succession By Death

As we have noted, since the adoption of the Twelfth Amendment in 1804 the ratio of Vice Presidents who have succeeded to the Presidency by election in their own right has been one to eighteen. But the chances have been much greater for a Vice President to succeed to the Presidency on the death of the incumbent.

In all there have been thirty-three Vice Presidents since the Twelfth Amendment. We should exclude Mr. Nixon, since it is too early to say whether he will succeed to the Presidency. So there have been thirty-two fair chances to succeed, though even this is subject to some question. Of the thirty-two, seven —or nearly twenty-two per cent—have succeeded on the death of the President. So the proportion of Vice Presidents to occupy the White House because the President has died has been a little more than one fifth.

It is very significant that the seven who did succeed deceased Presidents served terms averaging almost as long as if they had been elected to the office. The Presidents who died in office were elected for a total of twenty-eight years. But the Vice Presidents who replaced them actually served for twenty-three of those years or better than eighty per cent of that time. Or for nearly one seventh of the time since George Washington was inaugurated we have been under the Presidency of a person who came to that office through the death of its occupant.

If the voter stopped to think about such facts he might be more concerned about his party's Vice Presidential nominee.

We now take it for granted when a President dies in office that the Vice President will assume not only his function but also his title. But when John Tyler, in 1841, became the first Vice President to fill out the term of a dead President, his accession gave rise to heated argument over a very important point of Constitutional construction. The succession clause quoted before states:

In Case of the Removal of the President from Office, or of his Death, Resignation, or Inability to discharge the Powers and Duties of the said Office, the Same shall devolve on the Vice President, and the Congress may by Law provide for the Case of Removal, Death, Resignation, or Inability, both of the President and Vice President, declaring what Officer shall then act as President, and such Officer shall act accordingly, until the Disability be removed, or a President shall be elected.

Controversy arose primarily over the meaning of the expression, *the Same shall devolve*. Did "the Same" mean the office of President, or did it mean the immediate antecedent expression, "the Powers and Duties"? If it meant the former, then the Vice President succeeding a deceased President would become President. If it meant the latter, the Vice President would only act as President. As we have seen, there was very little debate in the Constitutional Convention over the office of Vice President. So the records give us no positive answer which construction was meant.

Resolving this point meant a great deal in 1841, both to those who wanted clarification of the Constitution and to those who wanted to gratify partisan political ambitions. A brief review of history will help us to understand the significance of the debate.

The Whig Party, which assembled in national convention in Harrisburg, Pennsylvania, in December 1839, to prepare for the election of 1840, was a strangely mongrel political association. Its cohesiveness was so delicate that to undertake to agree on principles of public policy would have been too explosive. It had just one common denominator and no more: opposition to Andrew Jackson. It has been suggested that a more accurate name would have been the Anti-Jackson Party. Its membership included Adams Republicans, Nullifiers, Anti-Masons—in fact every element that could be rallied to the attack on the current administration.

The outstanding name as a possibility for the Presidential candidate was Henry Clay of Kentucky. But Clay was a Freemason, and he had pronounced and known views in favor of a protective tariff. To nominate him would have been to risk an explosive disruption of the party. Clay seemed to sense this. In a letter to the Kentucky delegation he announced his willingness to abide by the decision if the party nominated someone else.

The Whigs adopted no platform at all. They were so heterogeneous that they couldn't without losing their following. The convention passed up the able but controversial Clay and turned to a war hero whose views on public matters were not too well known—General William Henry Harrison, the hero of Tippecanoe. Harrison was already nearing his sixty-seventh birthday and would be past sixty-eight when inaugurated. But we had had good luck. Vice Presidents had died in office, but not Presidents. The Presidency was a charm.

For Harrison's running mate the Whig convention chose John Tyler of Virginia, a former United States Senator and former governor of Virginia. Tyler had little in common with Henry Clay. He was really a dissident Democrat. He was a stanch states' rights man and would have still been a Democrat but for the fact that he had broken with Jackson over the National Bank and the latter's vigorous opposition to nullification. The fact that all Tyler really had in common with the rest of the Whigs was his anti-Jackson stand wouldn't matter, for he would be placed in the innocuous position of Vice President, and he would pull a lot of Democrats into the Whig camp. He was a perfect ticket-balancing candidate.

Since they couldn't deal in principles, the Whigs put on a great song and dance and parade campaign. They showed pictures of log cabins and rolled out barrels of hard cider. They held picnics and barbecues. "Tippecanoe and Tyler Too" was their motto, and they won with it. The Democrats had renominated Van Buren without agreeing on his running mate. Harrison and Tyler won handily and brought in Whig Congressional majorities.

The Whigs got Old Tippecanoe, but they were to have him in the White House for just one month. They got "Tyler Too," but not according to plan. They intended to see him safely secluded in the Vice Presidency for four years, but the death of President Harrison on April 4, 1841, put Tyler in the White House for three years and eleven months.

When Tyler became the tenth President of the United States in this manner, the government was in for rough sailing. Tyler, being really an anti-Jackson Democrat rather than a Whig, differed with the Whig majority in Congress, led by Henry Clay. Tyler was not a brilliant man, but he was nobody's cream-puff. He had solid convictions and he stood by them, brandishing his veto in the face of the Whig majority, particularly on bank bills. His behavior caused such a row as has seldom been known in Washington. All Tyler's Cabinet except Daniel Webster resigned, and leading Whigs accused Tyler of betraying the party. Needless to say, Tyler was not renominated in 1844, and the party fuss made it easier for the Democrats, with James K. Polk and George M. Dallas, to win the election.

But the important point to remember is that when John Tyler was hastily summoned from Williamsburg, Virginia, to Washington on the death of President Harrison, he thought he had become President. And though he believed his oath of office as Vice President enabled him to occupy the Presidency, he took no chances. He took the Presidential oath.

But the Whig Congress had another view of Tyler's status. Before his death President Harrison had issued a call for a special session to convene on May 31. Congress convened all right, but it now had to deal with John Tyler, not William Henry Harrison. On June 1, 1841, this message from the House was received in the Senate:

Resolved, that a committee be appointed on the part of this House, to join such committee as may be appointed on the part of the Senate, to wait on the President of the United States, and to inform him that a quorum of the two houses is assembled, and that Congress is now ready to receive any communication he may be pleased to make.

Senator Jabez W. Huntington, a Whig from Connecticut, moved that the Senate concur in the above resolution, making it a joint resolution of both houses. Democratic Senator William Allen of Ohio moved that the resolution be amended by striking out the words "President of the United States" and inserting instead the words, "the Vice President, on whom, by the death of the late President, the powers and duties of the office of President have devolved."

In the ensuing debate Senator Allen assured the Senate that he meant no offense to Mr. Tyler and that he would not wish to interfere with his powers. He said he assumed that the Congress would go ahead and vote Mr. Tyler the same salary he would get if he really were President. He pointed out, however, that the clause cited above " . . . classified all the contingencies under which the Vice President shall discharge the duties and exercise the powers of President, and it made no distinction whatever between removal by death and removal by a temporary inability to discharge the functions of the Presidential office."

Allen feared that if it were decided that the Vice President succeeding by death became President rather than merely acting President, a future Vice President might undertake to oust a President by taking over his duties during a temporary illness and then asserting that he had become President. Senator Allen's point could not be laughed off. Suppose, he argued, that we come on a time of bitter partisan rivalry, with the two parties about equally strong. Suppose further that, at the time, the President is a member of one party and the Vice President is a member of the other. The President becomes temporarily ill, whereupon the Vice President takes over his powers and duties. Later the President recovers and undertakes to resume his functions. The Vice President might then assert that he had become President. Allen dreaded that Congress might set a precedent that would allow this to happen.

Senator Huntington countered that he presumed every member of the Senate to have made up his mind and to be prepared to vote without further debate. Even at that early day, apparently, it was becoming evident that debate on the floor seldom changes a vote.

Senator Robert J. Walker, a Mississippi Democrat, opposed the Allen amendment. He thought Mr. Tyler had become the President and saw a significant distinction between the first part of the succession clause and the rest. In the first contingency, the death of the President, he thought the office of President would devolve on the Vice President. He thought "the said Office" and not "the Powers and Duties of the said Office" was the real immediate antecedent and that therefore the words "the Same" refer to the "said Office." But in the second contingency, according to Senator Walker, where there is neither President nor Vice President to serve, the clause makes a clear distinction: that an officer designated by law "shall act accordingly." This officer would merely be acting as President.

Senator Calhoun observed that since none of the circumstances existed as supposed there was no point in further discussion.

In the end the Allen amendment was beaten by a vote of thirty-eight to eight, a rather decisive margin. The original motion was then adopted, and the joint committee appointed to wait on "the President of the United States." A very important precedent had been set. Since then six other Vice Presidents have succeeded to the Presidency in the same manner as did Tyler. Every one of them has regarded himself President, and the country has accepted this status. The language of both the Twentieth and the Twenty-second

Amendments bolsters this view, though it doesn't nail it down as a settled Constitutional point. It is doubtful that the matter is open to question now, however legitimately debatable it was in the beginning.

In 1844 the Whigs named Henry Clay their candidate for President, and they were not successful. In 1848 they had another aged general in readiness, and they took him. They nominated General Zachary Taylor, hero of the Mexican War and the battle of Buena Vista. If elected, he would be nearing his sixty-fifth birthday on inaugural day and would be nearly sixty-nine at the end of his term. They nominated as his running mate a person with some ability but no extraordinarily conspicuous talents—Millard Fillmore of New York. The Whig ticket won, but again death struck a Whig President. General Taylor died on July 9, 1850, having been in office for a little more than a year and four months. For the second time a person whom no one intended for the office of President went to the White House. Millard Fillmore became the thirteenth President of the United States.

What sort of person was this second accidental President? There is not much to be said. He certainly had some admirable qualities. He had started life as a farm boy in a very poor New York family. His opportunities for formal education had been practically nonexistent, but he was ambitious and persistent and acquired a good bit of learning by his own efforts. For any person with as little opportunity as Fillmore to rise to the Presidency in any way on earth was quite an achievement. But it is better that we should not go into the history of his administration.

It was not conspicuously bad or conspicuously good. The country drifted along ever nearer to the great conflict of 1861-1865. The cleavages were getting sharper. We needed in the White House a man of decision and extraordinary ability. Instead we had a man of extreme caution and little more than moderate ability. When the time came to prepare for the election of 1852, Fillmore was not an old man. He was fifty-two. Certainly age did not bar his way to another term in the White House. But his party did not nominate him. He had served as a passable spare when Taylor expired, and that was about all. The Whigs went back to their old ways and nominated another old soldier, General Winfield Scott, who was sixty-six years old. This time the old soldier charm failed. Franklin Pierce, the Democratic candidate, paired with William R. King, won rather easily.

History has been neither harsh nor generous with Fillmore. It has mostly ignored him. Had he not become President there would be scarcely a line about him in the history of the nation. Had he not become Vice President, he would never have become President. And had it not been a matter of expediency at the Whig convention to throw out a small consolation prize to the Clay following in 1848 Fillmore would never have become Vice President.

Andrew Johnson, the sixteenth Vice President and the seventeenth President of the United States, provides us a true life story as amazing as any Horatio Alger or any of his kind could invent. Born in a very poor but respectable North Carolina family, fatherless after the age of three and with a mother who could neither read nor write, Andrew Johnson never had the chance to go to school a single day in his whole life. He was apprenticed at an early age to a tailor, learned that trade and at the same time learned a great deal from educated people who frequented the tailoring shop.

Moving to Tennessee with his people, he became a tailor at Greenville. He was scarcely twenty years old when he married Eliza McCardle, and this fine young woman set out to teach her husband to read and write. Eliza did a good job— such a good job that her husband eventually managed to become President of the United States.

As a plebeian Democrat, Andrew Johnson was always interested in politics, and at an early age he took a plunge of his own. This unschooled tailor came up the hard way, from city councilman to mayor to the state legislature, and then on from there to the United States House of Representatives and to the office of governor of Tennessee. Remembering his own struggle to acquire learning, he became, as governor, a strong champion of a more effective system of public education. In 1857 he went to the United States Senate and held a seat there when secession and Civil War descended on the nation. All other Senators from the seceding states went with the Confederacy. Andrew Johnson had a hard decision to make. The rift in the Union was so severe that one with good conscience and honor could go in either direction. Johnson made his decision and stayed with the Union. President Lincoln made him military governor of Tennesee, and he was serving in that capacity when preparations got under way for the election of 1864.

When the Republican national convention met at Baltimore on June 7, 1864, in accordance with the views of President Lincoln it did not call itself a Republican convention. It needed a broader base, so it met as a National Union convention. There were War Democrats at the convention who were not ready to affiliate with a Republican Party but were eager to work with a Union Party. Abraham Lincoln was renominated for President. There were some anti-Lincoln delegates, particularly from Missouri, but in the end they gave in and made Lincoln's nomination unanimous. The big question, of course, was the selection of a Vice Presidential candidate. Without playing an open and dictatorial hand President Lincoln appears to have worked behind the scenes for Andrew Johnson. He had great respect for Johnson and felt it would give the party the broadest possible national base to put on the ticket a Southern "Democrat for the Union." While there was opposition to Johnson, his nomination was finally made unanimous. Andrew Johnson's own analysis of the result demonstrates excellently his political acumen. "What will the aristocrats do with a rail-splitter for President and a tailor for Vice-President?" he asked.

As inauguration time approached Andrew Johnson was in Tennessee, weak from overwork and ill with fever. He didn't feel up to the trip to Washington, so he wrote to the office of the secretary of the Senate to find out whether it was necessary for him to be there for the inauguration. The reply was that several Vice Presidents had been sworn in after the inauguration of the President. But President Lincoln both wrote and wired Johnson that he wished him to be present. Johnson, though very weak from his spell of typhoid fever, complied. He made the trip to Washington, where on the day before the inauguration he attended a party given in his honor by the secretary of the Senate.

There was plenty of wine at the party, and Johnson may have taken on too much for his weakened condition. The next day, March 4, he was very shaky. He went up to the Senate to be sworn in as Vice President. According to accounts he had taken no intoxicants that morning, but when he got to the Capitol he didn't feel equal to what was ahead of him. He was still very weak from his illness. Going up to Vice President Hannibal Hamlin's office, he complained that he needed something to drink. Hamlin sent for whisky or brandy, and Johnson took a few drinks.

A little later, with the Senate galleries packed with dignitaries, Hamlin administered the oath of office to Andrew Johnson. Johnson then proceeded to address the august gathering without a manuscript. It was clear to the audience that he was drunk. He uttered some of the greatest truths ever delivered to the Senate, and his intoxication completely emancipated him from all impediments of decorum.

Johnson had come up from nothing to the second office in the nation. He believed that this country was a great nation for making such a rise as his possible, and he appreciated it from the bottom of his heart. That a poor boy could climb the ladder to success in this Union was one of the big reasons for his decision to stand by it when secession came. Now he made a good speech, but at the wrong time and in the wrong way.

"Deem me not vain or arrogant," he said, "yet I should be less than a man if under such circumstances I were not proud of being an American citizen, for today one who claims no high descent, one who comes from the ranks of the people,

stands, by the choice of a free constituency, in the second place
of this Government." He continued, "The people, in short, are
the source of all power." He vigorously reminded the Senators
and the bench of the Supreme Court that they were " . . . but
the creatures of the American people."

He poured on his belief in popular sovereignty with even
more force. "You, Mr. Secretary Seward, Mr. Secretary
Stanton, the Secretary of the Navy, and the others who are
your associates—you know that you have my respect and confidence—derive not your greatness and your power alone
from President Lincoln. Humble as I am, Plebeian as I may
be deemed, permit me in the presence of this brilliant assem-
blage to enunciate the truth that courts and cabinets, the
President and his advisors, derive their power and their greatness from the people."

Then a pretty pointed suggestion of his views on reconstruction came out. He proclaimed proudly that his own state
of Tennessee had become loyal once more. "She has bent the
tyrant's rod, she has broken the yoke of slavery, and today
she stands redeemed. She waited not for the exercise of power
by Congress; it was her own act, and she is as loyal, Mr.
Attorney General, as is the state from which you come." No
state could withdraw from the Union, he declared, and "Congress cannot eject a state from this Union." He proudly announced that soon Tennessee's Representatives and Senators
would be back in that body.

Of course Johnson's inebriation became the talk of Wash-
ington. The Senate was greatly perturbed both by the affront
Johnson had offered its dignity and by concern for its reputa-
tion. On the Monday following the Saturday inauguration of
Lincoln and Johnson, the prohibition movement hit the
Senate. Let the *Globe* tell the story, for it is very brief.

Mr. Wilson. I submit the following resolution. I do not
propose to call it up for action today, but shall do so to-
morrow:
Resolved, That the Sergeant-at-Arms be, and he is hereby,
directed to remove forthwith from so much of the Capitol as

is under his care all intoxicating liquors, and hereafter to exclude liquors in every form from the Senate portion of the Capitol.

Mr. Sumner. Why not consider it at once?

Mr. Wilson. I did not know but that some Senators might wish time to consider it. I am ready to act upon it.

Mr. Pomeroy. I am ready.

By unanimous consent a vote was then taken, and the resolution passed. So it was that prohibition conquered the Senate in a matter of moments—and all because one sick man took a little too much on an empty stomach. Needless to say it was a most inauspicious start for Vice President Johnson. Every thirsty Senator would from then on blame him for the enforced abstinence. But Johnson was not to impose his presence on the unhappy lot very long. He went out to Silver Springs to recuperate until the short special session of the Senate was over on March 11.

He never had to preside over the Senate again, for in the early morning of April 15, 1865, President Lincoln died from the wounds John Wilkes Booth had inflicted the night before at Ford's Theatre. A few hours later Andrew Johnson took the oath of office as the seventeenth President of the United States.

The Republican national convention of 1880, meeting in Chicago, was a wide-open affair. President Hayes had previously made a pledge that he would not be a candidate for a second term. The Stalwart wing of the party, led by Roscoe Conkling, was booming General Grant. The general appeared perfectly willing to go back to Washington for a third term if the country so desired. The so-called Half-Breeds wanted James G. Blaine nominated. In the end the nomination for President went to Congressman James A. Garfield of Ohio, a dark horse. As a consolation prize to the Stalwarts Chester A. Arthur of New York, famed machine politician, was nominated for Vice President. The Republican ticket won.

Hardly had President Garfield taken the oath of office when the patronage miseries besieged him. Dealing with office seekers had become an ever-increasing burden on the President. Civil-service reform was being agitated by those who favored efficiency over party spoils. The reformers had great hope that they might gain support from President Garfield. In the early days of his administration Garfield found himself in a patronage fight with Conkling and his Stalwarts. Vice President Arthur was more inclined to support his old machine pals, the Stalwarts.

Garfield complained that he had to take up so much time deciding whether this person or that would be rewarded with an office that he didn't have enough time to consider public policy. William Starr Myers relates that one day President Garfield came out of his office and said to one of his children, "When I am gone, always be fair to the President. He is the last person in the country to know what the people really want and think. Not a person comes to see me but has some axe to grind or some personal favor to ask."

President Garfield had been President for scarcely four months, struggling with patronage problems for a large part of the time, when he went to the Pennsylvania Railroad Station in Washington to board a train for Williamstown. He was planning to attend the commencement exercises of his alma mater, Williams College. As Garfield waited at the station, Charles J. Guiteau, a somewhat deranged disappointed office seeker, shot him, shouting "I am a Stalwart, Arthur is now President of the United States." Garfield lived for several weeks but finally succumbed, on September 19, 1881. His death made Chester A. Arthur the twenty-first President of the United States.

The hour seemed dark indeed for the reformers. Chester Arthur had been a thoroughgoing spoilsman and machine man. He had held but one federal job—collector of customs of the port of New York. Though he had probably not been personally dishonest, he had so used his position for patronage and had so padded his payroll that President Hayes had removed him from his post in 1878. Arthur had certainly been kicked upstairs now. He was occupying the same position from which the order for his removal had come.

Civil service reformers, of course, used the dreadful tragedy of President Garfield's assassination by an office seeker as a dramatic argument for reducing spoils in filling federal positions. But they had to deal with an old, experienced spoilsman in President Arthur.

Still, there seems to be something about the Presidency that brings out the best one has to offer for his country. President Arthur went a long way on the path urged by the reformers. During his administration an act designed for civil service reform, sponsored by Senator George H. Pendleton, Ohio Democrat, passed both houses of Congress. It was a bipartisan measure, with Republicans and Democrats alike supporting it. President Arthur signed the bill.

The Pendleton Act, as the public generally knows, is the very heart of our merit system. It brought under the merit system only a small portion of the federal payroll, but it authorized the President to extend the list of merit appointees from time to time. Though it has been supplemented with other statutes, it is still the basic law.

President Arthur not only signed the act, but also gave it administrative support. The President was to appoint three members of a Civil Service Commission, of which no more than two could belong to the same political party. By appointing so-called practical politicians not in sympathy with the merit system to the Commission he could have robbed the reformers of victory. But as the first Chairman he appointed Dorman B. Eaton, a pioneer in the reform movement who had served as secretary of the Civil Service Reform Association. Senator Pendleton, the father of the law, wanted to select the Democratic member. He recommended a young lawyer, Leroy D. Thoman of Ohio. President Arthur accepted the recommendation and appointed Thoman. For the third position Arthur named his old college friend John M. Gregory.

This is not to imply that President Arthur completely forgot his old comrades the Stalwarts. At times he did lean in their direction. But it must be said that considering his background, he did surprisingly well. Nevertheless the Republican Party did not nominate him for President in 1884. The party liberals could not forget his machine past, and the regulars were displeased by his treatment of their legislation, especially his veto of a pork-barrel rivers and harbors bill.

So far we have observed all sorts of ticket-balancing techniques, geographic and otherwise, at work in determining the party nominee for Vice President. John Tyler's selection was a bid for the votes of dissident followers of another party. Andrew Johnson was picked to give the ticket a broader national balance. Chester Arthur was named as a consolation prize to a strong disappointed faction of the party.

Now we come to the most amazing case of all—a case of cold, calculated, premeditated conspiracy for the political exile of a governor who did not suit the big corporations bossing the big political bosses of New York State. In ancient Greece when a rising political star seriously threatened the leading politicos' hold in the council they got a state decree of exile against him and sent him beyond the border. This, of course, could not be done so openly in America—not even in New York. But there was a way, if the political bigwigs would take on the role of political undertakers and ply the trade with skill and cunning. All they had to do was to measure their man carefully for a ready-made vault in the political cemetery the Constitution obligingly provided. To understand this analogy thoroughly we need to look at both the situation and the man.

The situation is the simplest to explain. When the Republican national convention of 1900 met in Philadelphia, there was no great problem about a Presidential nominee. President William McKinley was serving his first term. He would undoubtedly be renominated for President. But Vice President Garrett A. Hobart had died in office, creating a propitious opening on the ticket.

Now we had best look at the measured man. Theodore Roosevelt was able and vigorous, and he was giving plenty of headaches to the machine of Senator Thomas C. Platt, the big Republican boss whose rank in the party high command of New York State was somewhat comparable to that of the Democrats' Tammany king, Boss Richard Croker. Theodore Roosevelt was a battler and had been all his life. He had won his boyhood fight against physical weakness and had developed into a pretty durable man. He was a Harvard graduate, but he didn't mind getting on the ground floor with the common masses in the political organizations.

He had served for a time as a member of the United States Civil Service Commission and had infused new life into that body. He had been president of the Board of Police Commissioners of New York and had gained favorable publicity for his good work in suppressing corruption and raising efficiency in the police force. He had been Assistant Secretary of the Navy and had applied his usual energy to that post. He had distinguished himself further as leader of his Rough Riders in the Spanish-American War. Now he was governor of New York.

Roosevelt knew Boss Platt all right. In fact Platt had helped to make him Governor, not because he particularly wanted Roosevelt, but rather because he had figured that the party would win the state with Roosevelt at the head of the ticket. Platt thought Theodore would be a little softer touch than he proved to be after getting into office. On the surface it seemed that Teddie and Platt were making out all right. They often had breakfast together. But the governor was actually refusing to allow Platt to determine what appointments should be handed out. More disturbing than this, Governor Roosevelt had insisted that corporations should pay their fair share of the state taxes. That was rank heresy. The corporations put the pressure on Platt and his machine, and the bosses had to do some planning. They saw that empty place on the Republican national ticket—the Vice Presidency, just what the doctor ordered. Platt's crowd would have to sell the idea to some

influential political guardsmen from other states, but that
wouldn't be so difficult. After all, Theodore Roosevelt was
only forty-two years old. He was dangerous, and if he weren't
put into seclusion right away he might in the near future break
out of New York and become President. Then he would be
everybody's problem.

Interestingly enough, Theodore Roosevelt knew he was
being measured by the Platt crowd, and he knew why. They
simply wanted to get him out of New York politics. Roosevelt
didn't enjoy the prospect of being their victim. If Platt was to
succeed he would have to get a fairly early start. Roosevelt's
correspondence reveals that he understood Platt's motives and
that Teddie knew he would not fit well into the Vice Presidency. Writing to Henry Cabot Lodge on January 22, 1900,
Roosevelt mentioned the fact that Platt had just urged him to
take the Vice Presidency and then remarked, "I believe Platt
likes me, though I render him uncomfortable by some of the
things I do."

This would appear to be a most correct presumption. On
February 1 he wrote Platt, "I can't help feeling more and
more that the Vice-Presidency is not an office in which I
could do anything and not an office in which a man who is
still vigorous and not past middle life has much chance
of doing anything." He would be a mere presiding officer,
" . . . and that I should find a bore."

By February 3 Roosevelt fully understood the situation. On
that day he wrote Senator Lodge, "I have found out one
reason why Senator Platt wants me nominated for the Vice-
Presidency. He is I am convinced, genuinely friendly, and indeed I think I may say really fond of me, and is personally
satisfied with the way I have conducted politics: but the big-
monied men with whom he is in close touch and whose campaign contributions have certainly been no inconsiderable
factor in his strength, have been pressing him very strongly
to get me put in the Vice Presidency, so as to get me out of the
State. It was the big insurance companies, possessing enormous
wealth, that gave Payne his formidable strength, and they to a

man want me out. The great corporations affected by the franchise tax have also been at the Senator. . . . I find that they have been at Platt for the last two or three months and he has finally begun to yield to them and to take their view."

When convention time came Teddie was a delegate from New York. He had consistently refused to give the green light to the Platt crowd to put him up for Vice President. But Platt had by this time won over enough bosses from other states to make it a matter of little moment whether New York sponsored Roosevelt or not. In fact, by convention time things had got completely out of hand so far as Theodore Roosevelt was concerned. Rank and file delegates who wanted a new and more vigorous spirit in the party joined in the clamor for Roosevelt, unwittingly playing the role the big wheels had designated for them. Theodore Roosevelt had resisted the imprecations of the bosses, but he couldn't turn a deaf ear to the call of the masses. He accepted the nomination.

On March 4, 1901, Theodore Roosevelt became the twenty-fifth Vice President of the United States. He presided over the Senate for just one week in its extra session—not long enough for him to get bored. He said he enjoyed that week but that doubtless he would get tired of it in the future.

The great Platt plan was working fine. Theodore Roosevelt was out of New York politics and in a safe position. He was pleasantly and humanely entombed in the Vice Presidency. Then a man named Leon Czolgosz, until then unknown and unimportant, came along and spoiled all the plans. On September 6, 1901, this anarchist shot President William McKinley at Buffalo, New York. McKinley lingered on a few days but died on September 14.

So Theodore Roosevelt became the twenty-sixth President of the United States. The vigorous New York battler, though grieved at the President's death, had now broken out of exile. Czolgosz with his pistol had produced the funeral of one and the resurrection of another. The carefully sealed tomb had been opened, and Theodore Roosevelt stepped forth to become one of the ablest of all our Presidents.

If past precedent was to be followed, then Theodore Roosevelt would merely serve as the spare tire to run in on until March 4, 1905, when he would be replaced by someone elected in his own right. All four of the other Vice Presidents who had reached the Presidency on the death of the incumbent had been set aside as soon as they finished out the deceased Presidents' terms. Nothing would have pleased the bosses better than to cook up the same deal for Theodore Roosevelt. But their plans had no chance to work out.

The new President captured the imagination of the people. He gave them action. He attacked monopoly by more vigorous application of the Sherman Anti-Trust Act. He secured legislation strengthening the hand of the Interstate Commerce Commission in dealing with the railroads. He made conservation of the nation's resources a major project. He got rights to the Panama Canal by methods that could hardly be termed immaculately ethical, but the country knew that whatever he did sprang from his patriotism and not from selfish ambition.

When the Republican national convention of 1904 met at Chicago the conservative wing of the party wrote the platform, but the progressive wing won the Presidential nomination. Theodore Roosevelt was nominated by acclamation, with Charles W. Fairbanks of Indiana as his running mate. In American politics the candidate has meant much more than the platform, so we would have to say that the progressive element of the party got the better of it.

Theodore Roosevelt served another vigorous term as President, saw to it that his anointed successor, William Howard Taft, was safely established in the White House, and then set sail for Africa to hunt big game. By 1912 Roosevelt was badly dissatisfied with the way things had been handled by President Taft, his adopted political son. He tried to win the nomination for a third term for himself, but the Taft crowd was in control of the Republican convention and renominated him. Roosevelt therefore led a third party, the Progressive or Bull Moose ticket, with Hiram Johnson of California. Of course Roosevelt and Johnson lost, but they did defeat Taft and enable

Woodrow Wilson, the Democratic condidate, to become President. Theodore Roosevelt remained a force to be reckoned with right up to the time of his death, on January 6, 1919. Few will deny that he was one of our greatest Presidents, however accidental was his reaching the White House.

As the presidential contest of 1920 neared, political diagnosticians of both major parties undertook to feel the public pulse. That pulse had been going at a rather high rate for nearly eight years. Changes of party administration, efforts at neutrality, war, with all its idealism and its practical ugliness, and the thorny problems of peace had all been packed in that period. All the while the people had enjoyed or suffered or tolerated a scintillating brilliance adulterated with a touch of unfortunate vanity and a dearth of tact emanating from the White House, occupied by the once vigorous but now broken Woodrow Wilson. Apparently the people were a bit fed up on brilliance and wanted to slow down to a pace of serene normalcy.

Both parties sensed this feeling and, to some extent, accommodated themselves to it. The Democrats nominated Governor James M. Cox of Ohio for President and Franklin D. Roosevelt, Assistant Secretary of the Navy, for Vice President. The head man on the ticket had considerable ability, but he was not likely to exhibit anything like Mr. Wilson's offensive brilliance. The second man didn't matter much anyway. Usually the Vice President has little opportunity to exhibit extraordinary talents even if he possesses them.

The Republicans performed the more masterful job. They took no chance on extra intellectuality from either end of the ticket. They nominated Senator Warren G. Harding of Ohio for President and Governor Calvin Coolidge of Massachusetts for Vice President. As far as they were concerned the country would be thoroughly insured, two deep, against the White House's being occupied by anyone with any appreciable taint of intellectualism.

Senator Harding had few enemies for the simple reason that

he had taken few firm stands. He was not regarded as a heavy-weight by his fellow Senators. With him in the White House Congress would be safe from any spirited executive intrusion into legislative matters. Governor Coolidge doubtless would have passed off the stage without national attention as most other governors do had it not been for his cryptic statement during the Boston police strike of 1919— that nobody has a right to strike against the public safety. How much Mr. Coolidge had to do with the suppression of the police strike is a matter of disagreement, but in the public mind he got credit for it.

Let no one infer that Mr. Coolidge is presented here as a weak man. He had considerable ability and much practical good sense. He graduated from Amherst College *cum laude*. He had a great deal of political experience. He had served as Mayor of Northampton, Massachusetts, as a member of the Massachusetts legislature and as lieutenant governor and governor of Massachusetts. But if he possessed brilliance he certainly managed to remain silent enough to prevent many very discerning people from discovering it. It has been very difficult for political observers both in his own day and since to evaluate Mr. Coolidge's aptitudes and abilities.

At any rate, on March 4, 1921, Calvin Coolidge was sworn in as the twenty-ninth Vice President of the United States. While the Vice Presidency would have been, to use his own words, a bore to a man of Theodore Roosevelt's temperament, the inactivity didn't bother Mr. Coolidge. He found presiding over the Senate a fascinating duty.

But destiny had a different role for this undramatic person. And he was to begin that role in such a dramatic way that his career began to assume the character of legend from the very first moment that he became President. At shortly after mid-night August 3, 1923, he was in bed in his father's farm home in the little village of Plymouth, Vermont, when he heard his father coming up the stairs and calling his name. Newsmen had arrived saying that President Harding had passed away. Calvin Coolidge's father was the first person to address him as

President of the United States. After getting confirmation of the news from Washington, there in his father's home Calvin Coolidge found a copy of the Constitution, located the pre-scribed oath of office for the President and took the oath by the light of a kerosene lamp in the sitting room. His father, in his capacity as a Vermont notary public, administered the oath.

Mr. Coolidge served the balance of the Harding term. The country was prosperous, and he was extremely popular. In 1924 the Republican party nominated him for President. Sharing the ticket with Charles G. Dawes of Illinois, he won easily. In 1928 he was still popular. Had he made a serious effort he could possibly have been nominated and elected to a third term. He never did state positively that he would under no circumstances accept the nomination, but with his char-acteristic brevity he made the celebrated statement, "I do not choose to run." The party took him at his word and nominated Herbert Hoover, who was elected, with Senator Charles Curtis of Kansas as his Vice President.

On January 3, 1935, Harry S. Truman, escorted by his Missouri colleague, Senator Bennett Clark, walked up to the Vice President's desk and took the oath of office as the junior United States Senator from Missouri. No one had the slightest notion that in just a little more than ten years this man would be inaugurated President of the United States. Had Mr. Truman risen no higher than the Senate he would doubtless have felt quite content with his position. The new Missouri Senator had been raised a farm boy. He had finished high school but didn't go on to college. According to his own account he was ambitious for an appointment to West Point or Annapolis but was thwarted in this by his poor eyesight. After he finished high school, he worked at several jobs, including one as time-keeper for a railroad company. He undoubtedly acquired some of his sympathy for the working man at this time. He says that in this job he lived in hobo camps and learned what it meant " . . . to work ten hours a day for $1.50, or fifteen cents an hour." He also worked in the mailing room of the Kansas City *Star* and as a bookkeeper in a bank. In World War I he saw overseas service as a Captain of Field Artillery.

Returning to civilian life in 1919, Harry Truman married Bess Wallace and went into the men's furnishing business with his friend Eddie Jacobson. After the business failed, in 1922, Truman was elected a judge of the Jackson County court, in those days more an administrative than a judicial agency. Though in his campaign he had Pendergast support, he contends that his whole course was honorable and that he participated in no machine corruption. And there seems to be no reason to doubt his words.

Anyone familiar with the operation of big-city machines will attest to innumerable evils inhering in them but will recognize also that they arose largely out of society's default. In the years of rugged individualism society frowned on social security measures until they were long past due. The big-city machines stepped into the breach and supplied a kind of under-the-table social security, meeting a definite need but meeting it in a *sub rosa* and unwholesome way. The machines did not sponsor only dishonest men. If every person they put into power had been from the underworld the public would have swept the machines from power. To assume that every person who had the support of the powerful machines of the Pendergast vintage was a crook would be to brand unfairly many capable and honest public servants.

It should be said here that when finally, in 1939, old Tom Pendergast was indicted and entered a plea of guilty on the charge of income tax evasion nothing pointed toward any guilt on the part of Mr. Truman. Many people, among them Jonathan Daniels, who have carefully studied the machine have asserted that Truman's innocence is above question. But the affair did bring out one of Truman's most characteristic traits —whether we like it or not—never to run out on a friend. When he heard the news of Pendergast's indictment, he said, "Pendergast has been my friend when I needed it. I am not one to desert a ship when it starts to go down." This statement, made by Truman when he was a United States Senator, might have proved fatal to his political career.

Harry Truman was defeated for re-election as county judge in 1924 but made a comeback in 1926, when he was elected presiding judge of the county court. Meantime he had entered evening classes at Kansas City Law School. Now larger horizons began to open. In 1934 he was elected, again with Pendergast support, to the United States Senate. He was re-elected in 1940. During this second term in the Senate he became nationally known as chairman of a Senate committee investigating defense production.

Then came the Democratic national convention of 1944. Everyone assumed that Roosevelt would be nominated for a fourth term, even though the strain of three terms under trying conditions had worn him badly. Henry Wallace was Vice President, but the more conservative elements of the party, particularly those from below the Mason-Dixon line, opposed him stubbornly. It was not easy to find someone who would suit FDR and labor and the South and the conservatives. In the end the Vice Presidential raiment fell on Harry Truman.

As the thirty-fourth Vice President of the United States Harry Truman sought to bring the executive and the Congress into closer harmony. Whether he would have succeeded we can never know. At about five o'clock on the afternoon of April 12, 1945, he was summoned to the White House, where Mrs. Roosevelt told him of the President's death.

In this way Harry Truman learned that he had just become the thirty-third President of the United States. He entered upon a time of great trouble. The San Francisco Conference to plan the United Nations Organization was already scheduled, and it must go on. The atomic age would soon break forth. The problems of peace and the cold war with the Soviet Union were around the corner. How Truman met them is not our purpose to debate. Mr. Truman is still a controversial figure. But without trying to take away any of the fame of the late President Franklin D. Roosevelt, we must observe that death came at the moment most propitious to perpetuate his fame. Had he survived he would shortly have faced the problems of peace and reconstruction, and they always bring more controversy than do war efforts.

When a country is struggling on the battlefield it must muffle political animosities and partisan complaint. Once a war is over, however, all these suppressed animosities break out with intensified fury. It was so after the Civil War. It was so after World War I, and it was again to be so after World War II. Mr. Roosevelt, had he lived, would have faced many of the Congressional criticisms now to be directed at the administration of Harry Truman. That Mr. Truman was nominated in 1948 and scored his amazing upset victory speaks well for his handling of his problems.

So we see that these seven men—Tyler, Fillmore, Johnson, Arthur, Theodore Roosevelt, Coolidge and Truman—have firmly established that a Vice President shall assume the Presidency, not just its powers and duties, when the President dies in office. Though the intent of the succession clause of the Constitution is not entirely clear, there is no longer any doubt of its operation.

Vice President John Tyler, taking over for deceased President William Henry Harrison, was addressed by the Congress as President of the United States. As we have seen, the decision to so address him was made after considerable debate in the Senate. The precedent Tyler set has been followed by each of the other six Vice Presidents who have taken over on the death of a President.

It would appear that the Constitutional issue has been settled beyond revocation. The Vice President becomes the President, not merely the Vice President performing the duties of the President. Those who favor this precedent argue that when a President has died he has obviously vacated the office permanently and that there is no reason for considering the acceding Vice President as a mere acting President.

There is incontrovertible reason for this view: a nation needs an officer of supreme dignity and prestige at its head. This is very important for obvious reasons. It will be recalled that Tyler, Johnson, Arthur, Theodore Roosevelt and Truman served for almost the full terms of the Presidents for whom they took over. It would have been most unfortunate in each case to have the country headed for nearly four years by an executive with a title of only secondary stature.

VI

Succession By Removal

Following the reasoning presented in the previous chapter it would appear then that a Vice President taking over the powers and duties of a President who has been impeached and removed from office would also become President. We assume that a President dismissed under these conditions would certainly have vacated the office permanently. There would, however, be a slight difference. A dead President can never return to office. But it is possible, though extremely unlikely, that a Congress could impeach, convict and remove the President and then before his term expired, discover by new evidence that the removal was patently wrongful and revoke its action. Such a revocation is not considered in the Constitution and would pose problems so difficult that it would require a whole book to discuss them, but the situation is certainly not beyond all possibility.

There is no precedent to give us exact guidance concerning the status of a Vice President coming to the Presidency on the removal of the President. No President has ever been removed from office. One President, Andrew Johnson, was impeached, but his adversaries were, by one vote, unsuccessful in securing a conviction and removal. Even had President Johnson been removed, no Vice President would have succeeded to the Presidency, since there was no Vice President. Johnson had been called from the Vice Presidency to the position of chief executive on the death of President Lincoln. By the law of succession then prevailing Senator Benjamin Wade of Ohio, president pro tempore of the Senate, would have been in line to assume the powers and duties of the President.

Although a removal of Johnson would not have opened the way for a Vice Presidential succession, it nevertheless seems appropriate that we consider the process involved in impeachment proceedings and the particular case of President Andrew Johnson. Impeachment and removal is one possible route from the Vice Presidency to the Presidency.

The Constitution, in Article II, Section 4, states: "The President, Vice President, and all civil Officers of the United States, shall be removed from Office on Impeachment for, and Conviction of, Treason, Bribery or other high Crimes and Misdemeanors."

It appears from the above language that the impeachment process was intended only for "civil Officers." Precedent established by the Blount case in 1798 deems that members of Congress are not considered to be officers within the meaning of the impeachment provision. Expulsion from either house by a two-thirds vote is the Constitutional process of removing a member of Congress. Military officers also are not subject to impeachment. Court-martial is regarded as a more appropriate method of dealing with military personnel.

It is most significant to note that the Constitution is quite specific about the grounds for impeachment. It specifies " . . . Treason, Bribery, or other high Crimes and Misdemeanors." One is therefore certainly not supposed to be impeached for poor judgment or for political considerations. It is the clear intent of the Constitution that criminal action on the part of the accused officer is the only proper basis for impeachment. But, as we shall see, this view has not always been honored completely in Congress.

The mechanics of impeachment proceedings involve two separate and distinct processes. Article I, Section 2, clause 5 of the Constitution provides: "The House of Representatives shall chuse their Speaker and Other Officers; and shall have the sole Power of Impeachment." So whether or not an officer should be impeached is strictly the business of the House. The Senate officially has nothing to do with this decision at all. Ordinarily the process follows a pattern of this sort:

A member of the House presents to the House charges against a federal officer. The charges are then referred for investigation to a committee of the House, more appropriately to the Judiciary Committee. If the committee, at the conclusion of its findings, believes the charges, or some of them, to be substantial and true it makes a report to the House recommending impeachment of the officer. The committee in such a report usually recommends that the House vote in favor of formal charges incorporated in one or more "articles of impeachment." If the House then agrees with the findings of the committee it casts a majority vote in favor of the articles of impeachment. Then the House notifies the Senate that it has impeached the officer, at the same time providing the Senate with a copy of the charges.

At this point the officer has already been impeached. He may not be convicted and removed when his trial comes before the Senate, but the House has surely impeached him. Impeachment by the House is not conviction; it is somewhat analogous to indictment by a grand jury. It merely prefers official charges adopted by the House against the officer and notifies the Senate that the officer should stand trial on the charges before that body. Hence President Andrew Johnson was impeached. On February 24, 1868, the House passed, by a vote of 126 to 47, a resolution (the Covode Resolution) of impeachment against him. On March second and third, 1868, the House adopted eleven articles of impeachment against him and then provided the Senate with a copy of the charges.

Article I, Section 3, clause 6 of the Constitution provides, "The Senate shall have the sole Power to try all Impeachments. When sitting for that Purpose, they shall be on Oath or Affirmation. When the President of the United States is tried, the Chief Justice shall preside: And no Person shall be convicted without the Concurrence of two thirds of the Members present."

When the Senate receives an official certified copy of the articles of impeachment passed by the House, it provides the accused officer a copy of the charges and sets a day for the beginning of the trial. When the trial begins the regular presiding officer presides unless the President is on trial, in which case the Chief Justice presides. The House cannot try the case. Only the Senate can do that. But the House has made the charges, and it can prosecute. The House names a few of its members as managers. These managers present the case against the accused before the Senate. The Senators are placed under oath, or affirmation, to do impartial justice. Evidence is presented and witnesses are examined and cross-examined. The accused is entitled to counsel, who presents his defense.

Normally an impeachment trial is very similar to a court proceeding. The public is allowed in the galleries while the evidence is being taken and while the arguments are going on. But once the evidence is all in the galleries are cleared and the Senate deliberates behind closed doors. If the Senate, by a two thirds vote, returns a finding of guilty on any one of the charges, then the officer is convicted and removed from office. If no charge is sustained by a two thirds vote of the Senate, then the officer is acquitted and retains his office.

Only once has the President of the United States been impeached. This episode, arising from political conflict in a time of national stress, will long remain a mark to our discredit as a nation. And our unwise arrangement for selecting a Vice President can, in part, be held responsible.

When Andrew Johnson succeeded Abraham Lincoln as President on April 15, 1865, the power of the Confederacy had already been broken. A few days before, on April 9, General Robert E. Lee had surrendered to General Grant at Appomattox Courthouse. The war would soon be over; reconstruction would be the big problem. Any President who attempted to carry out a reasonable reconstruction in the former Confederate states would run into trouble with the radicals in Congress. Before his death even President Lincoln seemed due for rough times.

Mr. Lincoln was truly a great man and undoubtedly among the foremost of our Presidents, but, like Franklin Roosevelt, he died at the right time to preserve his fame. This is not to say he would have experienced all the difficulty Andrew Johnson got into. Lincoln was a more tactful man, and he had the advantage of four years' experience in dealing with Congress. There is little chance that he would have been impeached. But his views on reconstruction were so much more reasonable than those of the Congressional leaders that there is no doubt he would have quarreled with them. In fact he had already antagonized Congressional extremists.

In July 1864, toward the close of a session, Congress had passed the Wade-Davis Bill, which carried much more severe provisions for reconstruction than President Lincoln had planned to use. Lincoln killed the bill by a pocket veto but was tactful enough to say that if any state proceeded toward restoration under the Wade-Davis plan it was all right with him, though he did not believe that one plan of reconstruction should be considered the only proper way in all circumstances. In spite of Lincoln's diplomacy he was roundly scored by some Congressmen, who accused him of trying to get into position to dictate the electoral votes of the rebel states.

There is no doubt that a serious rift between the legislative and executive departments was developing during the latter part of Lincoln's life. It could hardly have been otherwise. During a major war there is always a tendency to follow the leader, and Congress is caught in and carried along with the general course of events. The executive necessarily over-shadows the legislative branch. All the while Congress is jealous of its powers, and the desire to control, pent up for the duration of the war, breaks out in full once the war is over. After the Civil War Congress was already beginning to turn on Lincoln. When he was assassinated it confronted Andrew Johnson with fury and overpowering strength.

The same thing has happened after every major war. After World War I the Senate turned on Woodrow Wilson and broke him. President Franklin D. Roosevelt's death spared him from facing pent-up Congressional hostilities, but Mr. Truman, his successor, got them in full measure. The seriousness of the threat from Moscow prevented open Congressional war on Mr. Truman's policies but it certainly did not halt a fusillade of bitter verbal attacks.

When Lincoln died a man came to the Presidency whom nobody had groomed for such a post. President Lincoln, it is true, had favored Andrew Johnson for a running mate in 1864, but he was not thinking of his successor in the Presidency. He was thinking of the good political strategy involved in having a loyal Southerner and a former Democrat on the ticket. The convention that nominated Johnson for Vice President would scarcely have done so if it had thought there was even a slight prospect that President Lincoln would not survive a second term.

Few would deny that Andrew Johnson was a very able man. But the Presidency, particularly in critical times, requires more than mere ability and character. It requires in addition rare tact, judgment, a fine sense of decorum and an art of graciousness. In these qualities Andrew Johnson was in default. He had all the ability, energy and rugged honesty necessary to make a success of just about any office in the United States except the Presidency, and he probably would have succeeded rather well in that office in normal times. To add to his woes, it was his ill luck to follow not a merely successful President, but one of the very greatest of them all and one whose greatness radiated with a more brilliant glow because of his martyrdom and because he never had to face the full force of the animosity Johnson faced. The contrast made Johnson appear a man of much smaller stature than he really was.

The death of Lincoln suddenly tossed Andrew Johnson into the waters of a political sea turbulent with the storms of vindictiveness. After a brief flirt with Stanton and the radical crowd in Congress Johnson soon turned toward the more reasonable and more constructive view of reconstruction that Lincoln had held. Seward was back in operation again, and the President was taking wiser counsel. The Southern states, he concluded, should be brought back into normal relations with the rest of the Union under terms of full loyalty as expeditiously as possible. This policy clashed head on with the stern idea of the Congressional radicals.

In the Senate Charles Sumner of Massachusetts wielded tremendous influence. He held to the view that the Southern states had by their secession committed state suicide and had become a body of territory the fate of which Congress was free to determine. In the House the aged Thaddeus Stevens was one of the strongest leaders, if not the strongest. He was extremely vindictive. He made it known that he was ready to devote the remainder of his life to punishing the Southern traitors. Speaking to the House of Representatives on February 18, 1867, he declared:

Mr. Speaker, why is it that we are so anxious to proclaim universal amnesty? Is there danger that somebody will be punished? Is there any fear that this nation will wake from its lethargy and insist upon punishing by fine, by imprisonment, by confiscation, and possibly by personal punishment, some of those who have murdered our brothers, our fathers, and our children?

It was not long before the battle between Congress and the President was on in full force. Congress began enacting its own severe views on reconstruction into law. The President was a fighter, and he swung back with his veto, which the opposition in Congress was often strong enough to override. In the midst of this battle over reconstruction policy the President decided to appeal to the people. He made his famous "swing around the circle" speaking tour in 1866, visiting Philadelphia, New York, Cleveland, Chicago, St. Louis and other cities. In addressing crowds on this tour his sense of propriety sank to the lowest ebb. He referred to his enemies in Congress in strong, insulting language. Some of his invective was no doubt well deserved, but his remarks had best been left unsaid. He freely exchanged taunts and insults with members of the audience who did not care for what he said. He brought the Presidency down to the level of street-corner argument.

If the President put on a bad show, Congress staged one that by contrast makes him look good. On January 7, 1867, Representative James M. Ashley of Ohio rose in the House and declared, "I charge Andrew Johnson, Vice President and acting President of the United States, with the commission of acts which, in contemplation of the Constitution, are high crimes and misdemeanors, for which, in my judgment, he ought to be impeached."

Ashley thereupon offered a resolution that the Judiciary Committee should inquire into the matter of impeachment.

The committee was authorized by the House to make the inquiry. Ashley had undertaken to get an impeachment started in the previous December but without success. In this second effort he left no stone unturned. He even tried to dig up evidence that Andrew Johnson had been an accomplice in the conspiracy that took the life of President Lincoln, though the real fact is that Johnson was also an intended victim. Ashley went so far as to try to secure evidence of Johnson's association with the conspiracy from a convicted perjurer.

No matter how hard Ashley tried, he still could gather no proof that the President had committed treason, bribery or any other high crimes and misdemeanors. Johnson had used bad judgment, but bad judgment is not an impeachable offense under the Constitution.

On July 10, 1867, the committee reported that it had not found sufficient grounds for impeachment. But the committee had divided five to four on the proposition. Its report did not end the matter. Ere long one member shifted position, and the committee recommended impeachment. The House voted on the recommendation on December 7, 1867. The resolution to impeach was decisively beaten, by a vote of 57 to 108. This vote did not signify that the House had no desire to impeach. It meant merely that the House did not believe it had found charges with which to secure Johnson's removal. The President's enemies were desperately in need of evidence that he had engaged in actual criminality in office. Their opportunity was soon to come, but on most questionable grounds.

On March 2, 1867, Congress passed the famous Tenure of Office Act. This act was so drastic that it can hardly be interpreted as anything but an attempt either to take charge of the administrative branch or to goad Johnson into a violation, which would render him liable to impeachment—or, as is more likely, both. In order to avoid extraneous detail it is best to consider only the parts of this act that related to the President's power to remove members of his Cabinet.

The act provided that " . . . the Secretaries of State, of the Treasury, of War, of the Navy, and of the Interior, the Postmaster General and the Attorney General, shall hold their offices respectively for and during the term of the President by whom they may have been appointed and for one month thereafter, subject to removal by and with the advice and consent of the Senate." The seven mentioned were the only Cabinet officers of that day.

It is evident that the intention of the sponsors of the act was to put the Senate in a position to exercise a veto on the President's removal power. This was a sharp departure from past practice and from the prevailing view of the Constitutional powers of the President. The Constitution makes no reference to the President's power to remove his subordinates.

The question was debated pretty thoroughly in the First Congress. Some members of Congress then argued that such officers as the President appointed with the advice and consent of the Senate (and this includes Cabinet members) he could only remove in the same way. Others, including James Madison, the chief architect of the Constitution, took the view that the President could make such removals on his own initiative and without the consent of the Senate. The Madison view prevailed in the First Congress and in fact had been the commonly accepted view up to the time of the passage of the act we are now considering.

The Tenure of Office Act appears to be a patent and unconstitutional invasion of the executive power of the President. Its sponsors knew full well that they couldn't get away with their designs if they prevented the President's taking an unworthy person out of office while Congress was not in session. They therefore provided that the President during a recess of the Senate could suspend an officer shown "by evidence satisfactory to the President" to be guilty of "misconduct in office, or crime," or for any other reason "incapable or legally disqualified to perform" the duties of the office.

But the act went on to provide that the President must report any such suspension to the Senate within twenty days of the first day of its next session. Then, if the Senate concurred, it was all right to make the removal permanent. If the Senate did not concur the officer was to be restored to his office. Thus it was arranged that the President could not take advantage of a Senate recess to rid himself permanently of undesired subordinates. But the big payoff was the provision that any violation of the act would constitute a high misdemeanor punishable by a fine not exceeding $10,000 or by imprisonment not exceeding five years, or by both. So if Johnson made a removal in violation of the act he would be guilty of a misdemeanor—an impeachable offense.

When the act came to President Johnson for his signature, he consulted his Cabinet. Reporting this consulation, Johnson stated, "Every member of my Cabinet advised me that the proposed law was unconstitutional. All spoke without doubt or reservation; but Mr. Stanton's condemnation of the law was the most elaborate and emphatic." Johnson further stated that Stanton " . . . added the weight of his own deliberate judgment, and advised me that it was my duty to defend the power of the President from usurpation, and to veto the law." Johnson vetoed the act as an unconstitutional invasion of the executive power. Congress repassed it over his veto.

As the months passed, Johnson found Secretary of War Stanton more difficult as a member of his administration. Stanton was conniving with the radicals in Congress. Johnson let him know by every sort of hint that his resignation would be acceptable, but Stanton had no disposition to resign. Finally, on August 5, 1867, Johnson wrote him, "Public considerations of a high character constrain me to say that your resignation as Secretary of War will be accepted."

Stanton refused to resign, sending the President a most abrupt reply saying that "public considerations of a high character" constrained him "not to resign the office of Secretary of War before the next meeting of Congress." At this juncture President Johnson arranged with General Ulysses S. Grant that he, Grant, would serve as Secretary of War *ad interim,* and on August 12 notified Stanton that he was suspended from the office. Although he regarded the Tenure of Office Act unconstitutional, Johnson so far was obeying it. He did not remove Stanton during the Senate recess; he merely suspended him.

Stanton yielded the office to General Grant but wrote the President that he denied Johnson's right to suspend him without the consent of the Senate but was submitting "under protest, to superior force." When the Senate again convened Johnson complied with the statute and reported his suspension of Stanton. The Senate refused to concur in the suspension. General Grant promptly gave up the office of Secretary of War and turned it over to Stanton. Johnson was badly disappointed. He thought he had an understanding with Grant that the latter would hold on to the office, forcing Stanton to carry the matter into the courts, where he believed the law would be declared unconstitutional.

When Grant surrendered the office President Johnson was in a sense at the end of his rope. If he now complied with the law and permitted Stanton to remain as Secretary of War, his title as chief executive would be illusory. The Presidency would be captive to the radical element in Congress. Johnson appointed General Lorenzo Thomas Secretary of War and on February 21, 1868, wrote Stanton that he was removed from office. Stanton refused to surrender the office and for a time we were in the ludicrous situation of having two rival Secretaries of War. Stanton held the office and really exercised most of its powers, and General Thomas went to Cabinet meetings.

The fundamental question was whether Andrew Johnson had violated law when he removed Stanton in violation of the Tenure of Office Act. The better view seems to be that he had not. If the act was, as Johnson thought, unconstitutional, then he had broken no law, since an unconstitutional statute is not a law. There was never a judicial test of the validity of the Tenure of Office Act during its existence. Johnson was thwarted in every effort to secure one. But in 1926, in the celebrated Myers case to be noted later, the Supreme Court volunteered the opinion that the statute was unconstitutional.

And even assuming that the statute was Constitutional, had Johnson actually violated it? That he had not would still seem the better view. If removing Stanton was a violation we must consider Johnson still Vice President, merely acting as President. Stanton's statutory tenure under the act was for the term of the President by whom he had been appointed and for one month thereafter. Now Stanton had been appointed by President Lincoln. If Johnson was merely acting President it might be said that this was still Lincoln's term and that under the law Johnson could not remove Stanton without Senate approval. But if on the death of Mr. Lincoln Johnson became President, then Lincoln's term had ended on the day he died.

Stanton had no formal appointment from Johnson. He had merely continued to serve under him by virtue of his appointment by Lincoln. So if Johnson was President, Stanton's statutory tenure had ended long before his removal. And most people thought the Congressional decision to call John Tyler President had settled that matter.

Now that President Johnson had removed Secretary Stanton, or at least had issued a removal order, his enemies moved with lightning speed. On the same day that Johnson notified Stanton of his removal, February 21, 1868, Representative John Covode of Pennsylvania introduced his celebrated impeachment resolution: "Resolved, That Andrew Johnson, President of the United States, be impeached of high crimes and misdemeanors."

The resolution was promptly referred to committee—not the Judiciary Committee this time, for it might be too deliberate, but to the Committee on Reconstruction, whose Chairman, Thaddeus Stevens, could be trusted to move it along with dispatch. The Reconstruction Committee came near setting a world's record for speedy deliberation and investigation. On the very next day, February 22, the committee reported the Covode impeachment resolution favorably and without change. The committee offered scarcely anything in the way of evidence except the order for Stanton's removal. It didn't even have articles of impeachment (the formal charges) drawn up. It just recommended that the House go ahead and impeach the President, then dig up the charges later.

This procedure was so injudicious and so patently an effort to railroad the President out of office, right or wrong, that Representative William S. Holman of Indiana most appropriately called attention to the fact that it was George Washington's birthday and requested that his famous farewell address, with its warning against rank partisanship, be read. "I suppose, Mr. Speaker," said Holman in the course of his remarks, "the Constitution of the United States would scarcely be in order."

Holman was right. The Constitution was not in order. The radicals had only one thing in mind—to get Johnson whether the means were constitutional or unconstitutional, fair or foul. The spirit of the majority was well exemplified by Representative George Washington Julian of Indiana. Speaking on February 24 on the President's removal order against Stanton, Julian declared that the President had perpetrated " . . . an act which on its face settles the question of law, and shuts us up to the absolute necessity of taking the recreant usurper by the throat."

Julian had no regret for the President's behavior. "On the contrary," he said, "I rejoice in the madness of this last act of his brazen defiance of the Constitution and the laws, and that in this, as in all the previous trials of our country since the year 1861, the devil has come to our rescue just at the point where the courage and virtue of men gave way."

On the day of Julian's speech the House passed the impeachment resolution, by a vote of 126 to 47. For the first time a President had been impeached, and he had been impeached without formal charges. On motion of Thaddeus Stevens the speaker was authorized to name first a committee of two to notify the Senate that Johnson had been impeached and second a committee to draw up and report articles of impeachment.

This was a strange procedure indeed. In substance the House was about to say to the Senate, "We have impeached President Andrew Johnson. Now we don't know just what charges formed the basis of the impeachment, but you can trust us. We will find some charges." It was like a grand jury's indicting a person for felony without stating the particular offense.

Finally, on March second and third, the House adopted eleven articles of impeachment. To analyze all eleven would involve too much detail. Suffice it to say that most of them—in fact the only ones on which the House had any real hope of securing a removal—grew out of the order for the removal of Secretary of War Stanton and the appointment of General Thomas as a successor. These acts, the articles alleged, were high misdemeanors in violation of the Tenure of Office Act.

The irregularities of the House procedure are well illustrated by the title of the committee that reported the articles of impeachment. Created on February 24, the same day on which the impeachment resolution was passed, it was designated not a committee to investigate charges or to find out whether there were charges, but a "Committee to declare Articles of Impeachment against the President of The United States."

On March 2, 1868, the House elected by ballot seven managers to present the case against President Johnson to the Senate. The seven elected were John A. Bingham of Ohio, George S. Boutwell of Massachusetts, James F. Wilson of

Iowa, Benjamin F. Butler from Massachusetts, Thomas Williams of Pennsylvania, John A. Logan from Illinois and Thaddeus Stevens of Pennsylvania.

One of the very first issues to be posed in the trial of President Johnson's impeachment was whether the Senate in trying articles of impeachment is a court or whether it can operate under its usual discretions as a body. Fortunately for Johnson, the Constitution expressly provided that when the Senate is trying the impeachment of the President the Chief Justice shall preside. Had it not been for this provision, the presiding officer for the trial would have been the president pro tempore of the Senate. Senator Benjamin F. Wade would have been a most biased presiding officer. He was bitterly opposed to President Johnson. Furthermore, as we have seen, under the succession statute then existing, had President Johnson been removed Wade would have been next in line to take over the functions of the Presidency, there being no Vice President.

On March 4, 1868, Chief Justice Salmon P. Chase, fully aware that he was about to preside over a body with strong preconceived notions and political biases, sent a communication to the Senate in which he most emphatically stressed his belief that the Senate would constitute a court. On the next day the Chief Justice entered the Senate chamber and took the chair. He again showed clearly that he believed the Senate was now a court by saying, "I attend the Senate in obedience to your notice, for the purpose of joining with you in forming a court of impeachment for the trial of the President of the United States, and I am now ready to take the oath." Mr. Justice Nelson then administered the oath to the Chief Justice.

The Constitution requires that the Senators while trying an impeachment must be on oath or affirmation. The Chief Justice administered the following oath to them: "I do solemnly swear that in all things appertaining to the trial of the impeachment of Andrew Johnson, President of the United States, I will do impartial justice according to the Constitution and laws. So help me God."

The trial itself got under way on March 30. Johnson had

been summoned to appear, but he elected to make his appearance by counsel. He had named former Attorney General Henry Stanbery, Benjamin R. Curtis, Jeremiah S. Black, William M. Evarts and Thomas A. R. Nelson to defend him.

From the very start of proceedings the House managers, operating under the theory that the Senate was not a court, addressed the Chief Justice as "Mr. President." Their interpretation would make it easier to secure a conviction and removal, as they could feel free to submit all kinds of evidence that would not be admissible in a court of law. Also, they would be in better position to get the President removed on grounds of mere bad behavior if their legal case broke down. In a nutshell, if the Senate was not a court, then it could operate with all the biases of a political body, and Johnson's chances of acquittal would be scant indeed.

Counsel for the President consistently addressed the chair as "Mr. Chief Justice." Their theory, in line with that of the Chief Justice, was that the Senate constituted a court to try the impeachment. No direct decision was ever made on the matter.

In his opening statement of the case to the Senate as a House manager, Representative Benjamin F. Butler declared, "We claim, and respectfully insist, that this tribunal has none of the attributes of a judicial court as they are commonly received and understood." What he was driving at became clear as he went on, "We suggest, therefore, that we are in the presence of the Senate of the United States, convened as a constitutional tribunal, to inquire into and determine whether Andrew Johnson, because of malversation in office, is longer fit to retain the office of President of the United States, or hereafter to hold any office of honor or profit."

The key word in Butler's statement is "malversation." If the Senate could vote to remove Johnson on that ground—merely very bad conduct—then it would not be necessary to prove that he had committed such crimes or misdemeanors as would render one liable for punishment in court. The managers would not have to establish indictable offenses on the part of the President. There was a good deal of precedent in English constitutional history—and indeed in past practice of the Congress in impeachment proceedings—to support the Butler view.

But to follow that interpretation completely would place the executive department in eternal peril at the hands of the legislature. The final practice of the Senate, established during the trial, placed that chamber somewhere between the position of court and that of political body. The Senate decided that the Chief Justice could make the initial rulings on points of law but that his decision could, on the request of a Senator, be referred to the Senate for final support or reversal. Had the Senate taken the position that it had none of the attributes of a court, President Johnson's removal would have been a virtual certainty.

One of the most significant issues arose at the beginning of the preliminaries to trial, as Senators were being called to take the oath on March 5. When the name of Senator Benjamin Wade was called, Senator Thomas A. Hendricks of Indiana, later to become Vice President, questioned the competence of Senator Wade to take the oath since if the President should be removed Wade would succeed him. There was much debate over the matter. Those in favor of having Wade step aside argued that the Constitution excludes the Vice President from presiding when a President is on trial for the simple reason that he would have a direct interest in the outcome. Wade, as immediate successor, had the same interest.

Supporters of Wade's right to take the oath and participate in the trial denied that the Senate was acting as a court and insisted that to deprive Wade of a vote would violate the Constitution by denying a state its equal suffrage in the Senate. They also contended that objection to Wade should come, if at all, from a party in the trial, not from a Senator. Hendricks finally withdrew his objection and Wade took the oath. In the end he voted for the conviction of Johnson, as everybody expected him to do.

If the Senate was a court, it surely was no impartial court. The radicals in that body were just as anxious to convict as the House leaders were to impeach. And they were prepared to put on similar speed in condemning Johnson. In the early stages of the proceedings Johnson's counsel pointed out that the eleven articles involved many questions of both fact and law and that they needed forty days to prepare the defense. There is no question but that they needed at least that much time, but the Senate saw it otherwise. It granted ten days for preparation.

If Johnson had not violated the Tenure of Office Act, then the House had no plausible grounds for impeachment. Looking back today, the case for the House seems inexcusably weak. In all the official proceedings both the House and the Senate recognized Johnson as President, not a mere acting President. The House impeachment resolution was directed against the President of the United States. The Stevens resolution calling for a committee to notify the Senate that the House had impeached Johnson and for another committee to prepare articles of impeachment spoke of him as "President of the United States." The House managers were elected " . . . to conduct the impeachment of the President of the United States." The Senate notified the House that it was ready to try the impeachment of the President of the United States.

If Johnson was President, then a reasonable person might conclude that Lincoln's term was over by far more than one month and that therefore Stanton's statutory tenure was gone at the time of the removal order. But the House managers could not concede this. If they did their case was exploded. Benjamin Butler in his opening argument, in which he gave just about everything the House had to offer, tried to hold that it was still Lincoln's term.

"Whose presidential term is the respondent now serving out?" Butler asked. "His own or Mr. Lincoln's? If his own, he is entitled to four years up to the anniversary of the murder, because each presidential term is four years by the Constitution, and the regular recurrence of those terms is fixed by the act of May 8, 1792. If he is serving out the remainder of Mr. Lincoln's term, then his term of office expires on the 4th of March, 1869, if it does not before."

That argument, resting entirely on the four-year matter, was the very best that Butler could do. But he could and did do a great deal more emoting. "By murder most foul he succeeded to the Presidency," he said, "and is the elect of an assassin to that high office, and not of the people."

In his emotional venture, Butler inadvertently testified that Stanton was a spy in Johnson's official household. Stanton, by the way, had barricaded his office and maintained physical possession in spite of Johnson's removal order. Speaking of him Butler said, "Is it not known to you, Senators, and to the country, that Mr. Stanton retains this unpleasant and distasteful position, not of his own will alone, but at the behest of a majority of those who represent the people of this country in both Houses of its Legislature, and after the solemn decision of the Senate that any attempt to remove him without their concurrence is unconstitutional and unlawful?"

Defense counsel more than countered Butler's argument that the Tenure of Office Act covered Stanton's case. By that act Cabinet officers were protected against removal without the consent of the Senate " . . . for and during the term of the President by whom they may have been appointed and for one month thereafter." By whom was Stanton appointed? they asked. He had been appointed by President Lincoln in 1862 and had never been reappointed by either Lincoln or Johnson. He had just held over. Johnson, they argued, had been President since Lincoln's death. In every legal sense Lincoln's term was terminated by his death, when Johnson's term began. Far more than one month had elapsed since that time, so the act could not apply to Stanton.

But even if Butler was right in his contention that Johnson was merely serving out Lincoln's term, the House managers' case would be no better. Stanton had been appointed by Lincoln in his first term and had not been again appointed. His tenure as defined by the act would therefore not carry over beyond one month in Lincoln's second term. If the act were to apply to Stanton it would have to read "during the term of the

President and any other term for which he may afterward be elected."

Besides contending that the President had not violated the Tenure of Office Act, the defense further argued that even if he had, he was justified, as he believed it unconstitutional. Johnson's desire to secure a judicial test of the act, maintained his counsel, was proper.

The House managers, speaking through Butler, had sought from the start to head off argument on the Constitutionality of the act. Butler maintained that the question was "totally irrelevant." He argued that if the President believes a bill to be unconstitutional, vetoes it and states his objections and Congress passes it over his veto, the President has exhausted his power to judge its Constitutionality. His duty then is to execute the law. If he refuses to execute it, Butler said "It may be said that he may do this at his peril. True; but that peril is to be impeached for violating his oath of office, as is now being done."

The innate fallacy of this position was demonstrated by defense counsel B. R. Curtis. He pointed out that in ordinary laws affecting the general public it is freely admitted that a private person may raise the question of Constitutionality and that in many cases he is performing a duty when he does. In the law in question, Curtis said, the President was the only one who could raise the Constitutional issue before the courts, since the problem was whether it had " . . . cut off a power confided to him by the people through the Constitution." Since only the office of President was affected by the law, only the President could raise the issue.

On April 17 defense counsel William M. Evarts moved to introduce the following most pertinent evidence:

We offer to prove that the President at a meeting of the Cabinet while the bill was before the President for his approval, laid before the Cabinet the tenure-of-civil-office bill for their consideration and advice to the President respecting his approval of the bill; and thereupon the members of the Cabinet

then present gave their advice to the President that the bill was
unconstitutional and should be returned to Congress with his
objections, and that the duty of preparing a message, setting
forth the objections to the constitutionality of the bill, was devolved on Mr. Seward and Mr. Stanton; to be followed by
proof as to what was done by the President and Cabinet up to
the time of sending the message.

Mr. Evarts was prepared to present Cabinet witnesses to
prove that this discussion had taken place and that Stanton
had been present. The Chief Justice ruled that since the articles
of impeachment charged that the President had issued his removal order with intent to violate the Tenure of Office Act and
in violation of the Constitution, Evart's evidence was admissible " . . . for the purpose of showing the intent with
which the President has acted in this transaction."

The Senate then staged a most amazing exhibition of bias.
It promptly overruled the decision of the Chief Justice and
voted, 29 to 20, not to admit the evidence.

Evarts further offered to prove that " . . . it was considered by the President and Cabinet that a proper regard to
the public service made it desirable that upon some proper
case a judicial determination on the constitutionality of the
law should be obtained." The Chief Justice offered no ruling
on this. Perhaps he had learned that on points so devastating
to the position of the House managers the Senate would rule
against him. He referred the matter to the Senate without
opinion, and the Senate voted, 30 to 19, not to hear the evidence. We know now that Johnson's enemies in the Senate
were so clearly stacking the deck against him that they were
beginning to harm their own cause.

On April 18 Evarts offered evidence, supported by witnesses, that the Cabinet had expressed the opinion that the
"Secretaries appointed by Mr. Lincoln" were not within the
provisions of the Tenure of Office Act. This statement also
had, according to Evarts, been made in Stanton's presence.

The Chief Justice declared that in his opinion this evidence
was proper for the Senate to hear. But the Senate voted, 26

to 22, that it was inadmissible, again directly flouting the opinion of the Chief Justice of the United States.

As the trial proceeded witnesses were examined for both sides and countless arguments were presented. It became quite clear that a vote of guilty or not guilty was going to follow party lines fairly closely. Though we have tried to avoid party controversy, at this point the narrative demands that we take account of party position. This affair is so far removed from present issues that it can scarcely affect anyone's voting.

The Republicans believed that Johnson had betrayed his party and his country. Republican Senators would in the main stand for conviction. The Democratic Senators, a small minority group, would stand for acquittal. With a two thirds vote necessary for conviction, the problem of the radicals was to hold the Republican ranks firm. They could still convict if six Republican Senators voted not guilty, but if seven deserted the ranks Johnson would probably be cleared.

There were fifty-four Senators, and all would doubtless cast votes. Thirty-six would have to vote guilty in order to remove Johnson. As the trial neared an end every sort of pressure was exterted to put doubtful Republican Senators in the anti-Johnson column.

The most badgered of all was Senator Edmund G. Ross, a Kansas Republican serving his first term as a Senator. Ross was told that to vote not guilty meant his certain defeat at the polls and that he would even be charged with accepting a bribe. He even faced threats of assassination. His Kansas colleague, Republican Senator Samuel C. Pomeroy, kept after him constantly to vote guilty. Ross, however, was a man of principle and courage. He decided that under his oath to do impartial justice his duty was to vote not guilty. He did so, even though he knew that he was in all probability digging his political grave.

On Saturday, May 16, the first vote was taken, on article eleven of the charges. This was a sort of omnibus article. It charged a variety of misconduct, but its most important part was the allegation that Johnson had unlawfully sought to pre-

vent the execution of the Tenure of Office Act. When the chief
clerk called the name of the first Senator, Henry B. Anthony,
Rhode Island Republican, the Chief Justice put the question:
"Mr. Senator Anthony, how say you? Is the respondent, Andrew Johnson, President of the United States, guilty or not
guilty of a high misdemeanor, as charged in this article?"
Senator Anthony answered, "Guilty."

So it went through the roll of Senators, in alphabetical order.
At the close of the roll call thirty-five had voted guilty and
nineteen had voted not guilty. Conviction and removal on this
article had failed by one vote. Seven Republican Senators had
voted not guilty along with the Democrats. Senator Ross had
stuck firm to his convictions in spite of all the pressures on
him.

With the failure to convict on the eleventh article the Senate
adjourned until Tuesday, May 26. In the ten-day interval the
radicals sought to mend their fences. The chief target was
again Senator Ross. Just about every sort of political and personal pressure the radicals could think of was brought to bear
on him. They had to break his will.

When the Senate convened again on May 26, a vote was
taken on the second article. This article charged an intentional
violation of the Tenure of Office Act and a similar violation
of the Constitution in authorizing General Thomas to act as
Secretary of War *ad interim*. All eyes were on Ross when his
name was called. Again he voted not guilty. The vote still stood
35 to 19.

Then the Senate voted on the third article—a charge that
Johnson had attempted to violate the Constitution by appointing General Thomas Secretary of War *ad interim*. The nineteen
who voted not guilty held firm. No votes were taken on the
remaining eight articles. The radicals saw that they were
defeated. The Senate, sitting as a court of impeachment, adjourned without day.

Andrew Johnson had been acquitted by one vote on each
article on which a poll was taken. The seven Republican
Senators who found Johnson not guilty were William Pitt

Fessenden of Maine, Joseph S. Fowler of Tennessee, James W. Grimes of Iowa, John B. Henderson of Missouri, Edmund G. Ross of Kansas, Lyman Trumbull of Illinois and Peter G. Van Winkle of West Virginia.

These men acted with rare courage in defying partisanship for principle. Their reward, as is so often the case, was political death. None of the seven was ever again elected to the Senate or to any important office, for that matter. But the nation is grateful for what they did. Had they not stood by their principles, Andrew Johnson would have been removed from office on purely political grounds. Had that happened precedent would have placed the executive at the mercy of Congress and our *tri-parte* system of government would probably have suffered a mortal blow.

If there is to be one hero of the sordid performance of 1868, then Edmund Ross undoubtedly deserves the honor. He knew he was courting political extinction when he voted for Johnson's acquittal. False charges of bribe taking were still hurled at him after the trial was over. On May 27, 1868, the day after the acquittal, Ross addressed the Senate. He called attention to the slander and gossip that had been spread about him and the " . . . fierce storm of party denunciation which burst over the heads of the seven Republicans who voted not guilty." He said he had expected the attack and was prepared for it, and he urged a full investigation of the matter. Speaking of his critics, Ross said, "They have today at their back a large majority of the great patriotic party to which they and I belong, with nearly all its machinery of vengeance; while I have but a feeble voice here, backed, however, by that never-failing source of strength, my own consciousness of rectitude and patriotic, honest purpose." He made it very clear that he disapproved of the policies of the Johnson administration but had sought to cast his vote " . . . with the candor and courage of an honest judge."

Thus closed the ugliest chapter in our political history. Just one vote prevented the ousting of a President of the United States. Had that additional vote for conviction been forthcoming, it might well have been said that Senator Benjamin F. Wade had elected himself President. Despite his position he had voted, and he cast his vote for the conviction and removal of Johnson.

Then what would we have said in 1926? In that year the Supreme Court handed down a decision in the Myers case that provisions of an act of 1876 requiring the consent of the Senate for Presidential removal of first-, second- and third-class postmasters were unconstitutional. In reaching this decision, the court consulted history. It pointed out that the First Congress, which had as members a number of people who had just recently served in the Constitutional Convention, had decided after full debate that the President had unrestricted power to remove those executive subordinates he appointed with Senate confirmation. Historical precedent had regularly favored this view right up to the passage of the Tenure of Office Act. Then the Court, speaking through Mr. Chief Justice Taft, significantly observed, " . . . and it therefore follows that the Tenure of Office Act of 1867, in so far as it attempted to prevent the President from removing executive officers who had been appointed by him by and with the advice and consent of the Senate, was invalid, and that subsequent legislation of the same effect was equally so." Thus was Andrew Johnson given posthumous vindication for his view.

There were many reasons for the regrettable episode of 1868. One, of course, was that the recent and bitter Civil War had left emotion and prejudice at a high pitch. Another was the vast chasm between views of the President and the Congress on reconstruction. By no means the least reason, however, was a matter to which House manager Benjamin F. Butler alluded emphatically when laying the case against Johnson before the Senate. "Yes, we have an answer," said Butler. "We can say this man was not the choice of the people for the President of the United States. He was thrown to the surface by the whirlpool of civil war, and, carelessly, we grant, elected to the second place in the Government, without thought that he might ever fill the first."

To such a miserable pass we had come by ticket-balancing techniques in nominating candidates for Vice President. A Vice President had suddenly and unexpectedly advanced to the Presidency, and he was to go down in history as the only President up to our time impeached.

Often in human affairs at the subsidence of that which is plainly evil we manage to garner some results that are good. So it was with the Johnson impeachment proceedings,

The proceedings, first of all, provided the ultimate clincher in establishing the view that the Vice President succeeding a deceased President actually becomes President rather than an acting President. The House, the Senate and the Chief Justice all recognized Johnson's status. This added support to the Tyler precedent was no doubt a good thing for the country.

And thanks to the magnificent courage of those who chose certain political annihilation over sacrificing principles, the proceedings left a good precedent in their failure. The impeachment was clearly evil—inspired by monstrous political bias and intolerance—but its failure has no doubt established the principle that we cannot succeed in ousting a President on mere political grounds, however violent the political antagonisms may be. It will instead be necessary to produce substantial evidence of criminal behavior. Seldom, if ever, will a Vice President reach the White House through the impeachment and removal of a President. This result of Johnson's impeachment was most fortunate.

Had the President been removed on no more than political grounds the consequences would have been dire. The executive department might have become no more than a cautious captive of Congress. The tenure of the chief executive would have been at the mercy of large, hostile legislative majorities. A legislative department is by its very nature inclined to encroach on the executive powers, and had Johnson been removed, succeeding Presidents would have been left in a very poor position to resist Congressional invasion of their functions.

No speculation on what might have happened can be conclusive. But it is possible that the President could have become a mere figurehead while we drifted toward a cabinet or parliamentary system of government. But in that case we would have drifted without plan in an era of world politics in which it would have been very dangerous to go along without reasonably solid political institutions.

The development of a cabinet system like England's might not have been a great misfortune *per se*, but with our vast territorial extent, our many sectional differences and our large variety of cultural components, it is possible that we could have gone in the direction of French cabinet instability rather than British balance.

Those who believe it is entirely fantastic to suppose that removing Johnson would have started us on a course leading toward cabinet government might pause for a moment to remember that impeachment of ministers preceded the idea of cabinet responsibility to Parliament until votes of confidence and no confidence made impeachment obsolete.

Since the only impeachment of a United States President involved a Vice Presidential heir to the first office in the land, it might reasonably have led to a re-examination of the office of Vice President. But there was no substantial re-evaluation. The storm blew over and the nation proceeded with its former careless apathy toward the Vice President.

VII

Succession By Inability

What will happen if a President becomes so critically ill, mentally or physically, that he is unable to function, and a crisis arises requiring Presidential action?

The Constitution, we have noted, provides that if the President is unable " . . . to discharge the Powers and Duties of the said Office, the Same shall devolve on the Vice President." No clear distinction is made between the status of a Vice President assuming Presidential duties on the death of a President and that of one taking over because a President is unable to fill his role.

While practical considerations make the Tyler precedent seem wise, we must nevertheless concede that it has had an unfortunate effect on the application of the inability provision. Three Presidents have been disabled for considerable periods of time, but in none of these cases was the Vice President called on to perform full Presidential functions.

One of the reasons for not employing the Vice President when the President is incapacitated has been fear that he would become President in fact, permanently ousting the disabled executive. Some believe that this might be the inexorable legal result even if the Vice President wanted to return the robes to the elected chief executive. They contend that the Tyler precedent would obtain just as firmly as if the President had died, since the Constitution does not recognize a difference between succession by death and succession by inability.

121

A distinction, as we have seen, is made in the latter part of the clause, which covers the possible immobilization of both the President and the Vice President. In such a situation Congress may by law declare what officer " . . . shall then *act* as President, and such Officer shall act accordingly, until the Disability be removed, or a President shall be elected." Here is a clear implication of temporary tenure by an officer merely acting as President. But this language seems not to apply to the situation we are discussing now.

The whole problem of inability is, if we let it get involved in excessive legalism, a most perplexing one. The Constitution offers no definition of the term. It does not state whether it embraces physical inability or mental inability or both. Much ink has been spilled over this matter, though debate frankly appears absurd. The framers of the Constitution were practical men. It would have been senseless then, and it is senseless now, to assume that a nation can well go along with an executive head incapable of taking care of his office for any reason. Surely the Fathers meant any kind of inability that would preclude high-level executive action.

Common sense dictates too that temporary absence from the country does not constitute inability. We are getting rather used to having our Presidents go abroad to deal with world problems. Of course President Wilson's announcement in late 1918 that he intended to attend the Paris peace conference after World War I aroused heated opposition among his foes. Senator Lawrence Y. Sherman of Illinois introduced a concurrent resolution declaring that Wilson's departure and absence from the territory and the seat of government would constitute ". . . an inability to discharge the powers and duties of the said office of President" and would create a vacancy in that office. Sherman insisted that immediately on the President's departure the Vice President should take over his powers and duties.

Naturally this resolution got nowhere. Senator John Sharp Williams of Mississippi offered effective rebuttal by showing that in the past Presidents had left the country without having the inability clause invoked against them. In recent years Presidents Franklin Roosevelt, Harry Truman and Dwight Eisenhower have not hesitated if they thought their going abroad would best serve the interests of the United States. The provincial idea of Senator Sherman, bred by political bias and stillborn, is of little interest to anyone today but the political archivist.

The Constitution does not define the degree of inability required before the Vice President takes over. More important, it does not say who has the power or the duty to raise the question whether the President is able to continue his work. Nor is anyone expressly authorized to decide that question or to say when the President is ready to return to office. And of course no one can say whether the Vice President assumes a different status if the inability is permanent rather than temporary. We have had nearly a century and three quarters to clarify these questions, but we have neither answered them nor established any method for getting the answers. As we shall see in a moment, it may be that our prolonged negligence has already caused great misfortune to us and to other nations. Now, at long last, we have begun to bestir ourselves to attack the problem. No magic protects the President. We must prepare for a situation in which he may be totally disabled. The inability problem has faced us in a practical way on three different occasions in our history.

The first such situation arose out of the assassination of President James A. Garfield. The President was shot on July 2, 1881; he died on September 19. Thus for more than eleven weeks he hovered between life and death. He was, of course, totally disabled. In the entire eleven weeks he performed but one official act, the signing of an extradition paper. All the while public affairs drifted badly, though fortunately no crisis arose.

The Cabinet members carried on matters within their authority, but many things were left undone because only a President could do them. There was much talk of having Vice President Arthur temporarily act as chief executive. There is little question that Arthur would have been acting within his rights—and probably within his obligations—had he raised the question of President Garfield's inability. It is fairly clear that the Constitution imposes on the Vice President a positive duty to act in case the President is unable. But obviously no Vice President with a sense of propriety would wish to raise such a question. In some quarters his motives would be suspect, to say the least.

Chester A. Arthur certainly was not disposed to take any steps in that direction. Even had he deemed it his duty he would have found it extraordinarily embarassing to make such a move. What was already a difficult situation was made even worse by the fact that Garfield and Arthur had taken opposing sides in a heated political clash from which bad feeling still persisted.

It is highly probable that the Cabinet would have called on Vice President Arthur to take over temporarily in spite of the recent policy conflict had not some members been afraid that Arthur's temporary accession would turn out to be permanent. Congress was not in session and matters were allowed to drift until President Garfield died.

President Woodrow Wilson's collapse in the fall of 1919 precipitated an even more serious situation. Mr. Wilson had undertaken a strenuous speaking tour of the West in his effort to generate public opinion for American participation in the League of Nations. He was not well at the start, and his personal physician had advised him against the trip.

But the President was engaged in the battle of his life. He believed that without a successful international organization for peace mankind would within a generation or so be involved in another world war. So he disregarded his doctor's warning. When he returned to Washington on September 28 he was already a very sick man. On the morning of October 2 he suffered a stroke. For several months the President was so ill that he could attend to scarcely any public matters.

That Mr. Wilson was too ill to serve as President is quite clear. No one knows even how much of the time the President was conscious or unconscious. Few people were admitted to the sickroom from October to the middle of May—even Cabinet members were excluded. There were rumors that the President was insane and even that he was dead.

From the day he returned to Washington until April 13, 1920, Wilson did not meet with his Cabinet—a period of over six months. Neither the Cabinet nor Vice President Marshall was well informed about the President's condition. Some claimed that Mrs. Wilson was assuming the powers of the Presidency, but that was undoubtedly an exaggeration. Certainly she was careful to carry out the doctors' orders to permit only matters of the most urgent moment to be brought to the President's attention. It seems that she and Dr. Cary T. Grayson, the President's personal physician, kept guard and decided who could see Mr. Wilson, for how long and over what matters. But Mrs. Wilson insisted that she made no actual decisions on public policy, and Josephus Daniels, Secretary of the Navy for eight years under Mr. Wilson, confirms her.

Debate still continues on the degree of the President's inability. Though some have pictured him as helpless and dependent, Joseph Tumulty, Wilson's secretary, has vigorously denied that there was real disability. Yet after all is said and done it can hardly be argued that a President who was almost completely shielded from problems of state in order to preserve his life was not unable to discharge his duties.

Nor is there a positive answer to the claim that President Wilson was, for a time at least, mentally unstable. If he was, it must have been while he was unconscious, for people who were permitted to see him said he seemed altogether rational. One of Wilson's most bitter foes, Senator Albert B. Fall of New Mexico, was one of the ones who doubted the soundness of the President's mind. As a pretext to test his suspicions Fall managed to get the Foreign Relations Committee to send him, together with Senator Gilbert Hitchcock of Nebraska, to the White House to interview Wilson on Mexican relations. Wilson was astute enough to know why Fall was coming and was fully prepared for him. Though there are several versions of what happened at the meeting, it is quite clear that Mr. Wilson more than passed his test.

According to Mrs. Wilson, the President easily drew first blood and stayed in complete command of the interview. She says that Fall was so much surprised at the President's alertness that he even told reporters Wilson had gestured with both hands, when as a matter of fact his left arm was useless. Josephus Daniels' account of the episode bears out Mrs. Wilson.

But though the weight of the evidence indicates that the President was far indeed from insane, it is incredible that one so ill and so weak could exert his full mental power.

It is hardly too much to say that for several months during Wilson's illness the country was virtually without a President. No one knows yet who really exercised executive authority. That Wilson was extremely dependent on his wife is certain. For instance, when David F. Houston, Secretary of Agriculture, was made Secretary of the Treasury it was Mrs. Wilson who informed him of the shift.

And those months when the President lay ill were critical months—critical for the United States and for the whole world. The fate of the League of Nations was being sealed insofar as the United States was concerned. Senators friendly toward the League desperately needed to consult the President to explore compromises by which the United States might become a member. But the President was too ill to confer. And Mr. Wilson, already disgusted with the emotionalism that was beating the League, became all the more bitter because of his helplessness.

Perhaps if Vice President Marshall had taken over during the worst period a compromise might have been reached and the history of the world changed for the better. Surely the League had little chance to succeed without the world's most powerful nation, and without a successful League there was little reason to expect that the peace of 1919 would prove more than a few-decades' truce.

But there seemed to be no way to invoke the inability provision of the Constitution. Vice President Marshall certainly didn't feel that he was the man to initiate the question, though there was plenty of talk of having him take over. But the fear that a temporary replacement by the Vice President would prove to be legally permanent still prevailed. Those loyal to President Wilson would not listen to proposals for Marshall to take charge.

Wilson, while still quite ill, fired Robert Lansing, his Secretary of State. The immediate occasion for the dismissal was Lansing's calling Cabinet meetings without an authorization from the President. But Wilson and some of those close to him suspected Lansing of an attempt to oust him in favor of Vice President Marshall.

Whatever Lansing's motives, the incident serves to highlight the tragedy of Wilson's collapse. Anyone seriously ill in the midst of a crucial battle may become more sensitive and less tolerant. This human tendency will probably complicate all future efforts to solve the inability problem, however wise any statutory approaches may be, so long as the Vice President is an independent officer beyond Presidential control.

The third occasion for extraordinary interest in executive inability arose from President Eisenhower's attack of coronary thrombosis on September 24, 1955. The President, it is true, did confer while in the hospital with the Vice President, Cabinet members and his personal staff. On September 30 Vice President Nixon presided over a Cabinet meeting, after which a statement was issued saying that there were " . . . no obstacles to the orderly and uninterrupted conduct of the . . . affairs of the nation." Thus the business of the President's office was carried on more or less smoothly during his absence.

Neverthless, it was some sixteen weeks before President Eisenhower was able to resume a full work load. Then in June came the attack of ileitis, which put him out of commission for some weeks more. It is a conservative estimate that within less than one year's time the President of the United States was at least partially disabled for some twenty-two weeks.

It is probably true that President Eisenhower had organized an efficient working staff. But to claim that for these twenty-two weeks the staff looked after matters so well that the President was not missed is, of course, absurd. It is to say that if a President will just get a good staff he can go away for four years and everything will go along fine.

Certainly anyone, President or private citizen, may be attacked by coronary thrombosis or by Crohn's disease. But the second major illness of the same President surely should emphasize the need to find some satisfactory way to put the inability clause in operation.

We have been dodging this issue ever since 1787. But the delegates to the Constitutional Convention have earned clemency at the bar of history. They had so many problems to solve that it should be no surprise to find some remaining for us to fret with. The Fathers expected us to stand on our own feet and exhibit some of their self-reliance.

The matter did come up briefly in convention on August 27, 1787. At that time it was contemplated that the president of the Senate would be the temporary Presidential successor. According to Madison's journal, Hugh Williamson of North Carolina suggested " . . . that the legislature ought to have power to provide for occasional successors. . . ." He proposed that the matter be postponed. John Dickinson " . . . seconded the postponement, remarking it was too vague. What is the extent of the term 'disability,' and who is to be the judge of it?" No answer is recorded. Just one line follows. "The postponement was agreed to."

Well, the postponement has lasted a long time. There have been intermittent efforts to do something about solving the problem of Presidential inability, but so far to no avail. President Chester A. Arthur, remembering his own perplexity during the weeks when President Garfield lay ill, emphasized the problem in his first annual message to Congress on December 6, 1881. Some discussion followed the President's message, but no legislation was forthcoming. We waited then and we are still waiting.

The second session of the Eighty-fourth Congress made a considerable effort to find a solution. Representative Celler gained a great deal of valuable information and opinion from his questionnaire. Space permits only a brief examination of the more important questions and answers. The questions are not necessarily in the words or in the order in which they were presented.

What is the meaning of "inability" in the constitutional sense, and should a definition be enacted into law? Most answers defined inability as any incapacity, physical or mental, so serious as to render a President unable to function. Dr. Everett S. Brown of the University of Michigan suggested that it might include capture of the President by a foreign enemy. Most of those questioned opposed a statutory definition on the ground that it might produce unfortunate inflexibility and fail to embrace unanticipated situations. In the words of Dr. Edward S. Corwin of Princeton a legal definition could " . . . operate to embarrass determination of the matter in many actual situations." Dr. Joseph E. Kallenbach at the University of Michigan was among the few who thought there should be a definition, and he urged that it should be stated "only in the broadest terms."

Who is to initiate the question of a President's inability? Here the division of thinking is proof of the perplexity that would have rained down on the Constitutional Convention had it undertaken a detailed solution. Some suggested that the Vice President should bring up—or at least have a large hand in bringing up—the question, since he has a duty to perform when the President is unable. Others voiced serious objection to this view. Dr. David Fellman of the University of Wisconsin thought the Vice President's " . . . personal stake in the decision precludes general confidence [in his objectivity]."

Dr. Arthur N. Holcombe of Harvard thought it the Vice President's duty to raise the question but suggested that he might well be prompted by a request from the Cabinet or Congress. Former President Hoover suggested the Cabinet.

The Hoover view earned both support and opposition. Dr. Charles Fairman of Harvard Law School thought the Cabinet should be able to start the inquiry, but he cautioned that " . . . the natural tendency of a staff is to cover up their chief's inadequacy and to pretend hopefully that all goes well." He suggested, among other possibilities, that certain designated leaders in Congress might be authorized to start the inquiry.

Others proposed the Congress itself as the body to set things in motion, but opponents to this pointed out that Congress might not be in session at the time of need. Some expressed the feeling too that Congressional initiation would violate separation of powers. It was quite generally agreed that the President himself, if he were able, might be the best authority to raise the question, but of course his condition might be so bad that he couldn't. This is by no means an exhaustive list of the suggestions made, but only illustrative of the diversity of opinion.

Who should decide the question once it is initiated? Here again, there was a variety of answers. Dr. Stephen K. Bailey of Princeton, hoping to remove the matter as far as possible from partisan politics, suggested that the Chief Justice be authorized " . . . to appoint an *ad hoc* body of 7 private citizens, not more than 3 from any one party and including at least 2 men of outstanding reputation in medicine and psychiatry. At least 5 members of said body after deliberation and investigation should agree on the President's inability, and even their certification of inability should be finally decided upon by the Supreme Court of the United States." Dr. Bailey indicated that such procedures as he outlined would require Constitutional change.

Mark DeW. Howe of Harvard Law School and Dr. Arthur Holcombe said Congress should decide. Dr. C. Herman Pritchett of the University of Chicago would have the President make the determination if he could (many others agreed to this), but said in case the President was unable the Cabinet should make the finding. Dr. Roland J. Pennock of Swarth-more would have the authority to decide rest in two bodies, " . . . the Congress, with the concurrence of the Vice President; or the Cabinet acting by majority vote."

Dr. John Romani of Brookings Institution favored having the Vice President make the determination if the President cannot and suggested further that the President himself should decide when he is ready to return to office.

Dr. Richard G. Huber of Tulane Law School made this comment: "Thus one solution within the present setup is to make the Vice President a sort of chief administrative officer of the Government, and remove from him his duties as presiding officer of the Senate. Duties carried by the executive department could then at least be divided beween two men and, if one's capacity to govern diminished the other could take up the slack. This suggestion, of course, would require a considerably different approach to the selection of Vice Presidents, but that is not a constitutional problem." This would be pretty near two consuls, wouldn't it?

If the President should be temporarily disabled, would the Vice President succeed only to the powers and duties of the office or to the office itself? Here the answers were in substantial agreement. The Vice President would take over only the President's powers and duties, and that for no longer than the duration of the President's inability. Dr. Charles Fairman spoke of him as Acting President. Dr. James Hart of the University of Virginia suggested the title of President pro tempore. Dr. Joseph Kallenbach stated that as he interprets the Constitution, any succession by the Vice President is merely to the powers and duties of the Presidency. He believes the usage developing from the Tyler accession unfortunate.

What if the President is permanently incapacitated? Would the Vice President then succeed merely to the powers and duties of the office or to the office itself? The responses here indicated a fairly equal division of feeling. Dr. Charles Fairman would have the Vice President succeed to the office, to afford added moral authority. "If he is the only President we are going to have for this 4-year period," said Dr. Fairman, "it is better to accord him all that makes for strength."

Dr. David Fellman believed the Vice President would succeed to the office of President just as he does by the "unwritten Constitution" if the President dies. He assumed that no finding of permanent inability would be made unless every hope for the President's recovery was gone.

Among others Thomas K. Finletter, attorney and former Secretary of the Air Force, thought the Vice President would only succeed to the powers and duties of the office. He seemed to think that so long as the President is alive there is some hope.

If the President is found permanently disabled, does the language of the Constitution demand the immediate election of a new President? If it does would the election be for a four-year term or for the unexpired term of the disabled President? This question refers to the concluding words of the succession clause, " . . . and the Congress may by Law provide for the Case of Removal, Death, Resignation or Inability, both of the President and Vice President, declaring what Officer shall then act as President, and such Officer shall act accordingly, until the Disability be removed, or a President shall be elected."

The responses to the question were overwhelmingly in the negative, although some of the answers were qualified. If we go into a detailed discussion of this problem we shall never get out of this chapter. Why not just give the framers of the Constitution credit for some common sense—which they seemed to have in generous supply? They knew it was possible that at some time death or some other catastrophe might strike both the President and the Vice President, and they tried in plain English to make it clear that Congress can provide that we will always have someone who can exercise the executive power. When a Vice President succeeds a deceased President we do not hold a special election. There is no more reason to when a Vice President takes over for one who is a permanently disabled.

The final question on Representative Celler's list was: "Does Congress have the authority to enact legislation to resolve any and all of these questions, or will a Constitutional amendment or amendments be necessary?" Happily, the replies preponderently supported Congressional power to act, though there were some dissents. Some believed that an act of Congress dealing with the situation would be effective only insofar as it gained voluntary acceptance from those immediately concerned. Dr. Everett S. Brown gave a direct and unequivocal answer: "In my opinion any and all of the questions raised in the questionnaire could be settled by legislation." Dr. Charles Fairman thought Congress had authority to settle the inability problem, but he suggested that there is a larger problem, which does require an amendment to the Constitution. He referred to a possible ". . . knockout of national governmental leadership, perhaps both executive and legislative by a hostile power." Dr. Fairman's suggestion is certainly worthy of consideration in an atomic age.

Dr. Jack Peltason of the University of Illinois was very much in favor of a Constitutional amendment to cover the inability problem. He believed that "an act of Congress would still leave some basic constitutional questions unresolved and would not decisively clarify responsibility. Only a constitutional amendment could do these things." Professor Arthur E. Sutherland of the Harvard Law School thought that any legislation on the subject would depend for its effectiveness " . . . on voluntary acceptance, as any statute purporting to stop the functioning of a President elected for 4 years will run into constitutional obstacles."

On April 11 and 12, 1956, the special subcommittee of the House Judiciary Committee held hearings on the inability problem. Much credit is due Representative Celler and his colleagues for their hard work in attempting to clarify the problem. Perhaps their efforts may bear fruit in the near future. Nevertheless, a reading of the printed record of the hearings indicates that we are still a good distance from a solution. Opinions of competent experts are still badly divided.

Through no fault of the committee, the hearings were not concerned with a single proposal. Rather they involved a proposal to amend the Constitution—House Joint Resolution 442—introduced by Representative Peter Frelinghuysen of New Jersey, a bill, Senate Bill 2763, introduced by Senator Frederick G. Payne of Maine, several committee prints posing alternative plans and, in addition, particular proposals made by witnesses who appeared before the subcommittee. Very little information was added that had not been provided in the responses to the questionnaire.

We may readily sympathize with New York Representative Kenneth B. Keating, who remarked during the proceedings, "Mr. Chairman, the deeper I get into this the more difficult it seems to become. Every witness who appears seems to have a fairly plausible solution of this problem."

All the proposed plans had merit, yet each was subject to serious criticism. Chairman Celler appeared fully to recognize this when he remarked during the testimony of Mr. Frelinghuysen, "As I said in my opening statement, we cannot have a perfect answer to this problem. No matter what kind of solution you propound, you will find some difficulty with it. There will be no solution that will be perfect. You have probably gathered that from your research."

The Eighty-fourth Congress adjourned without enacting any legislation on the inability matter. But the information and the ideas gathered by Mr. Celler and his fellow committee members should give the Eighty-fifth a helpful start.

No serious student of government science could help thinking deeply about a national problem and trying to arrive at a solution. One possible, though admittedly imperfect, approach comes to this author's mind after careful study of the House questionnaire. It seems clear that a statute to deal with the problem is needed. That statute should cover several important points.

First, it seems wise plainly to declare recognition of the Tyler precedent that on the death, resignation or removal of the President the Vice President becomes chief executive in fact and serves out the remainder of the current term. Whatever the historical error may have been at the time Tyler won his point, the precedent is now firmly established and should be the subject of very little controversy.

It is probably also necessary to state that a Vice President taking over the duties of a disabled President becomes only an acting President and surrenders the full executive powers as soon as the President is able to return to work. There is no precedent to interfere with such a decree, since no Vice President has ever succeeded to Presidential duties for this reason. A declaration of this sort would be sensible and would relieve the fear that the elected President might be thrust out of office.

If the President and the Vice President are on cordial personal terms and in harmony with each other on public policy the President could at times feel free to declare his own temporary inability, making way for the Vice President to perform. He could then, somewhat free from the cares of state, enjoy a more rapid and complete recovery from illness.

However the experts may have disagreed on other matters, they come to common terms on one point: they agree that the Vice President should only act as President for the duration of the President's inability.

No statute should, however, attempt to offer a definition of inability. A legislative definition, however wisely drawn, might prove unduly restrictive and could rise up to haunt us at a time of crisis. The term as used in the Constitution is flexible and broad enough to cover any situation in which the President's inability to perform might reasonably involve national peril or serious jeopardy to the public interest. Most of the outstanding students of the problem either oppose a definition or insist that it should be most loosely stated.

The President should by all means be authorized to announce his own inability. Such an announcement should be conclusive and should empower the Vice President immediately to take over temporary performance of Presidential functions. The President should continue to draw his full salary, but the Vice President should also be paid at the Presidential rate for the time he serves as President. There would be Constitutional obstacles to reduction of the President's salary, and it would hardly be just to require the Vice President to shoulder the responsibility without full compensation.

If the President's voluntary announcement of his own inability enables the Vice President immediately to take over, his announcement that he is ready to resume his duties should also be conclusive. The Vice President would then return to his regular position. Again it should be emphasized that a good personal relationship and basic agreement in political philosophy between the President and the Vice President are essential. Without these factors a President would be tempted to rise prematurely from a sickbed in order to arrest changes of policy that might annoy him.

If there is substantial reason to believe that the President is disabled, but he is either unable or unwilling to make an official announcement of the fact, we reach a great dilemma. Opinions on how to handle such a situation differ widely. There is no perfect solution in sight, and we shall probably never get one.

One proposal that seems to this author to have much to recommend it is for the creation of a Presidential power commission. This commission as contemplated would include eight heads of executive departments—the Secretary of State, who would be chairman, the Secretary of the Treasury, the Secretary of Defense, the Attorney General, the Postmaster General, the Secretary of Interior, the Secretary of Agriculture and the Secretary of Commerce. These are the Cabinet officers given seniority, following the speaker of the House and the president pro tempore of the Senate, in the Presidential Succession Act of 1947. The Secretary of Labor and the Secretary of Health, Education and Welfare would be next in line to serve if any of these eight should for any reason be unable to sit with the commission at a particular time.

All eight of the officers listed would normally be of the President's political party or at least in political sympathy with him. Their positions in the Presidential Succession Act are so remote that they would hardly be suspected of ulterior motives in finding the President unable to serve.

The representation from the President's official family might well be balanced with eight members of Congress. These should be the majority and minority floor leaders of each house and the chairman and the ranking minority member of that standing committee of each charged with matters pertaining to Presidential inability. The two houses would, of course, have to see to it that proper committee jurisdiction was thoroughly settled.

In the Congressional component of the commission the majority and minority parties would be equally represented— there would be four from each. But the President's political party, assuming that the eight Cabinet members belong to it, would always have the preponderance of voting strength, which is as it should be.

Besides these sixteen voting members of the commission there might well be four non-voting members with the right only to sit with the commission and participate in its discussions. These would be the Vice President, the speaker of the House, the president pro tempore of the Senate and the President's wife. The issue of Presidential inability might be raised by any two voting members provided one is a member of the President's party, or by any four regardless of party.

The commission would then proceed toward a finding. It should be required to arrange for a report by qualified medical experts. If nine members of the commission voted in favor of a finding of inability, then the Vice President would stand advised of his duty to take charge of Presidential functions. Requirement of an absolute majority when the President's party would have controlling strength should give complete assurance that there would be no finding of inability unless the situation had become very grave.

The President or any three voting members of the commission might be permitted to raise the issue of when the inability had been removed. If nine members voted to restore the President to office, the Vice President would be notified to step down.

While this plan is far from perfect it does have certain advantages. The Cabinet is well represented on the commission, but it cannot block a finding unless its ranks are absolutely solid. Surely the Cabinet should not be left entirely out of the picture. Former President Hoover, with the advantage of four years' experience in the White House, wired the special subcommittee at the time of its hearings that he believed that "the determination of inability and its termination should rest with the Cabinet."

In support of his view Mr. Hoover asserted that the Cabinet " . . . are in intimate contact with the President during any illness" and they can " . . . appraise the national setting as to whether there is any emergency which requires any action beyond the President's abilities." Few would claim that Mr. Hoover's views on the situation are less than those of an expert.

On the other hand, various objections were raised at the hearings to having the Cabinet solely responsible for determining Presidential ability. The Cabinet, through loyalty, might undertake to cover up for an ailing chief. Too, some members might fear that if they tried to declare the President unfit for duty and failed they might be summarily dismissed. Or perhaps some Cabinet officials might be on poor terms with the Vice President and stall calling him as long as possible.

But if a power commission were created these hesitations would be impossible. In the first place, once the issue of inability was raised the designated Cabinet members would be under obligation to participate in a decision. The President would certainly hesitate to discharge an official for performing his legal duty. If he did there would be no particular stigma for the dismissed department head, who would doubtless meet a more sympathetic public reaction than the President.

Nor would the Cabinet members be in a position to conceal the condition of the President or the state of public affairs.

Eight members of Congress would have full voting privileges and they could doubtless provoke a discussion and insist on a medical report. Of course if Cabinet ranks remained firm and unanimous, then that contingent could block a declaration of inability, but that is probably as it should be. No official body should ever declare the President unfit to serve unless the need for such a declaration is urgent. If eight Cabinet members participating in a joint Cabinet-Congressional body—including the Secretary of State, charged with protecting our foreign relations, and the Secretary of Defense, largely responsible for the security of the United States—should, after full discussion, vote that the President is able, then we may be reasonably sure that no great disaster is likely to flow from the decision.

Congress, the representative body of the entire nation, has a natural and legitimate interest in this problem. Throughout the special subcommittee's search for answers, whether by questionnaire or by its hearings, Congressional interest was freely asserted. But any design to have the Congress make a total determination of inability also brought strenuous objection. The Congress, for one thing, might not be in session when a crisis arises. Furthermore, Congress is innately a political body, in which partisan rivalry plays a vital role. A hostile Congressional majority might raise the claim of inability solely to embarrass an administration.

The plan to include on the proposed commission eight Congressional leaders, representing both political parties equally, would recognize the rightful legislative interest and responsibility without posing any danger of a purely political Congressional attack. The Congressional delegation would be well matched by the equal number from the Cabinet.

It is scarcely imaginable that a Constitutional difficulty should arise regarding the commission. Membership on such a board would surely not constitute an office within the meaning of the provision of the Constitution prohibiting a member of Congress from holding " . . . any Office under the United States." Members of Congress have served right along as members of fact-finding bodies and as delegates to international conferences. Members of both houses, for example, represented the country at the San Francisco Conference of 1945, which drafted the Charter of the United Nations.

Nor would Congressional membership violate the principle of separation of powers. The commission would in no sense intrude into the functions of the chief executive. It would have only one role to play—seeing to it that we have someone who has the capacity to act heading the executive branch. If this is a serious breach of the separation of powers, then the whole Constitution from the very beginning has been a complete repudiation of that principle. Since the day it went into effect the Congress has been charged with some degree of responsibility for seeing that we have someone as chief executive. By both the original Constitution and the Twelfth Amendment if the electoral college fails to choose either a President or a Vice President, Congress is charged to make the selection, within certain prescribed limits.

While both major parties would be represented on the commission, the President's party would control. The rival party is interested, of course, and should have an effective (though we hope unbiased) voice in the matter. It is also entitled to all available information on the President's condition. But as Professor Arthur Sutherland so emphatically pointed out at the hearings, the American people have given the President's political party a four-year mandate to exercise executive power, and the representatives of that party should be in the controlling position to determine executive inability.

Professor Sutherland proposed a plan to exclude any representative of the opposite party from a body that would examine an allegation of inability. This plan does not go that far, but it does give the President's party enough strength to decide all issues. While the rival party could be held accountable by the American people for its behavior in an inability proceeding before the commission, the President's party would be accountable for the ultimate decision. All this seems quite proper if we are to have party responsibility in the United States.

It will be observed that the Supreme Court has been left

entirely out of the proposed commission. While an issue of Presidential inability should certainly be decided without partisan bias, it is nevertheless political in character. The Supreme Court has consistently resisted efforts to involve it in political issues. It is important for the high court to maintain the highest possible dignity and to enjoy maximum respect and esteem from the public. In our times the Supreme Court finds itself facing enough divisive issues when adhering strictly to its job of interpreting the Constitution and the laws, without going out of the way to seek trouble in political matters.

For the President's wife to be a non-voting member of the commission could turn out to be of tremendous advantage. But she should not be required to take part in its discussions. The First Lady would be the best judge of her qualifications. Knowing her own sensibilities, if she believed that proceedings would embarrass her she could simply decline to serve. If she should see fit to participate, her service would doubtless be valuable. Her presence would have a sobering effect.

A decision on Presidential inability should be divorced entirely from partisan considerations. It would require partisan bigotry of such proportions as few people in public life possess to play politics with such a grave situation in the presence of the President's wife. But her presence would hardly prevent frank discussion. After all, the First Lady would fully realize the deep public interest in the proceedings and would appreciate that if she is to serve she must face up to realities—realities she may comprehend better than any other member of the commission. Nor would any American worthy of public trust suppress his true convictions on matters affecting the welfare and security of the United States merely because of the presence of a member of the President's family.

The Vice President, the speaker of the House and the president pro tempore of the Senate should also be privileged to participate in the deliberations. They have a duty to keep themselves informed. But being immediately in line for succession, they should have no votes. This is not to insinuate that these offices are ordinarily filled by persons who would allow personal ambition to interfere with right and justice. Rather, it is proposed to protect them as well as the entire commission from suspicion and rumor. To take any kind of action with the practical effect of suspending for even a short time a person whom the American people have designated as their chief executive is most serious. A severe crisis might arise if motives were suspect.

One may wonder, then, why Cabinet members in line of succession after the above-mentioned three are allowed votes in the hypothetical commission. The reason is simple: according to the Presidential Succession Act of 1947 a Cabinet officer would have only temporary tenure in exercising Presidential functions. He would act as President only until a speaker of the House or a president pro tempore of the Senate qualified.

The commission should really never determine that the President is permanently disabled. In an age of remarkable medical achievement we should not mock progress by pronouncing sentence of chronic incapacity on the first citizen of the nation. Also, by refraining from a pronouncement of permanent disability we would avoid the anomalous step of attempting to remove the President without an impeachment proceeding. The Constitutionality of that would be dubious.

Of course if the best medical advice available said there was no foreseeable cure for a President's malady, the President might quite properly resign. And it would not be amiss for Congress to enact legislation providing that a President who resigns for medical reasons should receive full salary for the balance of his term. Fortunately we do not have to witness the spectacle of a chief executive whose health has been broken in our country's service leaving the White House without assured income for the remainder of the term for which we elected him.

It is extremely doubtful that we will ever have a President so base as to feign an illness, mental or physical, in order to resign and run out on the American people, drawing a salary for doing nothing. If we ever have, then it will be cheaper to pay him off and let him go than it will be to suffer his kind of public service. The whole revolting idea is far from the realm of probability.

A serious question arises whether we should rely entirely on a statute or whether we should seek an amendment to the Constitution to treat the inability problem. There is much to be said in favor of the statutory approach. Ordinarily, to pass a law takes much less time than to secure the proposal of a Constitutional amendment by Congress and its ratification by the states.

Furthermore, a statutory solution would be more flexible than a Constitutional one. The problem is difficult, and any procedure we may establish will of necessity be experimental. If we proceed by act of Congress it will be fairly simple to make any changes that further study or experience prove necessary. Congress can amend a statute whenever it sees fit, assuming that the President goes along with the change.

The disadvantage of this approach is that a finding of Presidential inability by a statutory body might lack binding force. It might rest for its effectiveness on voluntary compliance, according to some expert testimony. It is by no means certain that by a finding of a statutory commission we could compel either the President to step aside or the Vice President to take over.

The President might assert that the only way he can be involuntarily separated from his executive functions during his elected term is by impeachment. The Vice President might claim that since the Constitution places on him the duty to exercise the powers and the duties of the President in case the latter can't, he himself is the one to decide when his duty arises and when it does not arise. If he is not yet satisfied that the President is incapacitated within the meaning of the Constitution, he might insist that he is under no obligation to act.

It is very doubtful though that either a President or a Vice President would resist a finding of inability by an official body. Past Vice Presidents have refrained from any attempt to take over for a President, however seriously ill. The main reason for this has been the desire to prevent any possible charges of usurpation. But if he were backed by the finding of a statutory body the Vice President could act and still be protected from criticism by all but the most rabid extremists.

An amendment to the Constitution could, of course, make the procedures certain and the findings binding. But it might take several years to secure the amendment and, once ratified, whatever it said would remain fixed. If the solution it offered proved unsatisfactory, we would still be saddled with it until we could get another amendment repealing or modifying it.

Most of the government scholars questioned believe that Congress already has full power to legislate on Presidential inability. Congress has often in the past acted on a strong belief rather than an absolute certainty that it has authority. If it hadn't the Constitution could never have expanded to meet the needs of an ever-changing society.

But some experts do doubt that Congress can authorize mandatory decisions on the question. Therefore it might be best, to meet our immediate need, to enact legislation authorizing only advisory decisions by the commission we propose. We have already examined the reasons why the advice of the commission would probably be heeded.

Meantime, for the long-range need, Congress might well propose a Constitutional amendment clearly empowering itself to authorize compulsory decisions. Once such an amendment had been ratified by the states the Constitutional issue would be resolved.

But until we solve another and perhaps more basic problem we shall not get very far toward a lasting resolution to the inability riddle. Unless the President and the Vice President can work together as genuine partners in the executive department—with the President as senior partner and ultimate source of executive power—the inability problem can be no more than half settled no matter how carefully we devise statutes and Constitutional amendments. Without this partnership we are going to have a President reluctant to permit a Vice President to put a temporary hand to the executive plow and a Vice President reluctant to offer the hand.

VIII
Murder Without Malice

When coronary thrombosis attacked President Eisenhower on September 24, 1955, it missed by just one day the thirty-sixth anniversary of another fateful day in the same state.

The twenty-eighth President of the United States had carried the heavy cross of leading this nation through the trials of World War I and the subsequent peace conference at Paris. He had made bringing order out of chaos in the community of nations his supreme goal. He had worked many long hours for a League of Nations. American participation in the League was clearly the most important key to its success or failure. But now some half-dozen "irreconcilable" senators, able men but men with minds of rather limited, provincial range, had set out to wreck the President's plans.

President Wilson had summoned every ounce of his courage and strength to accept the challenge and fight back. He had decided to take the matter to the people. He had covered thousands of miles. He had given some thirty-seven speeches in twenty-nine cities, with senators William E. Borah of Idaho and Hiram Johnson of California trailing behind in rebuttal.

The strain proved too much for the President. On September 25, 1919, Mr. Wilson collapsed in Pueblo, Colorado. The President survived his term of office, but as an ill and broken man. How the history of this nation and of the whole world might have been changed had the President retained his health is locked forever in the vaults of the unknown.

Scarcely four years later tragedy struck once more at the White House door. Mr. Wilson's successor, President Warren G. Harding, was returning from a trip to Alaska when he died very suddenly in San Francisco on August 2, 1923. In all probability the death of the President had been hastened by his chagrin and embarrassment over the misconduct of men high up the scale in his administration—even some Cabinet personnel. But Harding was spared the grief of learning the full extent of their dishonesty.

April 12, 1945, is all too recent. On that day the whole nation, and indeed much of the world, was thrown into deep sorrow and shock at the news of the sudden death of President Franklin D. Roosevelt at Warm Springs, Georgia. Three terms as President and a few months of a fourth, four Presidential campaigns, depression, recovery efforts, World War II, the North Atlantic, Casablanca, Teheran and Yalta conferences and the rest had proved too much for his physical strength.

Now, scarcely more than ten years later, we have seen another stricken amidst the terrific exactions of office—a much-beloved President, struggling with problems of both national and world import. Summing up, we find that in slightly more than forty years, beginning with the inauguration of President Woodrow Wilson in March 1913, two Presidents met sudden death in office, one suffered permanent loss of health and a fourth faced grave illness.

A casualty list of four out of seven Presidents in four decades seems an alarmingly heavy toll. Looking at it another way, the statistics appear even more disturbing. If we merely count the Presidents who reached the White House by election in first instance, the burdens of office have smitten four out of five (our seven Presidents include two Vice Presidents who took over when the incumbent died), giving us an eighty per cent casualty record. It is altogether doubtful that a President may be regarded as a good insurance risk in our day.

The only one of the aforesaid five Presidents to escape unscathed was President Herbert Hoover. He served only one term and has so remarkably retained his physical and mental vigor that he has been able to perform important post-Presidential services for the country. And he evidently realizes that he was fortunate to come out as well as he has, since he is in spite of his advanced years just about the most persistent agitator for Presidential relief. Testifying before the subcommittee on reorganization of the Senate Committee on Government Operations on January 16, 1956, in behalf of his proposal for an Administrative Vice President to assist the President, Mr. Hoover gave us well-considered warning. "In any event," he said, "we are going to have to give the Presidents some relief if we are going to keep them alive."

Surely the nature of the Presidential office—not its efficiency or its honor—has become a major Constitutional problem. Beset as we are with grave problems of world-wide significance, and likely as we are to remain so beset for many years, its ever-increasing burdens promise to continue to grow. Considering the advanced ages at which people ordinarily occupy the White House and also the patent fact that none of us, whatever our station, enjoys a guaranteed immunity against stroke or embolism or heart attack, it may be somewhat hasty to attribute all the ills that have attacked our Presidents to the strain of office.

But as we note the mountains of work—some sheer routine yet all of tremendous importance—that we assign to our chief executive, it becomes clear that we must either alter the situation or leave a record through which future historians may account us guilty of a national crime, negligent national Presidentiacide.

It is not without significance that before World War I the Presidential office did not appear exceedingly perilous from a health standpoint. Up to that time, while there had been five Presidential deaths in office, only two of them, William Henry Harrison and Zachary Taylor, had died natural deaths. Three, Abraham Lincoln, James A. Garfield and William McKinley, were victims of assassins. By that time natural death had taken seven Vice Presidents, and few would assert that the Vice Presidents had succumbed to excessive burdens of office. It is since World War I that the Presidency has become a major health hazard. Significantly, it has also been since World War I that our Presidents have been saddled with world problems on top of domestic problems. Let us look briefly at a few of the duties of the President's man-killing job.

First, the chief executive is the ceremonial head of the nation. In this station he must perform the functions of a king in a constitutional monarchy or of the symbolic state head in a parliamentary republic. This takes an enormous amount of the President's time. A new ambassador arriving from a foreign country must be received by the head of the state. A scholar in the sciences has made a significant discovery; no person can lend so much to the promotion of interest in further research as the President, who stands commending the scholar with a friendly handshake and an encouraging word as cameras click on all sides.

A word from the President will help so much in the Red Cross drive, the March of Dimes, the Community Chest campaign and scores of other worthy social projects. Is there a monument to be dedicated? A power generator to be started in a new dam? Can the President give a brief audience to the winner of a spelling bee? To a delegation from the Boy Scouts or the Girl Scouts? Can he get out to the ball park and throw in the first ball to initiate a good season in the national pastime? Can he address the annual convention of the AFL-CIO? Of the American Legion? Can he get out to the graduating exercises of some college or university and give the commencement address?

It is not our intention to deprecate the importance of these things. On the contrary, the President's position as ceremonial head is perhaps the most supremely important of all his functions. For national health and strength it is absolutely necessary that we possess a high symbol of national unity, and no other office can possibly supply it. In England, and in fact throughout the British Commonwealth of Nations, the symbol is today their Queen, and what a beautiful symbol they have. Imagine the British public or the Commonwealth publics without a king or queen, whipping up national sentiment by singing "God save the Parliament," or Americans rising to the tune of "Hail to the Congress."

The President has to be, in a sense, two people. As a political figure he often antagonizes many of us. Congressmen attack him. Caricaturists make sport of him and editors fulminate against him. But the President as head of the state is something else. Let something serious happen to him and we all feel it deeply. Party lines are dropped as the nation prays for a stricken President or mourns his death.

In 1923 President Harding was by no means the idol of the deep South. He couldn't be, for he was a Republican and at that time the Solid South was really solid. It was as steadfast in its Democracy as a mountain of granite is defiant of the elements. In fact Southerners considered it sinful and antisocial to be a Republican. There were none of the species around except the so-called post-office Republicans, kindred souls of their counterparts in Maine, the post-office Democrats. Yet when the news came that President Harding had passed away, there was only grief. "We have lost our President," was the word at every hand. And though we have seldom had a more controversial figure than the late President Franklin D. Roosevelt, seldom has a person's passing been more universally mourned.

We have a Presidential republic, and we would not think of changing. We are very happy with what we have. But it does us no harm to admit that in one respect a cabinet or parliamentary government has an advantage. In England, for example, royalty plays a most useful ceremonial role. The Queen can dedicate the monuments. Everybody likes monuments and she can officiate without offending anyone. The Prime Minister can be spared for serious problems of state. Everybody can cheer, love and admire the Queen. She does only those things that signify the dignity and the honor of the state, and she stops right there. She takes no stand on divisive political issues.

Not so with our ceremonial head. One moment he is congratulating a child musician on her remarkable talent and accomplishment, and we all applaud. The next moment he sends a message to Congress about the Taft-Hartley Act, which results in loud applause from one direction and vigorous condemnation from the other. Back in the days of President Herbert Hoover the country was bogged down in depression. All the blame seemed to descend right on his head. From the way he was disliked at the time one would suppose that he planned to have the depression, which is to say that he conspired to commit political suicide. One day some college students brought to their campus a copy of a sheet that was then in circulation. It was called the *Nutty News* or something of the sort and carried this big boxcar headline: HOOVER KIDNAPPED! ABDUCTORS DEMAND $100,000 AT ONCE OR THEY WILL SURELY RETURN HIM. Imagine what the British would think if someone came up with a sheet like that about their King or their Queen.

But no matter how difficult it is for the President to play his double role he will have to remain our ceremonial state head. No other officer can be his substitute. And a nation without a high executive as the symbol of unity would be like an orphan adrift. At least a free nation would be so, for there the outward expression of the nation's purposes must spring from the internal spirit of the people, and that internal spirit must find its focus in the head of the state.

The President is also the actual state head, the one and only chief executive of the nation. As such he occupies the same station as a British Prime Minister, and more. The President is more nearly comparable to the British Prime Minister and his whole Cabinet. In England the Prime Minister is chief all right, in the sense that he is the first of the ministers. But it is often said with much truth that he is merely *Primus inter Pares*. He stands above the other members of the Cabinet but not too far above. He and his colleagues are jointly and severally responsible to Parliament or, particularly, to the House of Commons. They are all sailing in the same boat, and they are subject to common hazards.

If the Prime Minister drops one of his Cabinet members

arbitrarily and with little reason he may run into difficulty. The fallen colleague does not retire to private life and early oblivion. He still holds his seat in Parliament, perhaps as a very influential member. It may not be easy to write the whole thing off as a closed incident. Furthermore, the Prime Minister must be ever mindful of the fact that the power of his Cabinet, himself included, proceeds from no direct and specific constitutional grant. Rather it arises from his ability to maintain majority support for his program in the House of Commons. But the Prime Minister may have one satisfaction that is denied our President—the other Cabinet members, being not too far removed from him in rank, must share responsibility with him.

The position of the President of the United States as state head is much different. He derives executive authority directly from the Constitution. Article II vests not the *chief* executive power or *partial* executive power but "the executive Power" in the President. He is the sole executive officer created directly by the Constitution, since the Vice President is only a potential executive officer. It would be very much different if the Constitution had provided that the executive power be vested in the President and his Cabinet, but it says no such thing. It carries no mention of a cabinet. Thus it was that President Lincoln, on one occasion in which he had voted "aye" in Cabinet meeting and all the rest had voted "nay," was acting thoroughly within his Constitutional powers when he reported said, "Seven nays, one aye—the ayes have it."

Nor is the President confined to the powers vested in him by the Constitution. Faced with the vast numbers of new problems our ever more complex society produces, Congress has of necessity imposed a mountain of statutory duties on the chief executive. And even if Congress were to lift some of these duties from the President's shoulders and place them in the custody of department heads or other high officials or agencies, the President would still be responsible, since we hold him accountable for just about everything that goes on in his administration.

The President's executive duties have multiplied over the

years, and they are likely to keep on multiplying. A detailed analysis would perhaps require several volumes. We shall have to be content with a cursory glance at the high spots.

The President has an enormous number of appointments to make, both civil and military. According to data presented to the Senate's subcommittee on reorganization in January 1956 by Robert E. Merriam, assistant to the director of the Bureau of the Budget, President Eisenhower submitted to the Senate during the year 1955 a total of 40,686 nominations, of which 37,467 were military and 3,219 civil. This was a far cry from the year 1796, when President Washington sought Senate approval on a total of eighty-five nominations.

Of course the President cannot make a personal determination on each nominee, but he must bear the responsibility for the efficient operation of the process of selection and also for the success of each appointment. He must keep a watchful eye on the functioning of the entire executive branch of the government. This is a tremendous job; note how it has grown. According to the figures of the Bureau of the Budget as presented by Mr. Merriam, in 1790 President Washington had to maintain some degree of Presidential surveillance over military personnel numbering 1273 and civilian personnel numbering 1,000. In 1910 President William Howard Taft had to do the same for 135,403 military personnel and 391,350 civilian personnel. But in 1955 President Eisenhower had some degree of surveillance over 2,935,107 military personnel and 2,371,421 civilian.

As for the agencies the President must supervise, Mr. Merriam submitted data showing that while in 1790 President Washington had only nine and in June 1864 President Lincoln had eleven, President Eisenhower in January 1956 had at least nominal supervision of fifty-six establishments, including five units in the Executive Office of the President, ten executive departments and forty-one independent agencies.

Of course the President has staff officers, department heads and other high officials to assist him in his vigil, but if things go wrong he is still ultimately accountable. He alone of all the executive officers must face the people to give an account of his stewardship in a Presidential campaign. Even if he is not a candidate his record must be defended by his political party's anointed successor. If any Cabinet officer incurs public displeasure his critics shout for the President to dismiss him from his post. The trouble is right at the President's doorstep. He must bear the full weight of public, party and Congressional pressure. The President has full power to fire all right, but it is very difficult to decide whether and when to fire and, if the decision is not to fire, what other steps to take. The President's executive duties require endless hours of work, as well as intelligence, perseverance and plenty of backbone.

The President would have more than enough work to do if he were merely chief executive. But he is much more than that; he has a third great responsibility. The President has become, in every practical sense, the chief legislator of the United States. Time and circumstances have imposed this duty on him—the framers of the Constitution had no way of foreseeing the development. They gave him only a few duties pertaining to legislation.

The Constitution requires that the President "shall from time to time give to the Congress Information of the State of the Union, and recommend to their Consideration such Measures as he shall judge necessary and expedient." He has a qualified veto over acts of Congress, which veto may be overridden by a two thirds vote of both houses. He may call special sessions of Congress and may adjourn the two houses if they cannot agree on their own time for adjournment.

The Fathers contemplated some degree of interest on the part of the chief executive in things going on in Congress but could not have contemplated the role the President plays today. This is not surprising. It is extremely doubtful that any of them could have foreseen the tremendous growth of the country, its complicated and interdependent economic system and its assumption of world leadership in a day of atomic power and Communist imperialism.

The expansion of the President's legislative duties is partly illustrated by another statement of Mr. Merriam before the reorganization subcommittee: " . . . Research shows that in 1789 President Washington approved 27 laws and 3 Executive Orders, while in 1955, President Eisenhower signed 390 public laws, 490 private laws, 65 Executive Orders, and 42 proclamations."

Not only does the President today sign many more laws than former Presidents, but also he sponsors more laws. The major legislative program gets its inception from White House recommendation. The President is and must be the planner-in-chief. There are many reasons why this has become so, not the least of which is the modern necessity for economic planning through legislation. Economic planning is a very elusive term, and it is used with various connotations. It may be so feeble, halting and timorous as to let a nation drift into despair. It may be so arbitrary and philosophically omniscient as to provoke stagnation. The real issue is one of degree.

One glance at our history shows us that our national government has engaged in some degree of economic planning from the very day George Washington took the oath of office as first President. Since 1933 it has been one of the major endeavors of the government. What has been the purpose of a protective tariff? What do we hope to achieve with reciprocal trade agreements? Why do we have Federal Reserve Banks and a council of economic advisers? Why a National Labor Relations Act? A Labor-Management Relations Act? A Fair Labor Standards Act? A farm price-support program? A Social Security Act?

No sane person doubts that our government is going to continue to keep a watchful eye on economic conditions and is going to make plans for maintaining prosperity. The only questions now are how much national economic planning our government will attempt and what directions it will take. Of course the government will not do it all. The major responsibility still rests on the people themselves, as producers, distributors, investors, managers, workers and financiers. But our government is and will continue to be the co-ordinator of our several efforts. In other words, it will give us a chance to work together for common goals for the good of all.

The international situation dictates that our government be deeply concerned about economic conditions in the outside world as well as at home if the world is not to go to Communism by default. The legislative problems of our day are huge and baffling and do not stop at our national border. They are national and international. They require careful plans. We must have democracy, but we must also have unified leadership, which the President alone can supply. If the President does not offer effective leadership to the Congress, the Congress is not led but just drifts. No person in Congress is in a position to offer such leadership as the President can give. There are 435 members of the House of Representatives, each one ordinarily representing one Congressional district. Each Congressman is elected by and accountable to the people of only that small fraction of this vast country. If a Congressman plans a legislative program he can muster little public support for it and is, besides, tempted to confine himself to a rather narrow, local range. A United States Senator is, by the same token, accountable only to his own state. His view of national affairs too is often dimmed by the glow of local emotion and prejudice.

Only the President and Vice President are elected to represent the whole country and are thus answerable to the whole country. And, as we have seen, the Vice President has no active voice in national affairs. So Congress, by its very nature, is ill equipped to plan a national program. Congress is capable of doing a good job in debating, enacting, amending or defeating legislative proposals emanating from the White House, but it is not well constituted, with its vast membership, for initiating the program. Only the President is in a position to do this.

Experience in our time has demonstrated that either the President will offer effective leadership to Congress or else Congress will give us much debate, much drifting but little action. Consult your own experience. As a voter, are you more interested in hearing two rival candidates for the Presidency undertake to outvow each other over which will more conscientiously execute the law, or are you more interested in hearing them compare their legislative programs, their stands on such matters as taxation, farm prices, a balanced budget, federal aid to education, revision of the immigration laws and stand-by credit controls?

Our President has a much harder job in leading the legislative body than his British counterpart. The Prime Minister always enjoys majority support in the House of Commons. If he loses that support he either gets out or calls for a Parliamentary election. The President, on the other hand, must often work through a Congress in which his own political party is in the minority. The President serves for a fixed term of four years, and he must carry on regardless of the political complexion of Congress. In the years since 1929 we have had four Presidents. Three of them at one time or another had to undertake to lead the legislative body when the opposite party was in the majority in one or both houses.

From 1931 to 1933 President Herbert Hoover, a Republican, had to court the support of a Democratic majority in the House of Representatives. Franklin D. Roosevelt was blessed with Democratic Congressional majorities during all his many years in the White House, but his successor, President Truman, had to confront the celebrated Eightieth Congress, with Republican majorities in both houses, from 1947 to 1949. In 1956 Republican President Dwight D. Eisenhower faced Democratic majorities in both the House and the Senate.

The President's legislative role is not an easy one even when his own party enjoys a Congressional majority. Our political parties cannot hope to discipline their members. There is no guarantee that all the Republican members of Congress will support a Republican President's program, and the same may be said of the Democrats.

No one who followed the sessions of the Eighty-fourth Congress would venture to say that both Senator Knowland, Republican Senate floor leader and Republican Senator

McCarthy from Wisconsin always saw eye to eye with President Eisenhower. In fact the public needs not be reminded that from 1953 to 1955 Senator McCarthy gave more trouble to the President than all the Democrats in Congress. Yet, even in spite of a Senate vote of censure, Senator McCarthy held his chairmanship of the permanent investigations subcommittee throughout the Republican Eighty-third Congress and in the Democratic Eighty-fourth sat as ranking minority member, ready to resume the chair if his party should regain the majority in the 1956 Senatorial elections.

And President Franklin Roosevelt met so much opposition from some leading Democrats in Congress in the late thirties that he sought to purge them from the party by urging Democrats to defeat them in the primaries.

To return to our comparison, the Prime Minister works from the inside, while the President must operate from the outside. The former, with his Cabinet, goes into the Parliament (primarily the House of Commons), presents his program there, debates it face to face with his opponents, votes on his proposition and drives it through with the support of a pretty strongly disciplined majority. But while the President can and often does have experts from the executive departments or from his own staff draft a bill for him, the rest of the way is not so easy. He cannot even so much as introduce the bill, but must get a member of Congress to do it for him.

Oh yes, the President can send a message to Congress requesting favorable action on a bill. Or if he wishes to be more dramatic, he may go down and address the legislative body in person. But once he gives his speech he gets out, and Congress is again in command. He can send his department heads or other executive officers down to Capitol Hill to present his case to committees, but neither the President nor his Cabinet can participate in Congressional debates. Yet in some way the President must get his legislative program across, for unless he does the nation is undirected and the chief executive is accounted weak. The President's legislative job alone is enough to keep him well occupied.

And there is no prospect that it will become easier as the years roll on. We are more likely to get the opposite. Valuable as its functions are, Congress is just too big, and its membership represents too many diversified interests, to achieve a unified approach to the multitude of problems confronting us today.

A fourth major Presidential role is that of director of the foreign policy of the United States. The situation today is a far cry from that prevailing when President George Washington warned the infant nation against assuming too many political entanglements with the nations of Europe and when President Thomas Jefferson made his pronouncement against entangling alliances. The policy of isolation is gone for good. It has become simply untenable. Today the fate of the whole world may be decided by the race for power—physical and psychological—between Moscow and Washington. With the North Atlantic Treaty Organization, the Southeast Asia Treaty Organization, the Formosa Pact and the rest, the United States has entered into alliances in just about every great sector of the globe.

No one human mind would be capable of even remembering the list of international conferences in which this nation must now participate in a single year, some within and some without the United Nations. And the President is and must be the focal point of them all. He is not a dictator of foreign policy, but he is far and away at the head. Let a delicate international situation develop, and the whole world wants to know first of all what position the President of the United States will take. Of course he has the Secretary of State, the whole State Department, a foreign service and scores of experts to help him, but in all critical matters the President must make the ultimate decision. He must set the policy.

He can settle many matters by informal consultation with officials of other governments. On others he may proceed by an executive agreement that requires no Senate approval. If the matter is incorporated in a treaty he must get the consent of two thirds of the Senate, but even there the President takes the initiative. Hardly a week passes but he must make a decision of far-reaching international concern. And it is the President who gets the approbation or the criticism of press and public for foreign-policy decisions.

Once our nation felt secure from foreign attack. No power in the New World had either the desire or the strength to destroy us. And our ocean barriers protected us from outside attack. But with the development of long-range aircraft, guided missiles and atomic and hydrogen weapons that security has now vanished. The President must be sensitive to what is going on throughout the world—in Korea, in Indo-China, in Israel and the whole Middle East, in Argentina, in the Formosa Straits, in Quemoy, in Iceland—everywhere. From these duties too the President has no relief in sight.

The fifth great burden carried by the President is the responsibility to serve as commander of all of the armed forces of the United States. The Constitution makes him commander-in-chief of the American military forces. Time and circumstance have so catastrophically magnified that job that he is now virtually defender-in-chief of all the free men and women of the earth.

For many decades before World War I this country maintained but a meager army and only a very modest naval force. In those days the President's military responsibilities consumed only a minor fraction of his time. Modern developments have changed all this. The President must now devote a very great deal of his time to military matters. Of course he does not assume personal and immediate direction of the military forces either in peace or in war, but here again ultimate decisions of major consequence must be made at the White House. It is true that the President gets worlds of advice from the Department of Defense, the National Security Council, the Office of Defense Mobilization, the Joint Chiefs of Staff and others, but the highest-level answers must come from him. And to make his burden all the more exacting, he cannot but be conscious that a foolish decision on his part might constitute the beginning of the end for western civilization.

An excellent illustration of the expansion of the President's responsibility as commander-in-chief is afforded by the growth of the armed forces. On June 30, 1930, President Herbert Hoover commanded 255,822 people on active duty in the armed services. But on June 30, 1955, President Eisenhower was commander-in-chief of 2,935,107 men and women on active duty. Our armed forces are more than ten times as large today as in 1930.

As though these five responsibilities were not enough, circumstances have forced on the President another exacting and time-consuming function. He is regarded as supreme spokesman for his political party. Of course his party maintains a national committee with a national chairman at its head. The national chairman, along with agencies of the national committee, looks after administrative details of the party. But every schoolboy knows that when a party matter comes up the country is more eager to know what the President has to say than what the national chairman may express. After all, the political fortunes of Representatives, Senators, Cabinet members, governors, state legislators, county clerks and sometimes even lesser township and municipal officials may rise and fall with the popularity of the President and his program.

There are always party gatherings that would like to have the President address them. National committeemen and women are frequently in Washington. It helps them and the party a great deal if the President can see them. While the President is assuming open leadership of his own party, he must often try to carry the opposition party along with him, at least part of the way.

In recent years the relative strength of the two major parties has been so nearly equal in Congress and the cohesiveness of both parties has been so defective that the President has seldom been able to carry out an important policy solely with his own party's support. President Eisenhower in foreign matters leaned rather heavily on Senator Walter F. George of Georgia, Democratic chairman of the powerful Senate Foreign Relations Committee, just as the late President

Franklin D. Roosevelt sought and gained significant support from the late Senator Arthur Vandenberg, Michigan Republican.

It is evident now that the President's duties and responsibilities have increased steadily with the growth of the nation and particularly with its assumption of world leadership. No sensible person would deny that the President has a man-killing job and that he should be allowed to tap every possible source of help. The question is naturally what has been done to make his duties lighter.

For many years the amount of personal assistance provided for the President was so small as to be ridiculous and tragic at the same time. Until 1857 the only member of the executive staff supported by Congress was a clerk to sign land patents. The President himself had to pay his secretary's salary. In 1857 Congress appropriated funds for a private secretary, a steward to supervise the White House and a messenger. Though a few more clerks were eventually provided for, this was the President's staff until 1928, when the number of secretaries was increased to three.

The ludicrous part of this situation was that the heads of executive departments had a great deal of help. Well, when Congress didn't provide the President with assistance, he did the only thing he could do. He borrowed help. Dr. Louis Brownlow, former Director of the Public Administration Clearing House in Washington, gave an interesting statement along this line to the Senate subcommittee considering the Hoover proposal for an Administrative Vice President. Dr. Brownlow's statement follows:

For many years, down until 1947, when Mr. Truman was President, the clerks and stenographers, or many of them, in the White House were borrowed from other departments. I remember when Mr. Roosevelt, FDR, was President, I saw a clerk in the White House whom I had known to be there on the same job when Theodore Roosevelt was President. He told me that he came in under McKinley. I asked him, "Have you been on the White House payroll all the time?"

He said, "I have never been on the White House payroll. I am still a clerk in the Department of Agriculture."

In recent years Congress has been more readily inclined to provide assistance. We will consider only a few of the more significant advances. The Budget and Accounting Act of 1921 was an important forward move. It provided the President with a budget office to assist in both the preparation and the execution of the budget. This office was at first placed in the Treasury Department, but with the Director solely responsible to the President. It has since been moved to the Executive Office of the President. Since then by reason of both empowering legislation from Congress and executive orders of the President, the President has acquired a large staff in what is known as the Executive Office of the President. It includes the Bureau of the Budget, the Council of Economic Advisors, the National Security Council, the Office of Defense Mobilization and the White House Office.

The latter office is most personal to the President. It includes the assistant to the President, the secretary to the President, a personal secretary, the press secretary, legal counsel, several administrative assistants, the executive officer and various aides from branches of the military service.

Various administrative reorganization acts have given the President authority to take the initiative in reorganizing administrative agencies to secure greater efficiency and better supervision. In 1950 Congress passed the McCormack Act to make it easier for the President to delegate his statutory duties to his subordinates. Much more can and will be done.

But merely passing statutes and providing more staff members will not solve the problem. What the President needs is not so much *more* help but a different *kind* of help. He needs prestige help. He needs the help of someone whose prestige is above every other officer in the nation except the President himself.

A Monumental Failure

The Presidency, as we have seen, carries so many heavy responsibilities as to jeopardize the health and even the life of its occupant, a badly overworked man. The Vice Presidency, on the other hand, has carried such insignificant responsibility that it has not redounded either to the benefit of its holder or to that of the nation. It is not too much to say that the office has often been frightfully near a sinecure. Its flaws have been so glaring and so numerous that we cannot even attempt a complete analysis of them.

The Vice Presidency as an office has seldom been able to generate a healthy competition for its possession or a substantial degree of prestige for its possessor. Its creation was an afterthought in the Constitutional Convention. It was designed largely to prevent a chaotic scattering of the electoral votes for President, to provide a tie-breaker for the small and even-numbered Senate and to assure a stand-by for the President. It was accepted lethargically by homesick and weary delegates. There was some opposition to the very existence of the office, but the objection was held in restraint by the objectors themselves. Nobody wanted to create another big argument and prolong the Convention.

So the office of Vice President came into being like an unwelcome child. Nobody knew what to do with it. It had an inauspicious birth, and it was to suffer a most serious retardation on the adoption of the Twelfth Amendment in 1804.

The First Congress, we know, even hesitated to vote the Vice President a salary. The thought that we didn't really need a Vice President was also freely expressed in the Eighth Congress in the debates over the proposal to separate the electoral college ballots for President and Vice President—the proposal that in less than a year after the debates became the Twelfth Amendment.

Representative Samuel W. Dana of Connecticut, speaking on December 3, 1803, declared that he thought it would be best to let the Constitution stand as it was, but rather than go through with a plan for separate electoral balloting for the two offices, he would prefer to abolish the Vice Presidency. Of the proposed amendment he said, " . . . the Vice President under it being but a secondary character, that office will become a lure to ambitious men, who, by flattering the states, and by the exertion of undue influence, will enable particular states to make a bargain as to the possession of executive power. . . . "

Dana's Connecticut colleague, Representative Roger Griswold, supported his views. Griswold believed that if the plan should be adopted the office of Vice President would become "useless, worse than useless." He too would leave the Constitution as it was, but he thought it better to have no Vice President than to adopt the discriminating ballot. "The office of Vice President," he said, "will be carried to market to purchase the votes of particular states." A big state, Griswold thought, would say to another state, "Give us the President and we will give you the Vice President."

Dana's efforts to abolish the office were defeated by a vote of 85 to 27, but few can deny that he and Griswold made a forecast that has proved over the years to be more nearly right than wrong. The Vice Presidency was no more inspiring as an office when the nineteenth century was nearing its close. Writing his doctoral thesis on Congressional government, a brilliant young scholar named Woodrow Wilson said of the Vice President, "His position is one of anomalous insignificance and curious uncertainty. . . . And the chief embarrassment in discussing his office is, that in explaining how little there is to be said about it one has evidently said all there is to say."

Doubts about the usefulness of the Vice Presidency persist in our own day. Of course we cannot ignore the obvious fact that during the last twenty years or so the Vice Presidency has undergone a resuscitation, which has perhaps reached its peak in the extraordinary harmony between Vice President Nixon and President Eisenhower. But we shall see that the revival has been moving in channels that, while they would be entirely proper with fundamental Constitutional change, are somewhat perilous as matters now stand. Unless the present trend is halted or the Constitutional position of the Vice President is re-examined and changed to accord with it, a political explosion detrimental to both the Presidency and the Vice Presidency is bound to occur.

The Vice Presidency must, if it be accounted a success, be the position of second importance in the nation—second only to the Presidency in prestige and influence. Actually it is not and never has been second. There are, to say the least, a dozen or more officers who surpass the Vice President in power and influence: the speaker of the House of Representatives, the majority floor leaders of House and Senate, the chairmen of the more important Congressional standing committees, probably more than half of the Cabinet officers, the assistant to the President, the Director of the Budget, the Foreign Operations Administrator and the governors of the more populous states, to name a few.

If one doubts the propriety of including the governors in this list, he should go back to Theodore Roosevelt, who served as governor of New York and then as Vice President. Writing to Maria Longworth Storer on March 6, 1901, Roosevelt said of the Vice President, "He does not begin to have the influence that the Governor of New York has, and even that influence of course is simply extended by courtesy." A few weeks later he wrote to Bellamy and Maria Storer, "But I often wish that I could only manage to make my friends understand that I really have much less influence with the President now that I am Vice President than even when I was governor."

In fact the Vice Presidency as an office has lagged so far

in importance that many of our leading statesmen have shied away from the nomination. Beyond a doubt it has been the butt of more jokes than any other office in the land, if not in the whole world. Fortunately many of our Vice Presidents and ex-Vice Presidents have managed to escape embarrassment by joining in the sport. Thomas R. Marshall, Woodrow Wilson's Vice President, and the late Alben W. Barkley, Mr. Truman's Vice President, were both fond of telling this story: "Once upon a time there was a farmer who had two sons. One of them ran off to sea. The other was elected Vice President of the United States. Nothing was ever heard of either of them again."

The amazing Mr. Barkley when he accepted the Democratic nomination for Vice President in 1948 began his acceptance speech, "Inasmuch as I am about to enter upon the discharge of the duties of an office that requires four years of silence, I will be brief in my acknowledgement."

In January 1954 Mr. Truman related in *Time Magazine* that when he was first approached about becoming a Vice Presidential candidate in 1944 he objected, saying, "Look at all the Vice Presidents in history. Where are they? They were about as useful as a cow's fifth teat." Mr. Truman, of course, would be the first to admit that he had little idea what fate was storing up for him when he made that remark.

The one regular duty the Constitution assigned to the Vice President has turned out unhappily. Making him president of the Senate has placed the Vice President in a weak and boresome position in which he can attain little distinction and little sense of achievement. That the Vice President was to become an innocuous presiding officer was almost inevitable. The House maintains a strong chair by choosing for its speaker a leader of its majority party with years of legislative experience behind him. But the Senate must accept a presiding officer whom it does not elect. He may or may not have legislative experience and the personal qualities requisite for a good presiding officer, and he may or may not be affiliated with the Senate's majority party. In the Eighty-fourth Congress, for example, the Senate majority was Democratic, while Vice President Nixon was Republican. For the Senate to entrust much power and influence to its president would be to risk having action desired by the majority delayed or sidetracked by a hostile chair.

On paper the powers of the speaker of the House and the Vice President as president of the Senate may appear very much alike, but the similarity is more apparent than real. The power of recognition is a case in point. Both have the power to recognize members of their respective bodies who ask for the floor. But by practice the speaker may exercise considerable discretion. He may inquire the purpose for which the member rises. If he finds that purpose not in order, he may waive the representative off the floor. The Vice President, on the other hand, has by tradition very little latitude. He may not question the purpose for which the Senator rises. He may purposely notice one Senator on his feet before he discovers another, but the second Senator need only bide his time. There is no way for the Vice President to keep him off the floor if the Senator persists long enough.

The rules of the two houses also point up the difference in attitude toward the chair. Both chairmen interpret and apply the rules of their respective houses, subject to appeal, but the speaker is again in much the more advantageous position. He is popular always with the majority party and quite commonly with the minority too. He can usually count on the substantial support of his own party in sustaining his judgment. The Vice President, however, is sometimes not very popular with the Senate. Henry A. Wallace, for example, drew Senatorial wrath for his extremely liberal views, as did Charles G. Dawes in his first year for his expressed contempt for the Senate rules.

Moreover, the Vice President often has no Senate majority behind him, and the Senate is historically so individualistic that it has no feeling that a ruling of the chair should generally be sustained. Speaking of his experience as Vice President, Calvin Coolidge wrote, "At first I intended to become a student of the Senate rules and I did learn much about them, but I soon found that the Senate had but one fixed rule, subject to exceptions, of course, which was to the effect that the Senate would do anything it wanted to do whenever it wanted to do it."

All down the list of the powers of the two presiding officers the story is just about the same. The speaker is a member of the House, a leader in the majority party. He is expected by the House to assume leadership. The Vice President is not a member of the Senate and is sometimes regarded as an intruder. He must ever be aware of his alien status. Any effort on his part to exercise a dominant position in the affairs of the Senate would be deeply resented, and his energies would be spent in vain.

The speaker, as a member of the House, has the same right to vote as any other member. He may leave the chair and enter into debate whenever he chooses. He does not resort to this practice very frequently, but when he does his views are likely to carry great weight with the members, particularly with those of his party. The Vice President, by contrast, may vote only to break a tie, and with ninety-six Senators tie votes are very infrequent. Beyond his statements in defense of his own rulings he almost never enters into floor controversy. The Senate would naturally object to his active participation in debate since he is not a member.

A little further examination of the status of the Vice President in the Senate makes it evident that this officer unhappily just cannot be first in anything. Technically he is the first officer of the Senate, but actually he is not. The Senate elects a president pro tempore to preside when he is absent. Ordinarily the pro tem is a much more powerful figure in the Senate than the Vice President. When he is in the chair he exercises the same powers, but he enjoys advantages the Vice President does not have.

The president pro tempore can vote whenever he wants to. If he wishes to leave the chair and participate in debate he may freely do so. Some other Senator easily fills in for him in the chair. He is usually chairman of a powerful standing committee, which fact alone enables him to outshine the Vice President. He is ordinarily the senior member of the majority party and, by years of experience, one of its leaders. Thus his word usually carries great weight with the Senate.

Perhaps nothing testifies so effectively to the Vice President's appreciation of his relative powerlessness in the Senate as the frequency of his absence. Even as early as 1803 the Vice President had thoroughly ceased to be indispensable to the Senate. During the debates in the House over the Twelfth Amendment Roger Griswold observed that the Senate ". . . sit half their time without the Vice President, and I have not understood that the business is not as well done without him as with him."

In our time the Vice President has become completely disillusioned. He seldom appears in the Senate today. In the Eighty-fourth Congress Vice President Nixon is said to have presided just about ten per cent of the time. Senator Margaret Chase Smith of Maine, before the reorganization subcommittee of the Senate Government Operations Committee, repeatedly observed, without contradiction, that our Constitutional Vice President very rarely presides over the Senate. Senator Smith's statements were made when former President Hoover appeared in behalf of his proposal for the establishment of an administrative Vice President in addition to the regular Vice President.

Senator John McClellan of Arkansas remarked at the same hearing, "Today [the Vice President] is in the legislative branch of the Government, and, as has been pointed out by Senator Smith of Maine, he performs very little duties in that capacity. He does preside, is presumed to preside, over the Senate, but seldom presides. This is not criticism—it is just a practical experience that we have—Vice Presidents seldom preside."

Yet who can blame the Vice President? Who would enjoy presiding over a legislative body from day to day with the full realization that he has less actual power over the deliberations than the least-known member of the chamber? What would it do to the Vice President if he undertook to sit in the Senate chair every day? He just couldn't stand it. No human being could.

When there is a key issue before the Senate its debate is interesting and sometimes brilliant, but the Senate is more commonly dealing with routine matters. Then its proceedings are painfully boring. Things get so dull that occasionally the presiding officer actually goes to sleep and has to be awakened by the parliamentarian in order that a Senator may be recognized. The Vice President would lose his mind if he sat through all those proceedings. Not even the pro tem manages that.

Sitting in a weak chair of a parliamentary body is not suited to the talents of a man of proper character to be within one breath and heartbeat of the White House. To put an outstanding man in such a position is wrong for the man. To put a mediocrity there is wrong for the Presidency.

Imposing a Constitutional intruder on the Senate has often been unfortunate for that body too. We have already noted that it has produced relative impotence for the presiding officer. If the chair must be weak because the Vice President may occupy it, then it must likewise be weak for anyone else who may preside. One of the most eloquent testimonials ever given on the feeble estate of the Senate chair was by Senator Smith at the aforementioned hearing:

However, our history shows that since Vice Presidents rarely preside over the Senate, the Senate elects a President pro tempore to do such presiding, but even the President pro tempore seldom presides, for the simple reason that traditionally the Senior Senator of the majority party is automatically selected for that position, and inevitably is the chairman of one of the top committees, such as Appropriations or Foreign Relations and, as such, has little time from committee meetings and work to preside over the Senate.

The end result is that presiding over the Senate is a duty that, in practice as distinguished from theory, is assigned to freshman and junior Senators because, since they had not acquired sufficient seniority in the Senate to obtain chairmanships or high places on major committee assignments, they do not carry heavy committee burdens and, therefore, have more time for presiding.

So it has come to this pass. Presiding over the Senate is too unimportant compared with other Senate duties to justify calling on the president pro tempore or even senior Senators. Let freshman and junior Senators—or the Vice President, if he happens to show up—perform this chore while the senior members do more important things.

In a way the weakness of the chair is more detrimental to the Senate than to the Vice President. The latter does not have to suffer it. He can be absent, but the Senate suffers from it all the time. A feeble chair in any deliberative body is provocative of chaos and confusion. At its best the Senate is an orderly and effective legislative body, but at its worst it degenerates into the most conspicuous exhibit of sheer legislative anarchy that exists in any civilized country in the world. Weak chair means weak organization, and the Senate gets into its most helpless state during its celebrated filibusters, which could develop only through the lack of a vigorous chair. When the Senate gets into this state an insignificant minority—sometimes a single dissident Senator—can halt action.

Ordinarily, unless an advance unanimous agreement has been worked out, when a Senator takes the floor he may talk as long as his lungs will hold out. He may wander far from the subject at hand and the presiding officer is powerless to do anything about his obstructive tactics. The late Senator Joseph T. Robinson of Arkansas, for many years Democratic floor leader of the Senate expressed it well when he remarked, "When a Senator once takes the floor, nobody but Almighty God can interrupt him—and the Lord never seems to take any notice of him."

Adequate time for debate in the Senate is positively necessary to our democracy. The House, because of its size, has sometimes to use rather extreme measures to stop debate. No informed person would like to see the Senate adopt the rules of the House. But while adequate time to debate is one thing, sheer obstruction is quite another. Its advocates have tried to justify the filibuster on the ground that we need one great and free debating forum. The argument is nonsense. Filibuster and debate are in reality different and unrelated things. A minority must be given enough time to state its case in full and to alert the nation to what is going on. We should let them have ample time, generously measured in hours. But when Senators spend hours and even weeks arguing over the commas and semicolons in the Journal or reading the Bible or poems or market reports only to frustrate action while a helpless chair sits idly by, not merely the Senate but the American people stand immobilized. This is an absurdity that cannot be matched anywhere.

In 1903 Senator Benjamin Tillman of South Carolina took the floor to filibuster a deficiency appropriation bill because it failed to include a payment of a war claim to his state. He appeared with a copy of *Childe Harold* in his hand and threatened to read it through, along with other poems, until the end of the session. The claim in which he was interested was added to the bill.

Four years later Senator Stone of Missouri resorted to reading *Pilgrim's Progress* to the Senate in his filibuster against a ship-subsidy bill.

In 1935 Senator Huey P. Long of Louisiana undertook a one-man filibuster of a joint resolution to extend parts of the National Industrial Recovery Act after the Supreme Court had invalidated most of it. Senator Long took the floor shortly after noon on June 12. He spoke of the NRA a little while, then read the Constitution and lectured on it. He talked on his "Share the Wealth" plan. He read extensively from Victor Hugo's *By Order of the King* and from the books of Hosea and Ecclesiastes. He gave recipes for making pot likker and for frying oysters, as well as for the preparation of other dishes about which he appeared to be expert. The Senate beat his filibuster by staying in session all afternoon and all evening, until Long gave out. If he had got a handful of Senators to help him he would undoubtedly have succeeded. As it was, he spoke until nearly four A.M. To sustain his strength he frequently munched grapes and cheese as he spoke, washing them down with milk.

Incredible as was Senator Long's performance, his is not the longest speech on record. Filibusters have been most successful when several Senators have banded together and spoken in relays. A feeble gesture at controlling them was made in 1917, after the successful filibuster of an armed-merchant-ship bill by a small group of Senators whom President Wilson called a "little group of wilful men, representing no opinion but their own."

The Senate at this time adopted a rule providing that if sixteen Senators petitioned to close debate, on the second calendar day later the presiding officer was to call a vote on the petition. If two thirds of those voting favored it, then each Senator would be limited to a maximum of one hour for further remarks. This was an extremely mild form of cloture. From 1917 to 1949 nineteen efforts were made to apply the rule, but the attempts succeeded only four times.

To be sure, Vice Presidents have objected to filibustering, but they have been able to do little about it. After one siege, when the Senate session closed on March 4 (the day terms expired before the Twentieth Amendment), Vice President Thomas R. Marshall, instead of announcing the Senate adjourned *sine die* (without day), pronounced it adjourned *sine deo* (without God). Marshall could show his disgust, but that was all.

On March 4, 1925, Charles G. Dawes was inaugurated Vice President. Mr. Dawes was a man of energy and dispatch, with a background of business, banking and military activities. He hated to see people frittering away valuable time. He came to Washington all steamed up with the idea that he was going to reform the Senate and make it a businesslike body.

In Dawes's inaugural address he created a sensation that stole the show from President Coolidge. He lectured the Senate freely on the necessity to revise its archaic rules, especially the rule on cloture. He stated in no uncertain terms that he believed it the function of the Vice President to enforce expeditious business in the Senate. The Vice President, at least in his capacity as president of the Senate, was finally going to be a real force in government.

Dawes told the Senate, "Reform in the present rules of the Senate is demanded not only by American public opinion, but, I venture to say, in the individual consciences of a majority of the members of the Senate itself." He asked, "Who would dare to maintain that in the last analysis the right of the Senate itself to act should ever be subordinated to the right of one Senator to make a speech?"

The Senate listened in silence. What it did was just what Mr. Coolidge had found as Vice President that it would do—what it wanted to do. Just then it wanted to do just nothing. Dawes learned that he had joined the long line of pedagogues whose lectures have fallen on deaf ears. He learned the hard way that he was only the Vice President. While Senators might be somewhat amused at his views, they were not going to be too much concerned about whether or not he liked their rules.

In 1949 Vice President Alben W. Barkley, one of the most popular Vice Presidents we have ever had, tried to do something about filibusters. He came out no better than Dawes. In 1948 a motion was made in the Senate to take up an anti-poll-tax measure. A filibuster of the debate on the motion to consider the measure then began. A cloture petition was circulated, whereupon a parliamentary issue arose on whether cloture was applicable.

Senator Arthur H. Vandenberg of Michigan was then president pro tempore. While he did not approve the particular filibuster, he ruled that the cloture rule provided for a petition and vote to limit debate on a "pending measure." This, he said, was not debate on a pending measure but on a motion to take up a measure, so cloture was not applicable. Senator Vandenberg governed his ruling by what he thought the rule meant, and not by what he thought it ought to mean. He made an able defense, and there was no appeal from his decision.

The net result was that the cloture rule became a virtual nullity. In the future Senators who wanted to filibuster would not wait until a measure was pending. By starting their talk fest on a motion to take up a measure they would be secure against cloture.

The issue arose again in 1949. This time Barkley was in the chair. He held that the cloture rule was applicable to debate on a motion to consider. In justifying his decision the Vice President said, in part, "The chair has reached the conclusion that what the Senate was trying to do, what it thought it was doing, what it intended to do, was to adopt a rule which would enable it to transact its business." Barkley went on further to say, "A motion to proceed to the consideration of a bill is an absolutely indispensable process in the enactment of legislation."

Senator Russell of Georgia immediately appealed from the decision of the chair, and a spirited debate followed. If one took a literal view of the rule, then Senator Vandenberg was right. But if one took the practical view, then Vice President Barkley was. A Democratic Senate, by a vote of 46 to 41, overruled the decision of Mr. Barkley, a Democratic Vice President, thus confirming the opposite ruling Senator Vandenberg, Republican president pro tempore, had made the year before.

When all is said and done, the vote must be counted a great victory for those who espoused the right of filibuster. Unless it could be amended to cover motions to take up a measure the cloture rule would be an empty shell. The Senate would be at the mercy of any group of experts at verbosity. There would be no way to clear the floor for a vote against their will. A handful of Senators could at any time throw the Senate into a state of anarchy—not near anarchy but total anarchy.

This prospect was too frightening. The situation was so patently clear now that the public, the learned and the unlearned, would all understand and demand an end to obstructionism. In this state the Senate worked out a so-called compromise, the "Wherry substitute," which was an amendment to the cloture rule. It passed the Senate on March 17, 1949. The amendment closes one gap but at the same time vastly widens another. The cloture petition now applies to debate on "any

measure, motion, or other matter pending before the Senate."
The motion to consider is no longer exempt.

But the Wherry substitute makes the vote to close debate far
more difficult. Formerly two thirds of those voting could halt
a filibuster. The new formula, however, requires concurrence of
two thirds of the entire membership of the Senate, or sixty-four
Senators, no matter how many are present at the session.

The filibuster situation is worse than it has been at any time
since 1917, except for the brief interval between the Vandenberg ruling of 1948 and the adoption of the Wherry substitute
in 1949. The Senate is under perpetual threat of total stoppage
at the hands of a loquacious minority. It is almost as defense-
less against obstruction as it was in 1917, when it was para-
lyzed at a time of dangerous international crisis. The weakness
of its chair is, of course, not the sole nor even the major cause
of the sad plight of the Senate. But, weakness of a parliamentary chair is infectious. It militates to the confusion of any
legislative body. The imposition of an outsider as Senate president has certainly not improved its situation.

In the early days, when the Senate was small, the Vice President's vote was important in breaking ties. John Adams used
his vote twenty-nine times, which was clearly the peak. Now
that the Senate has become much larger tie votes are very infrequent. Over our history the country has been without a Vice
President for some thirty-six years (seven have died, seven
have succeeded to the Presidency and one, Calhoun, resigned).
In no case did the Senate find itself helpless for want of a Vice
President to preside and break ties. The Senate has run along
just about the same whether or not there was a Vice President.

The fundamental justification for keeping a Vice President
is to have someone actually and Constitutionally at hand to
perform Presidential functions in case the President can't.
Fortunately—more by luck than design—each time a President has died there has been a Vice President available to take
over. Prone as we have been to elect aged and infirm Vice
Presidents, this need not have been so. Seven Vice Presidents

have died in office but, by sheer good fortune, the Presidents with whom they were serving lived out their terms.

Of the Vice Presidents who did take over for deceased Presidents, it may be said that on the average they at least approached the stature of the men they replaced. But of the seven Presidents who met death in office only two, Abraham Lincoln and Franklin D. Roosevelt, are generally regarded as unusually strong Presidents. At least one stand-by, Theodore Roosevelt, proved to be an extraordinary President himself. Of Mr. Truman it is too early to say. Time must pass before the historian may assess his record in an atmosphere of calm and dispassion. Five certainly were not outstanding Presidents. One had the dubious honor of being the only President to be impeached, though he did not deserve such severe treatment. At any rate, we have pulled through.

At providing a stand-by in case the President is disabled the Vice Presidency has been a total failure so far. On three occasions, which we have already examined, Presidents were incapacitated for considerable periods of time. In the cases of Garfield and Wilson important public business was neglected or poorly transacted during their illnesses. Yet never was the Vice President called on to exercise Presidential powers. Things simply drifted along as though there were no possible temporary successor to Presidential powers.

This statement does not apply so forcefully to the period of President Eisenhower's illness. Mr. Eisenhower's office was well staffed, and although Vice President Nixon did not assume Presidential functions, he did preside over Cabinet meetings and was in close contact with the President. This unusual situation was due, no doubt, to the fact that there has existed a relation of cordiality between President Eisenhower and Mr. Nixon that has seldom been paralleled in our history.

But never has the failure to call on the Vice President in a President's illness been the personal fault of the Vice President. It has been, in part, the fault of the office. In a large measure Congress also is to blame, since it has provided no statutory method to determine either the existence or the termination of Presidential inability. Congress, however, should not bear all the blame. The detached position of the Vice Presidency has been tremendously complicating. The Congress has been fully aware that in many cases there has been little warmth between the President and the Vice President and that in some cases the two officers have actually been at odds with each other.

The problem is most delicate. Who would like to provide a method by which a stricken President or his family may be told that he is being temporarily replaced by a Vice President who takes a substantially different view of public matters? Had the Vice Presidency been attached to the executive department, where it truly belongs, rather than to the legislative department, the problem would have been simpler to solve. Even the early fear that a Vice President stepping in for temporary Presidential duty would oust the elected President would have been more nearly groundless.

As a stepping stone to the Presidency the Vice Presidency has, since the passage of the Twelfth Amendment, been a signal failure. Since that time, though eighteen have had a fair chance, only one Vice President, Martin Van Buren, has advanced by election to the Presidency, and his case, as we have seen, was largely accidental.

We have been so consistent in excluding Vice Presidents from the White House except when a President dies that we in effect tell a Vice President that in becoming theoretical second-best he has reached the top of his ladder. Any of the rest of us may be elected President, but not he.

After the third unsuccessful campaign of the so-called perennial Democratic candidate for President it was said that America is a country in which any natural-born citizen may some day become President except William J. Bryan. Now we may as well say that America is the country in which any natural-born citizen may be elected President except an already elected Vice President.

This is a most amazingly inconsistent and paradoxical fact.

We in America believe in fair competition. We believe that society gains most when each person makes maximum use of his talents and strives to reach the top. But we proceed by practice to make of the Vice Presidency an office whose occupant must be content with second best. We need to re-examine either our philosophy or the Vice Presidency. The two are not in tune.

If political parties are to render their greatest possible service to the public as genuine instruments of democracy then they must operate to promote true popular government. This means that they must make their respective stands on public issues clearly and positively. Otherwise the people will be denied the right to govern no matter how many officers they elect. They will not know what kinds of public policies they are voting for when they turn the reins of government over to a political party.

If democracy is to reach its highest peak a national election must serve as a mandate from the people to put into operation policies that they understand and endorse. To clarify issues is to promote democracy, but to becloud them with confusion and contradiction is to negate it. Blind voting can convey no mandate.

Unfortunately the Vice Presidency has often been used by political parties more for confusion than for clarification. To pull in votes party conventions have balanced a liberal Presidential nominee with a conservative Vice Presidential candidate and vice versa. By thus working both sides of the street the parties create confusion in the minds of the voters. In a national election the voter hasn't even the weapon he often has in state elections of being able to split his ticket. Since he actually is voting only for electors he has to take the Presidential candidate and the Vice Presidential candidate in a single package.

We have already mentioned former President Hoover's proposal for an administrative Vice President in addition to the Constitutional one. This officer, according to Mr. Hoover's plan, would be appointed by the President in the usual way, with the approval of the Senate. Once in office he would be subject to the President's direction and would be removable by him. He would relieve the President of many of his routine functions and would take over some important functions that the President, without violating the Constitution, might delegate to him. The Constitutional Vice President would still be the successor if the President died or was disabled. Mr. Hoover's purpose was to provide much-needed relief to an overworked President.

While all members of the senate reorganization subcommittee as well as all witnesses seemed to appreciate the service Mr. Hoover was rendering they indicated a great deal of doubt about his proposal.

Senators Smith and McClellan both suggested that since the Constitutional Vice President spends so little time in presiding over the Senate there should perhaps be a re-examination of his office with a view to bringing it within the orbit of the executive department. Their thinking seems to be going in the right direction.

But Mr. Hoover correctly pointed out that it would require a Constitutional amendment to make the present Vice President a truly executive or administrative officer. He would have to be subject to Presidential direction and removal, whereas he is now an independent elective officer. Nobody at the committee hearing had an immediate solution, but it was clear from the start that the existence of the Constitutional Vice President would make some intelligent people hesitate to create an administrative Vice President.

Clark Clifford, former special assistant to President Truman, in a statement before the subcommittee expressed grave doubts about the Hoover plan. He was afraid that the proposed new office would foster both confusion to the public and a loss of prestige for the elected Vice President. He made this significant remark:

Another thought or two with reference to the suggested plan. There is great value in historic precedent. The office of Vice President is an office of dignity. I believe that such an office would disappear under this suggestion because we would no longer have the Vice President of the United States; we would have both a constitutional Vice President of the United States and the administrative Vice President. So, then, it could be said, "Well, I was talking with the Vice President," and the other person would have to say, "Which Vice President? Do you mean the constitutional Vice President or do you mean the administrative Vice President?"

I believe that would be unfortunate. I think it would not constitute a move in the right direction.

Professor Emeritus Edward S. Corwin of Princeton, a nationally known authority on Constitutional law, in a letter to Senator John F. Kennedy of Massachusetts, chairman of the subcommittee, expressed a similar view. "The Vice President," he said, "is a creature of the Constitution, and no other should be endowed with that title." He also stated that in his opinion " . . . Mr. Sherman Adams [the special assistant to the President] has been doing satisfactorily the job intended for the proposed Administrative Vice President. Why continue to multiply aids and offices in the executive department?"

While it is probably true that Mr. Hoover's proposal is not the proper solution, what he had in mind should not be lightly turned aside. It seems probable that he was not after just another administrative aid to the President. He was trying to give the President some super-prestige assistance, which is just what he needs. It is nevertheless clear that the existence of the Constitutional Vice Presidency, as long as it is attached to the legislative rather than to the executive department, is going to interfere with providing for the kind of help the President really requires.

If the office of administrative Vice President is created it can never reach maximum usefulness for fear it will diminish the prestige of the Constitutional office. The Vice Presidency is definitely in a period of transition, but until it finds its base it will becloud with obscurity some very important issues of our time.

It would be both unfair and unrealistic to close this chapter without happily and freely acknowledging the patent fact that the office of Vice President has gained in stature and prestige during the last fifty-six years. In a sense the year 1900 was the turning point. In that year Theodore Roosevelt was elected Vice President of the United States. It is of course true that this good break for the Vice Presidency fell more by accident than by design.

As we have already noted, Boss Platt and other political bigwigs had no idea whatever of reviving the Vice Presidency. They put the remarkable Roosevelt in office simply to give him a quiet and dignified political burial. But an assassin's iniquity suddenly transferred Roosevelt to the White House. In 1904 he was elected President for a full term.

This broke a serious jinx. During the preceding century four Vice Presidents, Tyler, Fillmore, Johnson and Arthur had succeeded to the Presidency on the deaths of incumbent Presidents, but not one of them had been re-elected in his own right. When Roosevelt broke that precedent he appears to have set the style for the twentieth century. After Roosevelt two other Vice Presidents, Coolidge and Truman, were called on to fill out unexpired terms. Each was subsequently elected for a full term. This is indeed a wholesome change.

But during the ninteenth century, after the adoption of the Twelfth Amendment, only one Vice President was able to move to the Presidency by immediate election. This jinx still holds fast. No Vice President has since been promoted by initial election from the second office to the highest.

Another improvement has been that the Vice Presidency has been brought into closer relation with the Presidency. In 1919 Vice President Thomas R. Marshall at Wilson's request presided over several Cabinet meetings while the President was attending the Paris peace conference. During President Harding's brief term Vice President Coolidge, at Harding's invitation, regularly occupied a seat at Cabinet meetings. Mr.

Coolidge was the first Vice President to be a regular partici-pant in Cabinet meetings.

Vice President Charles G. Dawes had the same opportunity under President Coolidge but he declined. President Hoover invited Vice President Charles Curtis to attend Cabinet meet-ings, but little came of it since there was very little warmth between Mr. Hoover and the Vice President who had bitterly fought his nomination in 1928. President Franklin D. Roose-velt during his years of service had three Vice Presidents, Garner, Wallace and Truman, and extended a Cabinet seat to each of them. Vice President Alben W. Barkley attended Truman's Cabinet meetings.

Cabinet activity for the Vice President reached a peak during Mr. Eisenhower's Presidency. Vice President Nixon not only attended Cabinet meetings but also presided over them in the President's absence. Of course it is a valuable experience for the Vice President to have this association. Certainly if he is suddenly called to take over Presidential duties he will better understand the kinds of problems that he must speedily face.

But as long as the Vice President is Constitutionally attached to the Senate chair rather than to the executive branch he can be of only limited use to the President. Normally things are likely to shape up very much as former President Truman said: "The President, by necessity, builds his own staff, and the Vice President remains an outsider, no matter how friendly the two may be."

In recent years Vice Presidents have been of some assistance to Presidents in ways other than mere attendance at Cabinet meetings. Some of them have helped greatly to get the Presi-dent's program through Congress, though it must be said that not every Vice President has been in complete agreement with the President's legislative policies.

They have, in behalf of the President, made foreign tours that, though frequently spoken of as good-will tours, have often involved important missions. Vice President Wallace made several trips to Latin America, and in 1944 he went on an extremely important mission to the Far East. Vice President

Barkley in 1951 visited the troops at the front in Korea. Vice President Nixon's trips have taken him nearly all over the world—to Latin America, the Middle East and the Far East.

A beginning has been made at bringing the Vice President into an administrative relation to the President. President Roosevelt made Vice President Wallace chairman of the Board of Economic Warfare. In 1949 the Vice President was made a statutory member of the National Security Council, a post he holds today. This was a most significant step. This council is a sort of super-Cabinet for national defense. It includes the President, as chairman, the Vice President, the Secretary of State, the Secretary of Defense, the director of the Office of Defense Mobilization, the director of the Foreign Operations Administration and such others as the President may with the consent of the Senate appoint. It assesses and appraises the commitments and risks of the United States in military power, actual and potential, and advises the President on its findings. In President Eisenhower's absence Vice President Nixon presided.

The responsibilities of the Vice President have truly become greater. But we must repeat that there is a limit to his usefulness so long as he is attached to the legislative department.

Time To Re-examine

So far we have been merely examining the Vice Presidency —its history, its fluctuating stature, its occupants and its relation to the Senate and the Presidency. We have been looking at the past and at the present. Now let us consider the future.

Can the Vice Presidency be made more useful? Would a more intimate co-operation between the President and the Vice President be helpful to both? Would it make the Vice Presidency more attractive to men and women of first-class abilities? These are vital questions. Though they may be debated academically at length, only the American people can provide the ultimate answers.

Our survey of the Vice Presidency has made clear several grave weaknesses in its structure and has illuminated imperfections in the very operation of our governmental machinery. The most critical of these seem to be in the executive department itself. The President is grossly overworked. He needs the Vice President as an adviser and confidant and as an active administrative assistant. The Vice President needs the President even more. Only with the President may he the more fully employ his energies and talents, the more completely realize the great prestige inherent in his office.

This potential of interdependence has long existed. Obviously the times require that we exploit it now. World and domestic problems increase in numbers and in gravity. They impose an incessant pressure on the White House. A trusted Vice President could be of immense comfort to the President. Yet an ill-considered arrangement hastily made in 1787 by an able but weary body of men prevents the absolute co-operation between President and Vice President that might properly distribute the burden of the executive department.

The chief executive is indeed a lonely man. Those who have legislative responsibility can take much comfort from the presence of equal associates. The Supreme Court now numbers nine men and has never had fewer than five; there is no awesome loneliness in the ultimate judicial authority. But the executive power is vested in one man.

The Constitution provides no assistance for the President within his own department. All his executive and administrative associates hold positions that rest directly or indirectly on a statutory base. Their capacity to relieve the President is severely restricted. They are so far beneath him that they cannot provide any of the comfort of equals or near-equals. Adlai Stevenson, speaking in Iowa in late September 1956, defined their roles well when he referred to the Secretary of Agriculture as the President's hired man.

It was doubtless wise of the framers of the Constitution to center executive power. Concentrated authority avoids the confusion of divided responsibility in the arm of the government charged with translating public policy into action—the one branch that must operate every day in the year.

Exhausting though his duties are, sheer work is not the primary hazard to the President's well-being. Crushing responsibility in a lonely position makes the heaviest exactions on his strength and spirit.

The President ought not have his power divided. That would be detrimental to him and to the nation as well. But he does need someone close to him to carry some of his load. To add a few more aids to the White House staff would be simple. It would, however, not be adequate. The assistant to the President, for example, has been an enormous help, but his position cannot be given prestige near or in any way comparable to that of the Presidency.

It is hard too to see how the administrative Vice President suggested by Mr. Hoover could fill the bill. We have already discussed the possibility of a rivalry for prestige between that officer and the Constitutional Vice President. For any appointive administrative official to become the second executive officer would deliver a mortal blow to the vitality of the Vice Presidency. It would then be even more difficult than it is now to recruit for that office men with the qualities needed for taking over the responsibilities of the Presidency.

So we see that the President needs no one with whom to divide his power. But he does need someone with Constitutional standing similar to his own and stature and prestige not too far beneath his. He must have someone to help him to oversee national affairs and to confer with him constantly on fundamental decisions that often draft significant chapters in the history of the world.

And we also see that the Vice President has been excluded from a function that should naturally be his. For lonely as the Presidency is, the Vice Presidency is even more so. The Vice President has no firm Constitutional home. He has no executive role to play in our government. The White House door, so long as the President is alive and able, swings open to him, so to speak, only on the President's invitation. And all too often in our history that invitation has been forbiddingly cold and formal, if not entirely lacking.

The Vice President cannot claim even a casual connection with the judiciary. With the legislative department he suffers a most peculiar and unenviable relationship. He presides over but is not a member of the Senate. If that body does not like him he becomes a tolerated intruder. Even if he is popular he is little more than an enjoyable boarder whose services scarcely pay for his keep.

He has a vote only in the rare case of a tie. And then his vote is no more significant than that of any other Senator. Since a tie vote kills a measure the Vice President carries no more strength by voting negatively than by abstaining from voting—he is only whipping a dead horse.

It appears then that the Vice President can be complete and whole in nothing. He has been something like a child from a broken home, unhappily passed back and forth between separated parents. In the nineteenth century he was confined largely to his peculiar legislative home. His office seldom achieved importance or prestige. In the twentieth century, particularly during the past twenty years or so, the Vice Presidency has moved closer to the executive. As it has done so it has gained in stature and in public recognition. The 1956 conventions and campaign placed the Vice President's role in sharp focus. Public debate on the matter cannot fail to carry into the Eighty-fifth Congress, which will undoubtedly continue to explore the possibilities in the office.

The Vice President's gravitation toward the executive is not surprising. That department is the natural and logical base for him. The Senate chair certainly is not. The mounting responsibilities of the Presidency, the increasing harmony between the President and the Vice President and the strong hand given Presidential nominees in selecting their running mates have all strongly motivated the shift. And all the while the Vice Presidency has been attracting better qualified men. Few would dispute that our last five Vice Presidents—Garner, Wallace, Truman, Barkley and Nixon—have brought to the office a measure of ability distinctly above that of the average of their predecessors.

To give to the Vice President a permanent executive role would pose difficult and delicate problems. But if they could be worked out the change might well produce tremendous advantages.

Since his Constitutional rank is, in theory, second only to that of the chief executive, the Vice President might easily become the President's first assistant. This would surely help us to enlist vigorous and talented men to run for the office. Rescued from its orphan status the Vice Presidency would be more interesting, more significant and more dramatic and would carry more challenging responsibilities. Selecting Vice Presidential candidates would, in turn, become most important. We might easily see the end of the spare-tire era.

The President would have the prestige assistance he needs without the hazard of confusion involved in the Hoover proposal. And when his chief was ready to retire, good political strategy would place the Vice President among the first to be considered for nomination in his own right. This matter of prestige really seemed uppermost in Mr. Hoover's mind when he said during the hearings on his proposal, "I am sure that Presidents will find even more fields for an Administrative Vice President to be of service; and to accomplish this purpose it seems to me necessary to have an official who is clothed with dignity and prestige."

Transferring the Vice President to administrative duties would probably also place the Senate in a position to emancipate itself from the indigency engendered by its weak chair. There is no danger, however, that the Senate would ever become just another House of Representatives in its procedure. Its smaller size makes the traditions of privilege for an individual Senator and the firm attachment to the principles of free debate forces that would hardly be overcome. Free debate would remain, but there would be a greater opportunity to bring order to the forum.

Changing the status of the Vice President could, in addition, do more to solve the complicated inability problem than all the statutes or Constitutional amendments we might draft. The Vice President would be a member of the White House staff. For a member of his official family to take over his duties if he were ill would be so much more satisfactory to a stricken President than for an utter stranger to the administrative machine to be brought in just long enough to get things completely out of gear. Besides easing the President's mind it would also be much better for the country to have a well-trained apprentice President.

Finally, the shift would bring a tremendous improvement in

the situation that obtains when a President dies and the Vice President is suddenly called to the driver's seat. The Vice President would not take over as an utterly inexperienced hand. It was doubtless with this in mind that President Eisenhower reassured a gathering of Republican leaders at Gettysburg in mid-September 1956. "I feel fine," he replied to a question about his health. Then he continued, "I want to say this: there is no man in the history of America who has had such a careful preparation as has Vice President Nixon for carrying out the duties of the Presidency, if that duty should ever fall upon him."

Since the relationship between the President and the Vice President has never in our history been closer than during his administration, President Eisenhower's words can hardly be disputed. Mr. Nixon's personal qualifications for the Presidency are not for us to debate. Executive association like that he has been permitted to have is truly very important, but it is only one of the elements that make a good chief executive. The American people must assess many other factors to determine who is to be kept in readiness to succeed their President.

The idea of giving the Vice President important executive functions is by no means purely academic. It is not confined to the ivory-tower planners. Two seasoned members of the Senate, both highly respected and from opposite political parties, indicated thinking in that direction during the hearings on the Hoover plan.

The Maine Republican Margaret Chase Smith, after her remark that the Vice President seldom presides over the Senate, significantly added, "Whether this should be the practice or not is certainly one of the many questions that should be considered in arriving at conclusions as to what should be the functions of a modern-day Vice President, whether he be the present-policy one or the proposed administrative one."

The Arkansas Democrat John L. McClellan observed, "It does seem to me that the office of Vice President of the United States should be related to the executive branch of the Government, where the Vice President, in the performance of functions that might be assigned to him in that branch of the Government would become equipped from experience and from direct contacts with the problems involved to assume the duties of the Presidency in the event a vacancy should occur. I think some thought should be given along that line toward a solution of this problem."

If we conclude, along with many of our best political thinkers, that there is a need to alter the duties of the Vice President we must examine ways in which this might be accomplished. Four fundamental approaches suggest themselves. Each has its advantages, and each its drawbacks. The people must decide whether the former outweigh the latter in any course of action they may determine to take.

There is much to be said for simply relying on the current trend of the Vice Presidency toward closer executive relationship to continue without any formal redefinition of the office. Many students of government believe that we should let well enough alone. Not a single word of the Constitution has been changed, yet the Vice President today spends much more of his time working with the President than with the Senate.

He meets regularly with the Cabinet, and Mr. Nixon has even presided over Cabinet meetings when the President has been ill. Vice Presidents have traveled abroad to carry the good will of the President and to gather information for him. There is a strong argument that the Vice President is just as useful to the President as he would be if we amended the Constitution to transfer him completely and permanently to the executive. There is no need, say advocates of this view, to amend the Constitution just for the sake of amending it.

Though this reasoning looks pretty good on the surface, it demands a few reservations. In the first place, it is not true that the Vice President is as useful to the President as he might be. His assistance is now largely confined to consultation and ceremonial appearances. He is not really a part of the President's administrative organization, nor can we confidently expect him to become one by evolution alone. Mr. Hoover made that point in the Senate hearings. He expressed great satisfaction over the progress made in recent years but pointed out that the Vice President is still separately elected and is not responsible to the President. That, said Mr. Hoover, is the reason why he has not been made an administrative officer for the President. We shall see that the President's sole authority would be dangerously compromised by a delegation of a part of it to another elected official.

Until the impediment to placing the Vice President in administrative work is removed he cannot be of the greatest possible assistance to the President and cannot acquire the experience he needs to be able to take charge of Presidential functions should he be called on.

And there is no guarantee that the present trend will continue. Both parties still comprise divergent elements, factions they must satisfy. Party politicians will always be tempted to resort to ticket-balancing in their nominations. There is nothing to indicate that a major party will not again nominate Presidential and Vice Presidential candidates of viewpoints miles apart if the maneuver will call enough voters into the fold to bring home victory. Yet the present closeness of the President and Vice President depends on the harmony between them.

In tune with what we have been saying about these opposing factions within our major parties—which make for ticket-bal-ancing—Roscoe Drummond of the New York *Herald Tribune,* president of the Washington Gridiron Club, at its seventy-first annual dinner on May 12, 1956, summed up the problem in this jab. He said that President Eisenhower must be pleased ". . . to see among us so many fine conservative humanitarians—those Republicans eager to march forward with Eisenhower—protesting every step of the way." President Eisenhower was present and enjoying it all.

With equal sharpness and ease Mr. Drummond directed a similar quip at the Democrats. "Half of the Democratic Party," he said, "is intent on secession. The other half seems to prefer suicide. Republicans say that if the Democratic politicians were laid end to end—they would point in all directions." Returning to the Republicans, Drummond continued, "All the Republicans know what they want—just an unshakable grip on those coat-tails, and they can soar above principle." Mr. Drummond, of course, made these remarks in a spirit of fun, but there was enough truth in what he said to make his audience appreciate his wit.

If things are left to their natural course the recent progress of the Vice Presidency can quickly be undone. As soon as we get a President and Vice President in basic disagreement on vital issues we may again see the one exile the other right back to the Senate chair.

Hazards do inhere in depending on evolution alone to solve the problem of the Vice Presidency. To point them out is not to condemn the approach, to treat it lightly or to brush it aside. After all, this, like every major issue in a democracy, is for the people to decide. We seem now to have been awakened from our old indifference about the Vice Presidency. If we remain awake and develop a political climate in which ticket-balancing or using the office simply to further partisan ends will not thrive, our major parties will respond. They want to win.

If the voters put pressure on them party conventions will have to come around. They will be forced to nominate for Vice President able candidates in basic accord with the Presidential nominees. Neither party would go to market with a bill of goods it knew it couldn't sell. The electorate, the ultimate seat of all sovereignty, can have what it wants if it takes a firm stand.

But only by intensive and continuous effort can our alert citizens and civic organizations emphasize and sustain public interest in the true importance of the Vice Presidency. And this they must do if we hope to advance the influence of the office—or even to keep it at its present level—by simply permitting it to develop naturally, filling needs as they arise.

We must happily concede that evolution has made us one important gain. It is highly unlikely that a President will ever again leave his Vice President totally uninformed about high-level actions. The peril of such negligence is now evident to all concerned—to the President, to the Vice President and to the public.

A second approach, mentioned quite frequently, is to accelerate the present expansion of the Vice President's role by giving him statutory administrative duties, leaving his Constitutional status unchanged. Congress has already made a start in this direction. The Vice President is now, for example, a statutory member of the National Security Council. And President Eisenhower arranged for Mr. Nixon to preside over that group in his absence.

This device may well have wholesome possibilities, but to use it incautiously could be dangerous. We must be extremely careful not to give the Vice President statutory duties of an executive character *without a fundamental redefinition of his role*. The Constitution vests *the* executive power in the President. One of the President's most vital and effective instruments for the exercise of that power is his authority to appoint and remove his strictly executive subordinates.

The Vice President is an independent officer. He is in nowise responsible to the President or subordinate to him. It may be all right to confer on the Vice President an advisory function within the executive orbit. But to allow him authority for executive *action*—particularly should his acts not be subject to Presidential review and veto—would be a dangerous and doubtless unconstitutional intrusion into the domain of the chief executive. Ill-considered legislation of this sort might even destroy the unity of the executive, an essential property of our system of government.

A third approach involves a Constitutional amendment to divorce the Vice President from the Senate chair and remove him permanently to the executive department. He would still be elected just as he is today. Clark Clifford, speaking from four years' experience as President Truman's special assistant, advanced this idea at the Senate reorganization subcommittee hearings. Clifford urged that the Vice President be empowered to operate as an executive assistant to the President.

Clifford's plan would make the Vice President the primary administrative officer for the President. In this role he could relieve the chief executive of attending many ceremonial functions and making many speeches. This would be practicable, Mr. Clifford argued, since the Vice President would be known to be close to the President and quite familiar with the policies he favored.

And a Vice President actually functioning as an administrative aid could relieve the President of a great many of his political party activities. As an instance, Clifford said that much of the President's time would be saved if the Vice President just took over the obligation to meet with his party's national committeemen and state chairmen when they came to Washington.

Mr. Clifford ably defended his plan, suggesting that it would enhance the importance of the Vice Presidency, which would in turn attract more capable men. He said further that it would give the President all the assistance he would get through the Hoover plan but would carry the added advantage of greater prestige. And, he said, it would provide the ". . . process of preparing a man for succession to the Presidency."

Conceding that the President could not remove an elective officer, Clifford ran into his plan's greatest weakness. There would be no way to assure harmony between the President and the Vice President and there might be a threat to the undivided executive authority of the President.

On the first of these two problems Clifford said he felt that once a party knew its Vice Presidential candidate was really a nominee for the position of top assistant to the President it would change its timeworn tactics. It would be careful to seek a well-qualified man. "I believe," Clifford said, "that the presidential nominee would be sure that the vice presidential nominee would be one with whom he could work."

It is probably true that the new role for the Vice President would have some effect on nominating methods. But we would be taking a long chance if we expected a complete and thorough revolution. Often a party, wanting first to win, would trust victory to take care of itself. Ticket-balancing would hardly be abandoned.

Moreover, the policies of an administration cannot be static. It is entirely possible that at convention time a party's two candidates might be in complete agreement on the issues of the hour. Yet later, when facing in office different issues arising from changed conditions, they might find themselves in bitter discord.

Mr. Clifford's answer to the problem of maintaining undivided executive authority for the President seems somewhat vague and general. "I think," he said, "that the Presidential powers are so tremendous that if by chance a Vice President would get off the reservation, I have no doubt but that a President could trim him down to size in no time at all. I would not be concerned."

But really, should we not be concerned? If we were to amend the Constitution to make the Vice President the President's top assistant could we be sure that the President would still enjoy undivided executive power? In strengthening the Vice Presidency we dare not weaken the Presidency.

The Presidency has been throughout our history one of our most successful governmental institutions—perhaps the most successful. From George Washington to Dwight Eisenhower it has supplied strength, stability and symbolic unity to the nation. And nothing has contributed so much to its success as the fact that the supreme executive authority is not distributed but is concentrated in it. This has on the one hand enabled the President to perform as an effective and vigorous state head and on the other has made him more clearly accountable to the American people.

In order to equip him efficiently to exercise his executive authority the Constitution expressly granted the President much latitude in appointing subordinates and, by judicial interpretation, even greater freedom to dismiss them. The powers to appoint and remove are essential to directing the major policy-determining instrumentalities of the executive department. In building up the Vice Presidency we must not tear down any part of our basic political structure.

Mr. Clifford's proposal deserves much better than unsympathetic criticism. It is extremely thought-provoking. Beyond doubt it impressed the subcommittee. Many students of the problem thoroughly agree that the Vice President really should be the top assistant to the President. But the means Mr. Clifford suggests for accomplishing this objective are open to serious question.

It is, for example, altogether possible that some day we shall have a President and a Vice President of different political parties. Remember that President John Adams was a Federalist, while his Vice President, Thomas Jefferson, was a Democratic-Republican. The Twelfth Amendment, ratified before Jefferson left the Presidency, offers no positive assurance that the same situation won't be true again. Suppose a third party picked up enough electoral votes to prevent either the Democratic or the Republican ticket from commanding a majority.

The House of Representatives would then choose the President from the three candidates with the highest numbers of votes. The Senate would choose one of the top two nominees for Vice President. If each of the two houses of Congress was controlled by a different party the President and Vice President would almost certainly be of opposite faiths.

One way to preserve the fundamental ideal of Mr. Clifford's plan and still to avoid some of its pitfalls might be to amend the Constitution to place the Vice President at the President's disposal, limiting the President's obligation to make use of his services. The extent of administrative activity he would allow the Vice President might be left to the President's discretion. The President could be given veto power over any executive act of the Vice President and could be empowered to relieve the Vice President of any administrative activities for which he found him unsuited.

Discretionary authority of this sort would not disturb the primacy of the President. And if the Vice President worked well with the President he might indeed become a true second consul: one on whom would devolve responsibility and authority, not the inactive stand-in John Adams must have seen if he applied the term as he is reported to have done. Of course we do not urge that the Vice President ever be granted the authority of one of the two equal Roman consuls. But his office must be made a position of genuine importance to the state.

A fourth possible means to enhance the Vice Presidency might be to go all the way—really to make the Vice President the official second man in the administration. To follow this approach means to amend the Constitution to provide that the Vice President be appointed and removable by the President. This would securely preserve the unity of the executive power.

At the hearings on the Hoover proposal it became quite evident that many of the Senators present believed that the Constitutional Vice President should be doing just about the sort of thing Mr. Hoover had in mind for his special administrative Vice President. In response the former President said, "Of course, you might effect the same suggestion I am making if you changed the constitutional provisions with regard to the Vice President and required him by constitutional amendment to be entirely subject to the President, as the Executive, and then you would make him a sort of Executive Vice President. But I do not think you could maintain him as an elective officer and maintain any cohesion in administration. I think you would have to make him appointed."

Mr. Hoover did not advocate an appointive Constitutional Vice President. He would in all probability be much opposed to the idea. But in pointing out the difficulties of making the Vice President a real assistant to the President he did make quite clear the point of this fourth, drastic approach.

Whether authorizing an appointive Vice President would be consistent with the principles of democracy is clearly debatable. Each person can resolve the dispute only in terms of his own conception of the essence of political democracy.

If a definition of this term must include voting for people to fill high offices as an end in itself, not merely as a means to an end, then the personalities of the candidates must be of first consideration. To voters guided by this interpretation the idea of an appointive Vice President would be offensive. Someone the American people had never directly designated or intended for the position might succeed to the highest office in the land.

But if true political democracy can be considered the means by which the people may choose between rival policies—with the candidates standing primarily as instruments of the policies—then a strong defense may be made for an appointive Vice Presidency. If we accept this view, the people give their President a mandate for four years to put into effect policies he and his party have defined to them. If the voters change their minds about the policies when they have had a chance to see them in operation they may modify their mandate in the mid-term Congressional elections.

Should the President die or be disabled for any length of time a Vice President he had appointed would be more likely to follow consistently his policies—for which the people voted—than would an elective official independent of him. The President would hardly keep on hand an appointive aid not in basic agreement with him on major policy matters.

Thus far no academic discussion of its possible benefits has reconciled the idea of an appointive Vice President to American traditions. Certainly there can be no formal consideration of the plan until some questions posed by such a radical change in the structure of our government have had reassuring answers.

For instance, should either Senate or Congressional confirmation of the President's appointment be required? If so, what if Congress is controlled by the opposite political party? Then a popularly elected legislature might refuse to approve a man the President, also elected by the people, wanted to be his first assistant.

The Twentieth Amendment now provides that if the President-elect dies before he is inaugurated the Vice President-elect shall become President. If we choose to make the Vice President appointive should we continue to follow that amendment? (It would have to be amended to require that the President-elect designate his choice for Vice President as soon as he is elected.)

Strategy would almost surely dictate that political parties insist on their Presidential candidates' announcing their choices for Vice President immediately on their nominations. This would leave the voter just about where he is now—choosing between two two-man tickets.

Whatever desirable results might derive from it, this fourth approach affects basically so many political habits and structures that it must be entertained only for consideration in the future. It carries with it so many knotty problems that it can scarcely offer a practical solution to our immediate problem.

If we do seriously consider permanently transferring the Vice President to the executive division we should take note of two things. First, we would be leaving the Senate without its tie-breaker. In a normal situation this would be no serious hazard. Tie votes in the Senate are very infrequent. On fifteen different occasions this country has been without a Vice President. The Senate has gone along just about as well without as with him. But there is one important possibility. In recent years party division in the Senate has been very nearly equal. It is not at all inconceivable that the Senate might some time find that it contained forty-eight Republicans and forty-eight Democrats.

This would raise the puzzling problem of which party would provide the president pro tempore, the committee chairmen and the other Senate officers. A deadlock on this score could prove most unfortunate. Hence it might be wise, though he need no longer be president of the Senate, for the Vice President to retain one small relic of his traditional role. He might well keep the right to break a tie over organization. Of course he would cast his vote in favor of the President's party, which would settle matters in a way that would be happiest in the circumstances.

And while the President would gain much if the Vice President were added to his staff, he would suffer one significant loss. Recent Vice Presidents have often been able to serve as valuable liaisons with Congress. A Vice President, especially if he is a former, experienced member of Congress, may serve as a valuable link in getting the administration's proposals enacted into law.

Therefore the Vice President, serving in the executive division, might be given a legislative channel that would compensate for the Senate chair and would in all probability be much more useful. His Constitutional prerogatives might well include the privilege of the floor of either house for the purpose of explaining and defending the President's program. He should be permitted to take with him such department or other agency heads as he thinks will be helpful to his case. These officers would also be permitted to speak for the particular occasion. Of course the Vice President would never exercise his floor privileges without the complete approval of the President.

This change could meet a long-recognized need. Rules would have to be carefully worked out in Congress to assure that appearances of the Vice President with agency and department heads would serve to cast light on problems facing the executive and would not turn out to be mere political harangues. Many people, scholars and members of Congress included, have for many years expressed the belief that the executive and Congress, working in their separate compartments, are often poorly informed about each other's problems. The fact that there is little exchange of direct information has often resulted in misunderstanding and conflict.

It is true that department heads often appear before Congressional committees, but still the whole Congress gets the viewpoints of the administrators indirectly, as reported by the committees. Surely direct communication is more effective than indirect. Over the past century have come at various times proposals, in and out of Congress, to permit department heads to occupy Congressional seats without votes, but so far nothing has come of them.

Senator Estes Kefauver and Jack Levin in their 1947 book, *A Twentieth-Century Congress,* presented an interesting suggestion. They advocate a report-and-question period, in which

Cabinet members and federal agency heads would appear on the floors of the two houses in order to answer questions and clear up misunderstandings. They suggest safeguards to prevent the proceedings from degenerating into purely political bickering. The sole purpose of the Kefauver-Levin plan, say its authors, is to give the executive department both a right and an obligation to explain its problems to the legislative and to provide Congress with information about them.

There can be little doubt that the appearance of the Vice President, along with other executive officers, on the floor of a house of Congress would foster a spirit of co-operation on problems in which both the executive and the Congress are interested. It would also arouse tremendous public interest. People would follow such discussions much more eagerly than an ordinary Congressional debate. Alert civic interest is the very lifeline of democracy, and we need to utilize every means we can find to provoke and maintain wholesome interest in what the government is doing. The possibilities here are endless.

But some may ask why the President rather than the Vice President shouldn't go down to Congress. A little thought makes the answer clear. No matter how carefully the rules might be worked out, there would no doubt still be an occasional remark that had best never been expressed. The President might risk the supreme dignity of his office by indulging in a direct question-and-answer session with Congress. The Vice President would not face an equal hazard. He is not at the head of the nation. He can participate in give-and-take without injury to his office much more freely than can the President.

Whatever our thinking on these specifics, there is little doubt that the Vice Presidency is in for a re-examination. The Senate subcommittee that considered the Hoover proposal reported it out unfavorably. It based its decision primarily on the fact that President Eisenhower did not seek the establishment of such an office.

But at one place in the committee report appears this significant statement: "From the foregoing it is clear that there is considerable divergence of view concerning the suggestion to transfer the elected Vice President from the legislative to the executive branch. In any event, before a Constitutional change of this radical nature is undertaken, there should be extensive and thorough consideration of all aspects of the matter."

The subcommittee is certainly correct in that statement. Only after careful, serious thought should we even slightly alter the institutions on which the operation of our government rests.

Any success in renovating the Vice Presidency by Constitutional amendment is likely to come pretty far in the future. No fundamental change should be made without exhaustive debate and careful and intelligent public analysis. For the present our best hope would seem to rest in taking advantage of every opportunity to stimulate more widespread interest in the office and a more acute and lasting appreciation of its true importance.

From its very beginning it was plain that the 1956 campaign would generate extraordinary interest in the Vice Presidency. In their August conventions the two parties proceeded in much the same way to nominate Presidential candidates. In Chicago Democrat Adlai E. Stevenson, former governor of Illinois, scored such an easy and impressive first-ballot triumph over Governor Averell Harriman of New York, who was backed by former President Truman, that no one felt there was any real contest. In San Francisco President Eisenhower won the Republican nomination on the first ballot, without opposition. But in their methods of nominating a Vice President the two conventions offered a decided and significant contrast.

The Democrats held what is generally termed an open convention. Mr. Stevenson set the stage for this. Having won the Presidential nomination he was entitled by precedent to throw his most influential support to anyone he favored as a running mate. Instead he made a brief and businesslike appearance before the convention solely to make a statement about the forthcoming Vice Presidential nomination.

First of all Stevenson stressed the extreme importance of the office. He told the convention, "The American people have the solemn obligation to consider with the utmost care who will be their President if the selected President is prevented by a higher will from serving out his full term. It is a sober reminder that seven out of thirty-four Presidents have served as a result of such an indirect selection."

Mr. Stevenson went on to say, "The responsibility of the Presidency has become so great that the nation's attention has been focused as never before on the office of Vice President. The choice for that office has become almost as important as the choice for the Presidency."

Stevenson then announced that he would not express any preference for his running mate. He said he hoped the convention would of its own accord choose a man with whom he was congenial, but he wanted it to use its own judgment in nominating the best possible prospect.

As everyone who watched it knows, the convention changed face immediately. Up to that time it had been a rather tame, humdrum affair, with too little competition to keep interest alive. Now the fireworks started. For the first time the delegates went at their task with the enthusiasm that can be aroused only by a good contest.

A number of outstanding men were placed before the convention. The first ballot indicated a spirited battle—for the Vice Presidential nomination! It will be many a year before television viewers forget the exciting suspense of the thrilling second-ballot contest between Senator Estes Kefauver of Tennessee, the seasoned campaigner, and the youthful Senator John F. Kennedy of Massachusetts. Mr. Kefauver won out, but he will freely admit that he never had a closer call in his political life.

There is no doubt that Mr. Stevenson's move greatly stimulated public interest in the Vice Presidency. In fact he played his cards so well that the Vice Presidential race stole the whole show at the Democratic convention.

The Republicans, on the other hand, staged a fine example

of a closed convention. Long before the convention met President Eisenhower indicated that he would be quite happy to have Mr. Nixon as his running mate for a second time. Mr. Leonard Hall, the Republican national chairman, made no secret of his support of Mr. Nixon. He repeatedly expressed his confident expectation that the 1956 Republican ticket would be the same as the 1952.

A few weeks before convention time Harold Stassen, President Eisenhower's disarmament adviser, undertook a "dump Nixon" movement. He said he wanted to place on the ticket with President Eisenhower a person who would give the President a better chance to pull a Republican Congress over the wire in November. He urged that his party replace Nixon with Governor Christian A. Herter of Massachusetts. He soon found, however, that his Herter campaign had run into a formidable political blockade.

Chairman Hall arranged that Governor Herter place the name of Richard Nixon in nomination before the Republican convention. Governor Herter co-operated and announced further that if his own name were brought in he would ask that it be withdrawn. Party regulars, virtually to a man, frowned on Stassen's efforts, but Mr. Stassen stuck to his guns. His continued efforts to open the Vice Presidential nomination, even after the convention had begun, met disappointment at every turn.

Finally, after a conference with President Eisenhower in San Francisco, Stassen wound up seconding Mr. Nixon's nomination. In fact President Eisenhower announced that Mr. Stassen would request the convention to allow him that privilege. The Republican leaders were so decidedly determined on Mr. Nixon that the Vice President's only prospective opponent turned out to be a fictitious individual by the name of Joe Smith.

There had been so much unanimity in the Republican convention that it threatened to wind up without the slightest ripple of excitement. When the roll of the states was being called for announcements of intended nominations for Vice

President everything proceeded smoothly, with no opposition in sight for Nixon. Permanent Chairman Joe Martin was having a delightfully easy time in the chair—that is until Nebraska was called. Then business picked up for just one fleeting moment.

Mrs. Hazel Abel, the chairman of the Nebraska delegation, with little pleasure announced that one member of that delegation insisted on reserving the right to make a nomination. Joe Martin inquired who was to be placed in nomination. Mrs. Abel didn't know, but on Martin's request she asked the dissident delegate, Terry Carpenter. Carpenter said he wanted to nominate Joe Smith. Mrs. Abel relayed the answer to Chairman Martin, who quickly shot back, in consternation, "Joe Who?"

"Joe Smith," Mrs. Abel repeated, with equal consternation. Martin then announced that the Nebraska delegation reserved the right to nominate one Joe Smith, "whoever he is." The convention was now rocking with laughter. Delegate Carpenter never followed through with his nomination, but he did provide almost the only diversion from sheer routine. So the Republican show also was stolen—and salvaged, at least momentarily, in connection with the Vice Presidency.

Robert S. Ball, in the Detroit *News* on August 23, 1956, most appropriately remarked, "The darkest of all political dark horses was left at the post last night without ever knowing he was out of the stable." Mr. Nixon in his acceptance speech quite properly paid his respects to Mr. Smith.

In characterizing the Republican convention as closed we do not mean to suggest that a state delegation seriously wanting to nominate a competitor to Mr. Nixon would have been denied the right. But the convention was well described by an editorial in the August 22, 1956, New York *Times*: "It is a closed convention in the sense that the whole weight of the party machinery is and has for months been in operation to forestall any would-be rival of Mr. Nixon for the Vice Presidential nomination."

Lest we overdo our praise for the open Democratic convention let us remember that from both a political and a practical standpoint the Democrats were in much better position to keep the choice open. They had no incumbent to endorse or repudiate. There would be fewer political wounds to heal if the convention were left wide open than if the choice were dictated from above. Furthermore, a vigorous battle in an open convention would offer a most effective contrast to the Republican convention, which everybody knew would be cut and dried.

The Republicans faced an entirely different situation. Nixon was an incumbent. Since Eisenhower had expressed complete satisfaction with him both as Vice President and as a prospective running mate, for the convention to nominate anyone else would have been a virtual repudiation of Mr. Nixon.

The convention did, however, take far more precaution than was necessary. It didn't have to lock the shop and hide the key. Had President Eisenhower simply made a gesture in his favor at the convention the delegates would have nominated Mr. Nixon with all ease no matter how many opponents he had.

Be that as it may, it must be said that on many occasions the stalwarts in both parties have used pretty heavy hands to keep the political cart rolling smoothly down the road they have charted. Estes Kefauver proved amazingly popular in the 1952 Presidential primaries, but the party leaders did not favor him. Many Kefauver supporters at that time complained that pretty stiff foreclosure tactics were used against him.

On the other hand, should the convention be as open as the Democrats made theirs? Should we be content with merely opening the door, or should we tear if off the hinges? There is little doubt that Mr. Stevenson's step at Chicago was well timed. It brought great zest to the contest for Vice President and re-emphasized the importance of the office. Perhaps he felt he was taking very little chance. He may have calculated, as did many others, that the race would resolve itself between Kefauver and Kennedy, and he may well have surmised that he could work in reasonable harmony with either of them.

But the virtue of using the 1956 Democratic method as a perpetual precedent seems most doubtful. From our previous analysis we have seen that in order to make the Vice Presidency as useful and as important as possible we need to assure ourselves first that the Vice President will be eminently well qualified and second, that he will be congenial with the President. To make the office an object of spirited competition, without a suggestion from the Presidential nominee, may help to accomplish the first, but it may lead to total failure on the second. This is doubtless what the *Christian Science Monitor* had in mind in its August 17, 1956, editorial comment: "Mr. Stevenson has usefully focused added attention on this problem; he has not solved it."

The better answer seems to lie somewhere between the Republican closed convention and the Democratic open convention. The convention should be free from steamroller tactics. It is good to have competition for the nomination. But the competition should be among those whom the Presidential candidate has indicated as highly acceptable to him. The convention can be open without being rudderless.

We have sought so far to advance various means by which the full potential of the Vice Presidency might be developed. No matter which way we turn something arises to baffle us. The office has never had the public attention it deserves. Not even the careful and thorough delegates to the Constitutional Convention had the time or the inclination to fret with it. Through the years since then we have been generally disinterested in the Vice Presidency.

Today circumstance has handed us a supreme opportunity. Public interest in the Vice Presidency is now at a level it has not reached for many years. It may be many more years before it is so high again. This is a most propitious time for making the understanding, appreciation and improvement of the Vice Presidency a national project.

The problem is too complicated for any one mind to solve. We shall have to pool the best thinking of all our people. This has been our way of attacking public problems since our earliest beginnings as a nation. From the Albany Congress of 1754, twenty-two years before the Revolution, to the present day Americans have been coming together to exchange their views on matters that affect their government.

The celebrated Hoover Commission aroused intense interest in government reorganization. Why not create another national commission to make a careful study of the Vice Presidency? The office has really had very little directed study. A nonpartisan commission might gather information and ideas from all walks of life—from the farms, the factories and the marketplace as well as from academic cloisters. The commission's research could only be used as a prelude to a general referendum. After exhaustive study and analysis it might submit recommendations to the nation for its consideration.

Such a project would have infinite possibilities. Within only a few months Representative Celler with his subcommittee, was able to gather, by questionnaire and by hearings, a vast reservoir of data and opinions on the inability problem. They did not arrive at a solution, but they laid an excellent groundwork for future democratic action. Such a study would be well worth the time and the expense if it only enlivened our interest in a long-neglected office.

No sweeping Constitutional change should be made until the American people have done a great deal of thinking about it. If this book is provocative of thought it will have been worth while.

It would be idle to predict how the issues may be resolved. But we may devoutly close by considering again the last words of Alben W. Barkley, thirty-fifth Vice President of the United States: "I would rather be a servant in the house of the Lord than sit in the seats of the mighty."

The Vice President must serve. There is always the awesome prospect that he may ascend to the seats of the mighty. Surely it is unthinkable that his fitness should ever be in question. However vague the makers of the Constitution were, it is crystal clear that they created the office for a man who might be President.

Appendix

Roll Call of Vice Presidents

JOHN ADAMS, Massachusetts, Federalist. Vice President under George Washington, 1789-1797. Adams was born in Braintree, Massachusetts, on October 19, 1735. One of the outstanding patriots of the Revolutionary era, he graduated from Harvard, practiced law and served in the Continental Congress, where he supported the independence movement.

Adams was somewhat vain and sensitive, and his personality antagonized many people, but he was a man of extraordinary ability and the highest principles. His character is perhaps best demonstrated by his behavior in March 1770. Revolution was brewing, and British troops were stationed in Boston. The patriots resented their presence. On March 5 a crowd of Bostonians taunted, insulted and snowballed some of the troops. Finally the frightened soldiers, apparently thinking they were in grave danger, fired into the crowd. Before order was restored five people had been killed and several wounded. This was the famous Boston Massacre.

Adams was asked to serve as defense counsel for the soldiers, several of whom had been indicted for murder. Crown lawyers were afraid to take the case for fear of mob action. Adams was clearly on the side of the colonists in their quarrel with England, but he knew that if he didn't take their case the soldiers might go without adequate defense.

Though he knew the colonists would doubt his patriotism, he was dedicated to the principle that every accused man is entitled to counsel. He, with Josiah Quincy, successfully defended the soldiers. All except two were acquitted, and those two were given light sentences for manslaughter.

In 1796 Adams defeated Thomas Jefferson in a close race and, on March 4, 1797, became the second President of the United States. Adams died July 4, 1826.

THOMAS JEFFERSON, Virginia, Democratic-Republican. Vice President 1797-1801, under John Adams. Jefferson was born in Shadwell, Virginia, April 13, 1743. He graduated from William and Mary College, studied law and became one of the leading political figures of his day.

Jefferson was a man whose

genius was so great and whose accomplishments were so numerous as to make words about him unnecessary. He served as a member of the Virginia legislature, as governor of his state and as a member of the Second Continental Congress. There he was the prinicipal draftsman and one of the signers of the Declaration of Independence. He was Secretary of State under President Washington, then Vice President and, for two terms, from 1801 to 1809, President of the United States. The present Democratic Party looks on Jefferson as its founder.

Jefferson did not consider this or any of his many public offices his most important achievement. In the instructions he gave his daughter shortly before his death he asked that only three things be recorded on his gravestone: that he was the author of the Declaration of Independence, the author of the Virginia statute on religious freedom and the father of the University of Virginia.

Jefferson died on July 4, 1826, the same day as John Adams.

AARON BURR, New York, Democratic-Republican. Vice President 1801-1805, under Thomas Jefferson. Burr was born in Newark, New Jersey, February 6, 1756. He graduated from Princeton College, studied theology for a while and then gave it up for law.

In the Revolutionary army he distinguished himself for valor.

Moving to New York City, he became a member of the state legislature, attorney general of New York and United States Senator. As Vice President Burr presided over the Senate gracefully and skillfully.

His behavior during the contest with Jefferson for the Presidency in 1800, his shooting Hamilton in a duel and the events that finally culminated in his being tried for treason in 1807 disgraced him and ruined his political career. Much discredited in America, Burr went abroad for a few years. He resumed law practice in New York City in 1812. He died September 14, 1836.

The verdict of history has been that though Burr was a greatly talented man he lacked the character necessary to supplement his abilities.

GEORGE CLINTON, New York, Democratic-Republican. Vice President 1805-1812, during Jefferson's second term and Madison's first. Clinton was born in Little Britain, Ulster (now Orange) County, New York, July 26, 1739. He served in the Continental Congress and was a brigadier general in the Revolution.

Clinton was governor of New York when the Constitution was up for ratification. He opposed it and only yielded during the last moments of the campaign.

In 1804, at sixty-five, Clinton replaced the discredited Burr as President Jefferson's running mate. When Jefferson in 1808 declined to seek a third term Clinton naturally thought he was due for the Democratic-Republican nomination for President. But Jefferson preferred Madison to sixty-nine-year-old Clinton. Madison was nominated, and Clinton had again to take second place on the ticket, this time under a different leader.

Clinton thoroughly disliked Madison. In New York his followers supported him for President against Madison. Thus the regular party candidate for Vice President openly opposed the candidate for President. In the words of Henry Adams, "Clinton newspapers attacked Madison without mercy, while Madison's friends were electing Clinton as Madison's Vice President."

Madison and Clinton were both elected. Obviously Madison could have little reliance on his Vice President. Clinton died in office on April 20, 1812. Apparently the administration was not grieved at the loss of the Vice President. Clinton was the first Vice President to die in office.

ELBRIDGE GERRY, Massachusetts, Democratic-Republican. Vice President 1813-1814, in Madison's second term. Born in Marblehead, Massachusetts, July 17, 1744, Gerry was a member of the Second Continental Congress, a signer of the Declaration of Independence, a member of the Congress of the Confederation and a delegate to the Constitutional Convention.

In the Convention he opposed establishing an office of Vice President. He was one of three delegates who refused to sign the Constitution, objecting particularly to the extent of powers granted to the President. Later he supported ratification. Gerry was a member of the First and Second Congresses under the new Government and was later governor of Massachusetts.

As governor he caused a new word, gerrymandering, to be added to our language. The general assembly laid out legislative districts in such a way that the state senate was assured a Republican majority. This was by no means the first time such tactics had been used. The idea is to pack the opposition, in this case the Federalists, into a few districts, which they will carry with large and wasted majorities, and to spread your own party over many districts, which it can then carry safely.

On the occasion that provided the name one of the Massachusetts districts was drawn to resemble a dragon. The painter Gilbert Stuart is generally credited with having provided the drawing with head, wings and claws, saying, "That will do for a salamander." "Gerrymander!" replied some Federalist wit, and the term was born.

George Clinton's death created an opening on the Democratic-Republican ticket for the campaign of 1812. Gerry took his place and served until he too died in office, on November 23, 1814.

DANIEL D. TOMPKINS, New York, Democratic-Republican. Vice President 1817-1825, under James Monroe. Daniel Tompkins was born in Fox Meadows (now Scarsdale), Westchester County, New York, June 21, 1774. He graduated from Columbia College and practiced law.

Tompkins became an associate justice of the New York Supreme Court and was governor of the state from 1807 to 1817, serving during the War of 1812. In those days the states had to defend their own frontiers against the enemy. As governor, and thus commander of the state militia, Tompkins suffered severe handicaps from inadequate equipment, inadequate funds and inadequate staff. He was so busy with defense that some of his most important public records were lost.

As Vice President he was severely embarrassed because he could not supply vouchers to account for all the money that had passed through his hands as governor. He was technically in default, but few doubted his honesty. Both Congress and the New York legislature appropriated funds to help him out, but he remained depressed and humiliated. He began to drink and stayed away from the Senate much of the time. Tompkins died on June 11, 1825, shortly after his second term as Vice President.

JOHN C. CALHOUN, South Carolina Democratic-Republican. Vice President 1825-1832, under John Quincy Adams and Andrew Jackson. Calhoun was born March 18, 1782, near Calhoun Mills (now Mount Carmel, McCormick County), South Carolina. He graduated from Yale and from Litchfield Law School in Connecticut.

He sat in Congress from 1811 to 1817 and was Secretary of War from 1817 to 1825, during the two administrations of President Monroe.

In his earlier years Calhoun was one of the so-called War Hawks, strong nationalists who urged the war with England in 1812. The War Hawks' economic policies, including support of a national bank, led Josiah Quincy to remark that they had "outFederalized Federalism." Calhoun in those days supported a protective tariff and saw no need to argue about the Constitutionality of a National Bank.

But by 1828, the year Jackson was elected President and Calhoun Vice President for a second time, Calhoun had changed his position on the protective tariff. He saw it now as a discrimination against the South, unwarranted by the Constitution. As South Carolina deepened her opposition to the tariff and even began to talk of secession, Calhoun offered nullification as a substitute. From then on he was the champion of the nullificationists, who held that a state might declare a law of Congress null and void as applied to its citizens if it considered that law unconstitutional.

Calhoun resigned from the Vice Presidency in 1832 to become a United States Senator, which position he held until 1843. As Secretary of State under President John Tyler in 1844 and 1845 he was instrumental in arranging for the annexation of Texas.

He returned to the Senate in 1845 and remained until his death, March 31, 1850. While some of his views now seem untenable, there is little doubt that Calhoun was among the ablest statesmen this country has produced.

MARTIN VAN BUREN, New York, Democrat. Vice President 1833-1837, in Andrew Jackson's second term. Van Buren was born in Kinderhook, Columbia County, New York, December 5, 1782. He attended Kinderhook Academy, then practiced law in New York. He represented New York in the United States Senate from 1821 to 1828.

Van Buren was governor of New York from January 1 to March 12, 1829, when he resigned to become Secretary of State in Jackson's first administration. He resigned this post in 1831 to make it easier for his friend Jackson to reorganize his Cabinet. He was elected Vice President on the Jackson ticket in 1832.

In 1836, with Jackson's support, Van Buren was nominated Democratic candidate for President and was elected. He has been the only Vice President since the Twelfth Amendment to later be elected President in first instance. Van Buren died July 24, 1862.

RICHARD M. JOHNSON, Kentucky, Democrat. Vice President 1837-1841, under Van Buren. Johnson was born at Bryants Station, Kentucky, October 17, 1781. He attended Translyvania University and practiced law in Kentucky. He served as a member of Congress from 1807 to 1819.

Johnson commanded a regiment under General William Henry Harrison during the War of 1812. In recognition of his valor and that of his regiment Congress presented him a sword. He was United States Senator from December 1819 to March 1829 and a member of the House of Representatives from 1829 to 1837.

In 1836 he was nominated by the Democrats as Van Buren's running mate. After Johnson had been nominated at a national convention in Baltimore the Virginia delegation registered objection and announced that Virginia Democrats would not vote for him.

The Virginia delegation predicted correctly. That state's twenty-three electors all voted for Van Buren for President but cast their ballots for William Smith of Alabama rather than Johnson for Vice President. As a result Johnson received 147 electoral votes (Van Buren got 170) while Francis Granger of New York, John Tyler of Virginia and William Smith of Alabama together received the same total, leaving Johnson one vote short of a majority.

By the terms of the Twelfth Amendment the Senate had to choose between the highest two Vice Presidential candidates, Johnson and Francis Granger. On the first ballot the Senate chose Johnson by a vote of thirty-three to sixteen. This is the only case in which the Senate has chosen a Vice President.

Johnson was a candidate for re-election with Van Buren in 1840, but strangely, he was not officially nominated by the national convention. The convention left the choice of a Vice Presidential candidate to the Democratic electors.

Van Buren and Johnson were both beaten by the Whig candidates, William Henry Harrison and John Tyler. Johnson quite naturally took a worse beating than Van Buren. He then returned to state politics, serving as a member of the Kentucky house of Representatives in 1841 and 1842. He died November 19, 1850.

JOHN TYLER, Virginia, Whig. Vice President under President William Henry Harrison for one month, from March 4, 1841, to Harrison's death on April 4. Tyler was born in Charles City County, Virginia, March 29, 1790. He graduated from William and Mary College and practiced law.

He served in Congress from 1817 to 1821 as a Democratic-Republican. He was governor of Virginia from 1825 to 1827 and United States Senator from 1827 to 1836. He was elected president pro tempore of the Senate in 1835. Elected the tenth Vice President, Tyler became also the tenth President when Harrison died. Tyler was the first Vice President to succeed to the Presidency on the death of the incumbent. Since he had served only one month as Vice President, he was President for nearly four years. The Whigs did not nominate Tyler for President in 1844.

He became chancellor of William and Mary College in 1859. He went along with his native state when Virginia seceded from the Union and was elected to the House of Representatives of the Confederate Congress, but he died January 18, 1862, before the congress assembled.

GEORGE M. DALLAS, Pennsylvania, Democrat. Vice President 1845-1849, under President James K. Polk. Dallas was born in Philadelphia, Pennsylvania, July 10, 1792. He graduated from Princeton College and practiced law.

Before he became Vice President he served as private secretary to Albert Gallatin, minister to Russia, as mayor of Philadelphia and as United States Senator. After his term as Vice President he was, in 1856, appointed by President Pierce as envoy extraordinary and minister plenipotentiary to Great Britain. This post he held until 1861. He died December 31, 1864.

MILLARD FILLMORE, New York, Whig. Vice President 1849-1850, under Zachary Taylor. Fillmore was one of many unspectacular Vice Presidents. He was born in Locke Township (now Summerhill), Cayuga County, New York, January 7, 1800. His educational opportunities were quite limited; it is probably best to describe him as self-educated. He taught school while studying law.

Fillmore was a Whig Congressman from 1833 to 1835 and from 1837 to 1843. He ran for governor of New York in 1844 but was defeated. He was New York state comptroller in 1849, when he resigned to become Vice President.

When President Taylor died Fillmore became the thirteenth President of the United States and the second to succeed a President who died in office. In the Whig convention of 1852 he lost the nomination to General Winfield Scott on the fifty-third ballot.

Fillmore commanded a corps of home guards during the Civil War. He died March 8, 1874.

WILLIAM R. KING, Alabama, Democrat. Vice President under Franklin Pierce from March 4, 1853, until his death on April 18 of the same year. King was born in Sampson County, North Carolina, April 7, 1786. He graduated from the University of North Carolina, then practiced law in his home state.

King sat in the United States House of Representatives from 1811 to 1816. He served for a time as secretary of the American legations at Naples and St. Petersburg. He later moved to Alabama and represented that state in the United States Senate from 1819 to 1844. He was minister to France from 1844 to 1846 and returned to the Senate from 1848 to 1852. He served several times as president pro tem.

King was nearly sixty-seven years old when he was elected Vice President. His health failed completely between the election and inauguration day. He resigned as pro tem in December and went to Cuba to recuperate, but he was never able to return to Washington.

A special act of Congress enabled King to take the Vice President's oath in Cuba. The oath was administered by an American consul. King, in the last stages of tuberculosis, was so weak he could not stand up. The consul and Representative George Jones of Tennessee supported him while he was sworn in. Shortly thereafter King returned to his Alabama plantation, where he died on April 18, 1853.

JOHN C. BRECKINRIDGE, Kentucky, Democrat. Vice President 1857-1861, under James Buchanan. Breckinridge, who took office at thirty-six, is the youngest Vice President we have had. Born near Lexington, Kentucky, January 21, 1821, he graduated from Centre College, studied law in Transylvania Institute, then began his practice.

Breckinridge was a major of volunteers in the Mexican War and a member of Congress from 1851 to 1855. In 1860, while serving as Vice President, he was nominated by the Southern Democrats for President, but Lincoln defeated him. He was a United States Senator from March 4, 1861, until he was expelled on December 4 for entering the Confederate army. He became a major general and later secretary of war for the Confederate States.

Breckinridge was an able man. He had stood for maintaining the Union when he ran for President and had sought by compromise to avert civil war and disunion. But after hostilities started he chose the Confederate side. He died May 17, 1875.

HANNIBAL HAMLIN, Maine, Republican. Vice President 1861-1865, under Lincoln. Hamlin was born in Paris, Oxford County, Maine, August 27, 1809. He attended Hebron Academy, then practiced law in Maine.

Hamlin served as speaker of the Maine House of Representatives, as a Democratic member of the United States House of Representatives and as a Democratic member of the United States Senate. In 1856 he left the Democratic Party and, as a Republican, was elected governor of Maine. He was a Republican member of the United States Senate from 1857 to 1861.

Hamlin served only one term as Vice President. He was denied renomination in 1864 only for political expediency. The Republican party, wanting to strengthen its appeal for national unity, called itself the National Union Party for this campaign. After nominating Lincoln for a second term it passed Hamlin up in favor of Andrew Johnson of Tennessee to give the party a more national complexion.

Hamlin again entered the United States Senate, serving from 1869 to 1881. He was minister to Spain in 1881 and 1882. He died July 4, 1891.

ANDREW JOHNSON, Tennessee, Republican (National Union Party). Vice President from March 4 to April 15, 1865, under Lincoln. Andrew Johnson was born in Raleigh, North Carolina, December 29, 1808. He had no formal education and was by profession a tailor.

After moving to Tennessee he got interested in politics and was elected mayor of Greenville. He was a Democratic member of the United States House of Representatives from 1843 to 1853, governor of Tennessee from 1853 to 1857 and United States Senator from 1857 to 1862.

When Tennessee seceded Johnson adhered to the Union, refusing to endorse the secession movement. He resigned from the Senate in 1862 and was appointed military governor of Tennessee by President Lincoln.

Although he ran for Vice President on the Republican National Union Party ticket he was really a Democrat for Union. He was nominated to balance the ticket. When Lincoln died Andrew Johnson became the seventeenth President of the United States. In March 1875 he returned to the United States Senate, where he served until his death on July 31 of that year.

SCHUYLER COLFAX, Indiana, Republican. Vice President 1869-1873, under Ulysses S. Grant. Colfax was born in New York City, March 23, 1823. He attended common school there. In 1836 he moved with his parents to Indiana.

He affiliated with the Whig party in his earlier years but later became a Republican. He was a member of the convention to draft a new Indiana constitution, a member of the United States House of Representatives from 1855 to 1869 and three times speaker of the House.

That he was not renominated for Vice President in 1872 was not due to any failure in performing his duties. He had offended some Washington correspondents, who used their influence against him. His political career was nevertheless soon ended in a cloud of suspicion.

Just a short while before his term expired he was charged, along with others, with accepting stock in the notorious Credit Mobilier. The chief stockholders of the Union Pacific Railroad had offered the stock through Representative Oakes Ames of Massachusetts in a move to block Congressional investigation of their fraudulent transactions.

No one knows definitely how deeply Colfax was involved. He was not impeached, but his term was nearly up anyway. The *Biographical Directory of the American Congress* says he was fully exonerated. Whether he was guilty or just innocently shallow enough to get mixed up in the affair, the scandal halted Colfax's political career. He died January 13, 1885.

HENRY WILSON, Massachusetts, Republican. Vice President 1873-1875, in Grant's second term. Wilson was born in Farmington, New Hampshire, February 16, 1812. Born Jeremiah Jones Colbaith, on reaching adulthood he had the New Hampshire legislature change his name to Henry

Wilson. He attended common schools and later enrolled for short periods of study in several academies. In 1833 he moved to Massachusetts, where he became a shoemaker.

He served in both the state House of Representatives and the state Senate. In 1854 he was elected to the United States Senate by the Know-Nothings, with the help of the Free Soilers and the Democrats. He held his seat until he was inaugurated Vice President.

At this time the Know-Nothings, or American Party, a secret political organization both anti-foreign and anti-Catholic, had strong followings in some areas. It advocated an America run by Americans—what the Know-Nothings called "native stock." They got their name from their habit of replying to all questions about their party, "I dont know."

Wilson was also among those charged with complicity in the Credit Mobilier scandal. He died in office on November 22, 1875.

WILLIAM A. WHEELER, New York, Republican. Vice President 1877-1881, under Rutherford B. Hayes. Wheeler was born in Malone, Franklin County, New York, June 19, 1819. He attended the University of Vermont and practiced law in Malone. He became a member of the New York state Assembly, the state Senate and the United States House of Representatives.

After his one term as Vice President, Wheeler retired from public life because of poor health. He died June 4, 1887.

CHESTER A. ARTHUR, New York, Republican. Vice President March 4 to September 19, 1881, under James A. Garfield. Arthur was born in Fairfield, Franklin County, Vermont, on October 5, 1830. He graduated from Union College, Schenectady, New York, and practiced law in New York City.

During the Civil War Arthur held a number of military positions, including quartermaster general of New York. Grant appointed him collector of the port of New York in 1871, but Hayes removed him after an investigation indicated that Arthur, like so many big New York machine politicians of his day, was using his position to build up an unwholesome patronage machine.

Without any particular claims to or qualifications for the office he was nominated by the Republican national convention of 1880 as Garfield's running mate. Arthur's nomination was in every sense a consolation prize, thrown out to Roscoe Conkling and the other Stalwarts, who had sought to nominate General Grant for a third term.

On the death of President Garfield Arthur became the twenty-first President of the United States. He died November 18, 1886.

THOMAS A. HENDRICKS, Indiana, Democrat. Vice President March 4 to November 25, 1885, in Grover Cleveland's first administration. Thomas Hendricks was born near Zanesville, Ohio, September 7, 1819. He moved with his parents to Indiana, where he graduated from Hanover College. He practiced law in Indiana and entered politics.

Hendricks served in the Indiana state House of Representatives and the state Senate and was a member of the United States House of Representatives from 1851-1855. He was United States Senator from 1863 to 1869 and was later governor of Indiana.

Perhaps the most significant thing Hendricks did in his short time as Vice President was to oppose President Cleveland's program of strict civil service reform. Hendricks was disgusted with Cleveland for trying to restrict the spoils of the Democratic party, so long out of office. He had won Tammany support for his nomination by promising Boss Kelly that Cleveland would be considerate of the Wigwam in his appointments.

It should of course be pointed out that many leading political figures of the day, both Democratic and Republican, had little sympathy with the effort to diminish party patronage.

Hendricks had served less than a year as Vice President when he died, in Indianapolis, on November 25, 1885.

LEVI P. MORTON, New York, Republican. Vice President 1889-1893, under Benjamin Harrison. Morton was born in Shoreham, Addison County, Vermont, May 16, 1824. He attended public schools and Shoreham Academy.

He taught school and went into the mercantile business in New Hampshire. Moving to New York, Morton entered the dry goods business and then banking. He was a member of the United States House of Representatives from 1879 to 1881 and minister to France from 1881 to 1885.

After his term as Vice President Morton became, in 1895, governor of New York, serving until 1897. He died May 16, 1920.

ADLAI E. STEVENSON, Illinois, Democrat. Vice President 1893-1897, during the second Cleveland administration. Stevenson, grandfather of the Democratic nominee for President in 1952 and 1956, was born in Christian County, Kentucky, October 23, 1835, but later moved with his family to Illinois. He attended Illinois Wesleyan University and Centre College in Kentucky. He practiced law in Illinois.

Stevenson served as a master in chancery and then as a district attorney in Illinois. He was a member of the United States House of Representatives from 1875 to 1877 and again from 1879 to 1881. From 1885 to 1889 he was first assistant Postmaster General. Stevenson was not renominated for Vice President in 1896. He was, however, nominated to run with Presidential candidate William Jennings Bryan in 1900, but both were beaten by McKinley and Roosevelt.

Stevenson died June 14, 1914.

GARRETT A. HOBART, New Jersey, Republican. Vice President 1897-1899, under William McKinley. Hobart was born near Long Branch, Monmouth County, New Jersey, June 3, 1844.

He graduated from Rutgers College, taught school, was clerk for a grand jury, studied and practiced law and was Paterson, New Jersey, city attorney and counsel for the board of freeholders.

Hobart served for a time as speaker of the state Assembly and, later, as president of the state Senate. He was also a member of the Republican National Committee. He died in office as Vice President on November 21, 1899.

THEODORE ROOSEVELT, New York, Republican. Vice President from March 4 to September 14, 1901, in McKinley's second term. Born in New York City on October 27, 1858, Roosevelt graduated from Harvard University.

He served as a member of the New York state Assembly, a member of the United States Civil Service Commission, president of the New York board of police commissioners, assistant Secre-

tary of the Navy, organizer of the famed Rough Riders in the Spanish-American War and governor of New York.

On the death of President McKinley, Roosevelt became the twenty-sixth President of the United States. In 1904 he was reelected in his own right. He died January 6, 1919.

CHARLES W. FAIRBANKS, Indiana, Republican. Vice President 1905-1909, in Roosevelt's second term. Fairbanks was born near Unionville Center, Union County, Ohio, May 11, 1852. He graduated from Ohio Wesleyan University and moved to Indianapolis, where he practiced law.

Before he became Vice President he was a trustee of Ohio Wesleyan and a United States Senator, from 1897 to 1905. In 1898 he was a member of the United States-British Joint High Commission for adjustment of Canadian questions.

Fairbanks was not nominated for Vice President in 1908 or in 1912, but was Charles Evans Hughes's running mate in 1916. The Republican ticket that year was defeated by Wilson and Marshall. Fairbanks died on June 4, 1918.

JAMES S. SHERMAN, New York, Republican. Vice President 1909-1912, under President Taft. Sherman was born in Utica, New York, October 24, 1855. He graduated from Hamilton College, then practiced law in New York.

Besides being mayor of Utica Sherman was a member of the United States House of Representatives, from 1887 to 1891 and from 1893 to 1909. He was renominated for Vice President in 1912 but died on October 30, before the campaign was over.

THOMAS R. MARSHALL, Indiana, Democrat. Vice President 1913-1921, under Woodrow Wilson. Born in North Manchester, Wabash County, Indiana, March 14, 1854, Marshall graduated from Wabash College in Crawfordsville, Indiana.

He later practiced law in Indiana and was governor of that state from 1909 to 1913. During his two terms as Vice President he was very popular with the Senate. He had a fine sense of humor and is the source of many anecdotes about the Vice Presidency and about what went on during his time in Washington.

When he left Washington he returned to law practice in Indianapolis. He served as a member of the Federal Coal Commission in 1922 and 1923. He died in Washington on June 1, 1925.

CALVIN COOLIDGE, Massachusetts, Republican. Vice President 1921-1923, under President Harding. Coolidge was born in Plymouth, Windsor County, Vermont, on July 4, 1872. After graduating from Amherst College he practiced law in Massachusetts.

He served in the Massachu-setts House of Representatives and the state Senate and became mayor of Northampton. He was lieutenant governor from 1916 to 1918 and governor of Massachusetts in 1919 and 1920. As governor he attracted national attention with a statement about the Boston police strike. "There is no right," he said, "to strike against the public safety by anybody, any time, anywhere."

On the death of President Harding, Coolidge became the thirtieth President of the United States. In 1924 he was elected in his own right. He died January 5, 1933.

CHARLES G. DAWES, Illinois, Republican. Vice President 1925-1929, under President Coolidge. Dawes was born in Marietta, Ohio, August 27, 1865. He graduated from Marietta College and took his law degree in Cincinnati.

He practiced law in Lincoln, Nebraska, then shifted his interest to public utilities and banking, primarily in Illinois. He served for a time in the United States Treasury Department, as comptroller of currency. A brigadier general during World War I, he was decorated by the American, British and French governments. He was the first Director of the Budget and was, in 1923, a member of the first committee of experts for the Reparations Commission.

Dawes, a very vigorous and able man, was not especially

happy to be Vice President. He tried to reform the Senate but got exactly nowhere. He is well remembered not only for his attack on filibusters but also for a famous afternoon nap.

President Coolidge had submitted to the Senate the nomination of Michigan's Charles B. Warren for Attorney General. When the Senate voted on it, Dawes was at his hotel "taking a snooze," as he expressed it. The vote tied at forty. Administration forces were frantic to get hold of Dawes to break the tie. Reached by telephone, he hurried into a taxi and sped down Pennsylvania Avenue.

But he was too late. While he was on his way Republican Senator David A. Reed of Pennsylvania, who had voted for confirmation, changed his vote and moved for a reconsideration. Democratic Senator Thomas J. Walsh of Montana immediately moved that Reed's motion be tabled and, on a second ballot, Walsh's motion carried. So the matter was settled for the day; Warren was not confirmed. A later effort in his behalf failed by a vote of forty-six to thirty-nine.

After his term as Vice President Dawes served as ambassador to Great Britain, from 1929 to 1932. He died on April 23, 1951.

CHARLES CURTIS, Kansas, Republican. Vice President 1929-1933, under Herbert Hoover.

Curtis was born in Topeka, Kansas, January 25, 1860. He practiced law in Topeka.

He was for many years a member of Congress, serving in the House from 1893 to 1907 and in the Senate from 1907 to 1913 and from 1915 to 1929. He was president pro tempore for a short time in 1911 and Senate majority leader from 1924 to 1929.

Curtis was nominated by the Republican Party for a second term as Vice President on Hoover's ticket in 1932, but both were defeated by Franklin D. Roosevelt and John Nance Garner.

After his term as Vice President Mr. Curtis practiced law in Washington, where he died February 8, 1936.

JOHN NANCE GARNER, Texas, Democrat. Vice President 1933-1941, under Franklin Roosevelt. Garner was born near Detroit, Red River County, Texas, on November 22, 1868.

A man of little formal education, Garner practiced law in Texas. He was a judge in that state and a member of its House of Representatives. He was a United States Congressman from 1903 to 1933, serving as minority floor leader in the Seventy-first Congress and as speaker of the House in the Seventy-second.

Because of his age he was not nominated for a third term as Vice President in 1940. He now lives in retirement at his home in Uvalde, Texas.

HENRY A. WALLACE, Iowa, Democrat. Vice President 1941-1945, under Franklin Roosevelt. Born near Orient, Adair County, Iowa, October 7, 1888, Wallace graduated from Iowa State College. He was editor of *Wallace's Farmer* from 1924 to 1929 and of *Wallace's Farmer and Iowa Homestead* from 1929 to 1933.

He was Secretary of Agriculture from 1933 to 1940. In 1945, after his term as Vice President, President Roosevelt appointed him Secretary of Commerce. On September 20, 1946, President Truman dismissed him from this post because of Wallace's outspoken disagreement with Secretary of State Byrnes's "get tough" policy toward the Soviet Union.

In 1948 Wallace was nominated by the Progressive Party for President of the United States. He got over a million popular but no electoral votes.

HARRY S TRUMAN, Missouri, Democrat. Vice President January 20 to April 12, 1945, under Franklin Roosevelt. Mr. Truman was born in Lamar, Barton County, Missouri, May 8, 1884. He attended public school and later studied law at night in the Kansas City Law School.

Truman was a captain in field artillery in World War I. Back in the United States, he spent a short time in the haberdashery business and then went into politics. Early in his career he was backed by the celebrated Tom Pendergast, political boss of Kansas City.

Mr. Truman served as a judge of the Jackson County, Missouri, court from 1922 to 1924 and as presiding judge from 1926 to 1934. From 1935 to 1945 he was a United States Senator. He attracted national attention as chairman of a Senate committee to investigate production for national defense.

When President Roosevelt died, on April 12, 1945, Mr. Truman became the thirty-third President of the United States. In 1948 he was re-elected in his own right.

ALBEN W. BARKLEY, Kentucky, Democrat. Vice President 1949-1953, under President Truman. Mr. Barkley was born near Lowes, Graves County, Kentucky, November 24, 1877. He graduated from Marvin College, Clinton, Kentucky, and later attended Emory University, Oxford, Georgia, and the University of Virginia College of Law. He practiced law in Paducah, Kentucky.

Among Barkley's positions prior to the Vice Presidency were prosecuting attorney for McCracken County, Kentucky, judge of the McCracken County court, member of the United States House of Representatives, 1913-1927, and United States Senator, 1927-1949. In the Senate he served several times as both minority and majority floor leader. He was undoubtedly the dean of the Democratic keynote speakers.

In 1952, because of his age, he was denied serious consideration for the Presidential nomination by the Democratic national convention. Invited to address the convention, he then astounded the delegates as well as the nation by giving such a speech as few men half his age would have the vitality to deliver.

In 1954, after his term as Vice President, Barkley was again elected to the Senate, becoming, ironically after his long years of service, junior Senator from Kentucky. He died on April 30, 1956, while addressing a mock Democratic convention at Washington and Lee University.

RICHARD M. NIXON, California, Republican. Vice President since 1953, under President Ei-senhower. Mr. Nixon was born in Yorba Linda, Orange County, California, January 9, 1913. He is a graduate of Whittier College and of Duke University Law School. He practiced law in Whittier, California.

During World War II Nixon served as a lieutenant commander in the Navy. He was a member of the United States House of Representatives from 1947 to 1951. In the House he attracted widespread attention through his part in investigating charges made against Alger Hiss, former State Department official, by Whittaker Chambers. Many people regard Mr. Nixon's efforts of primary importance in securing Hiss's indictment and conviction on a charge of perjury.

In 1950 Nixon was elected United States Senator. He is among the youngest of the thirty-six Vice Presidents, having taken the oath of office at forty.

NOTES

The passage in the text to which a note refers is indicated by page and by paragraph. The number of the page is followed, in parentheses, by the *final word* of the paragraph. If a paragraph carries over to a second page, the last page number is given here.

CHAPTER ONE (pages 11-26)

11 (government): Though Dwight D. Eisenhower was the thirty-third person elected to the office, he is generally accounted the thirty-fourth President, since Grover Cleveland served two nonconsecutive terms, from 1885 to 1889, and from 1893 to 1897.

12 (years): Of the thirteen original states only twelve sent delegates to the Constitutional Convention. Rhode Island was not represented. The cheap-money forces, debtors and small farmers, had the upper hand in that state, and the state legislature suspected that the Convention was going to try to stabilize the economy. The legislature was patently wrong in its position but dead right in its suspicions. Rhode Island was very reluctant to ratify the Constitution, which went into effect while she was still outside the Union. Finally, with hostile legislation pending in Congress against her, she ratified by a close vote, on May 29, 1790.

14 (Vice President): James

Madison, *Journal of the Constitutional Convention* (Chicago, 1893), p. 659. Madison, a leading delegate from Virginia, took careful notes on all speeches made in the Convention and summarized each one. His journal gives us an excellent account of the debates and is regarded as the most valuable single source of information about what went on in the Convention. The statements attributed to various delegates in this chapter are all taken from this journal. It is very fortunate that Madison kept these accounts, since the delegates were sworn to secrecy regarding their proceedings. The Convention elected an official secretary, William Jackson, but his record carries the bare minutes, with motions and votes by states. Hereafter the *Journal* will not be cited. The dates of the speeches are given, and quotations can easily be found under the dates indicated in this text. 17 (way): Patrick Henry declared that he "smelt a rat" and declined to serve as a delegate.

Tom Paine, whose pamphlet *Common Sense,* published January 10, 1776, had set the stage for the Declaration of Independence, was in Europe. Richard Henry Lee of Virginia, the man who had moved for independence in the Second Continental Congress, declined to attend because of his membership in the Congress of the Confederation. Samuel Adams and John Hancock were not elected delegates in Massachusetts. Thomas Jefferson was in Paris on a diplomatic mission.

17-18 (executive; country): Max Farrand, *The Fathers of the Constitution* (New Haven, 1921), pp. 134-135.

21 (third): The Connecticut Compromise reconciled the large-state support of proportionate representation in Congress with the small-state insistence on equal representation. It provided for proportionate representation in the House and equal in the Senate. The Three-Fifths Compromise resolved the conflict between the slave interest, which wanted the slaves to be counted in determining a state's quota of seats in the House, and the free states, which opposed the suggestion. The compromise stated that three fifths of the slaves would be counted as population both for determining a state's representation and for computing the amount of direct taxes to be raised in that state for the Federal government. Both of these compromises regulated the states' total representation in Congress. Since each state was allotted a number of Presidential electors equaling its total representation in Congress, the plan for the election of President and Vice President incorporated both of them.

The Commerce-Slave Trade Compromise made concessions to producers of raw materials and to the slave states. It provided that, while Congress could regulate interstate and foreign commerce and levy import duties, it could not levy duties on exports. Before 1808 Congress could not forbid the importation of slaves, and no tax or duty on them could exceed ten dollars per slave. This is not incorporated into the method of choosing the President. But since Article I, Section 1 vests all legislative powers in the Congress, the President could not exercise primary legislative authority and thus could not upset the terms of this third compromise.

25 (scene, opponents): Alexander Hamilton, John Jay and James Madison, *The Federalist* (Philadelphia, 1875), pp. 503-504, 508.

CHAPTER TWO (pages 27-49)

29-30 (proceed, people): Joseph Gales, Sr., comp., *The Annals of Congress: the Debates and Proceedings in the Congress of the United States,* 1st Congress, 1st Session, Volume I (Washington, 1834), pp. 16-17. The *Annals* do not carry a verbatim report of debates and proceedings in Congress, but they do carry very good summaries of both. Privately published, they cover the period from 1789 to 1824. They were compiled from the most authentic sources available and are regarded as a very good, though not absolutely perfect, account of what went on in Congress. Congress at the time did not keep a record of its debates. The *Annals* were superseded in 1825 by another privately published digest, the *Register of Debates.* In 1833 the *Congressional Globe,* a private publication, undertook to give a verbatim reproduction of the debates. Finally, in 1873, the *Congressional Record* was started as a government publication. It presents a verbatim, stenographic report.

33 (job): After the first session of the First Congress, President Washington began a tour of the states. He hoped to bring more solidarity to the Union and to stimulate psychological forces that might bring North Carolina and Rhode Island into the Union. On this tour, in which he carefully avoided getting into the "foreign country" of Rhode Island, he was usually shown great deference by state officials. But in Massachusetts Governor John Hancock seemed to feel that President Washington, who had arrived in Boston, should pay him the first call. Washington, standing on the superior position of his office of President, refused to yield. Hancock finally gave in and called on Washington.

33 (Republic): Thomas Jefferson, in a letter to Doctor Walter Jones dated January 2, 1814, gave a very penetrating analysis of Washington's qualities: "His mind was great and powerful, without being of the first order; his penetration strong, though not so acute as that of a Newton, Bacon, or Locke; and as far as he saw, no judgment was ever sounder. It was slow in operation, being very little aided by invention or imagination, but sure in conclusion. . . . He was incapable of fear, meeting personal dangers with the calmest unconcern. . . . He was, indeed, in every sense of the words, a wise, a good, and a great man." Paul Leicester Ford, ed., *The*

Writings of Thomas Jefferson, Volume IX (New York, 1898), pp. 446-451.

33 (States): *The Journal of William Maclay, United States Senator from Pennsylvania, 1789-1791* (New York, 1927), pp. 17-25.

34 (else): Henry Jones Ford, *Washington and His Colleagues: A Chronicle of the Rise and Fall of Federalism* (New Haven, 1921), pp. 17-18.

34 (salary): *Annals of Congress,* 1st Congress, 1st Session, Volume I, pp. 671-676. The debate is confirmed in John Bach McMaster, *A History of the United States from the Revolution to the Civil War,* Volume I (New York, 1931), p. 543.

37 (judgment, be): Maclay, *op. cit.,* pp. 71-72.

38 (conceived): Quoted in Clinton L. Rossiter, "The Reform of the Vice-Presidency," *Political Science Quarterly,* September 1948, Volume LXIII, pp. 383-403.

38 (say, Excellency, truth): Thomas R. Marshall, *Recollections of Thomas R. Marshall, Vice President and Hoosier Philosopher* (Indianapolis, 1925), p. 229. *See also* Edward S. Corwin, *The President: Office and Powers, 1787-1948* (New York, 1948), p. 73.

39 (one): Studies of methods of choosing Presidential electors in those early days sometimes vary a little in their conclusions. Edward Stanwood, in *History of Presidential Elections,* p. 20f, states that in nine states—Vermont, Rhode Island, Connecticut, New York, New Jersey, Delaware, South Carolina, Georgia and Kentucky—the legislatures elected the electors. In one, North Carolina, the legislature, divided into four membership districts, picked the electors by districts. In five states—New Hampshire, Massachusetts, Pennsylvania, Maryland and Virginia—the people elected them.

40 (Federalists): The groups opposing the Hamiltonian policies, consisting largely of those who had been termed Antifederalists, now assumed the title of Democratic-Republicans, apparently getting their name from Democratic societies that had sprung up over the country. The new name was more appropriate, for it did not imply a rejection of the Constitution.

40 (vote): Some claim that Jefferson won the Vice Presidency over Pinckney because some electors thought it wise to scatter the vote for the men intended for Vice President lest one of them beat out the Presidential favorite. Burr was much disappointed at his low tally of thirty on the Republican ticket. His

insistence in 1800 that he be supported equally with Jefferson no doubt played a vital part in bringing about that year's debacle.

40 (one): Stanwood, *op. cit.,* p. 28. *See also Annals of Congress,* 4th Congress, 2nd Session, pp. 1542-1543.

40 (Congress): *Annals of Congress,* 4th Congress, 2nd Session, p. 1543.

43 (President): Some students hold that the Federalists knew there was little hope that they could elect Burr. Rather, they thought that they could keep the situation in deadlock. For one presentation of this view see David Saville Muzzey, *The United States of America,* Volume I (Boston, 1933), p. 200.

44 (intentions): Charles A. Beard, *The Economic Origins of Jeffersonian Democracy* (New York, 1927), pp. 404, 410-414.

45 (result): John Bach McMaster, *op. cit.,* Volume II, p. 524. For an account of each ballot see *Annals of Congress,* 6th Congress, pp. 1022-1030.

46 (Senate): Allan Nevins, ed., *The Diary of John Quincy Adams, 1794-1845* (New York, 1929), p. 32.

CHAPTER THREE (pages 50-58)

51 (intrigue): Edward Channing, *A History of the United States,* Volume IV (New York, 1935), p. 295.

51 (successor): *See* Henry Adams, *History of the United States of America,* Book IV (New York, 1930), p. 227.

CHAPTER FOUR (pages 59-67)

60 (Rachel): James Parton, *Life of Andrew Jackson,* Volume I (3 vols.; Boston, 1876), p. 126.

62 (sight): Charles M. Wiltse, *John C. Calhoun: Nullifier, 1829-1839* (Indianapolis, 1949), p. 27.

62 (Eaton): William Graham Sumner, *Andrew Jackson as a Public Man* (Boston, 1833), p. 149, attributes Timberlake's suicide to his excessive drinking.

See also John Spencer Bassett, *The Life of Andrew Jackson,* Volume II (Garden City, 1911), p. 459.

63 (society): Allan Nevins, ed., *op. cit.,* p. 398.

65 (President): *Ibid.,* p. 400.

66 (victory): Frederick Austin Ogg, *The Reign of Andrew Jackson* (New Haven, 1919), p. 136.

66 (term): John Spencer Bassett, ed., *The Correspondence of*

Andrew Jackson, Volume IV (Washington, 1929), p. 405. 67 (candidate): Earlier, as we have seen, Congressional caucuses had nominated the Presidential candidates. In the 1820's they were supplanted by state legislative caucuses, which afforded little hope of party unity. In 1831 the Anti-Masonic Party held a national convention in Baltimore and nominated William Wirt for President and Amos Ellmaker for Vice President. In 1832 the National Republican Party, a faction of the old Democratic-Republican Party, led by John Quincy Adams and Henry Clay and formed in 1824 and 1825, and the Democratic Party, the followers of Jackson, followed suit. Thus was born the method of nomination used today.

CHAPTER FIVE (pages 68-93)

68 (fifth): Some might object to saying that Vice Presidents who died in office had fair chances. But never when a Vice President died in office did the incumbent President also die. So had all Vice Presidents survived their terms it would not have affected the ratio.
69 (nominee): See Peter R. Levin, *Seven By Chance* (New York, 1948), p. 3.
70 (administration): *See* George Pierce Garrison, *Westward Expansion, 1841-1850* (New York, 1906), p. 44.
72 (Senate): The resolution and debate will be found in the *Congressional Globe,* 27th Congress, 1st session, Volume X, pp. 4-5.
74 (administration): *See* Allan Nevins, *Ordeal of the Union,* Volume I (New York, 1947), p. 335.
75 (States): *See* Robert W. Winston, *Andrew Johnson, Plebeian and Patriot* (New York, 1928), p. 20.
76 (asked): *Ibid.,* p. 257.
77 (decorum): Winston, *op cit.,* p. 264, says that the oath was administered by the Chief Justice. The *Congressional Globe,* 38th Congress, 2nd Session, p. 1394, says he was sworn in by outgoing Vice President Hamlin.
78-79 (body, ready): *Congressional Globe,* 38th Congress, 2nd Session, Part 2, p. 1394; quote, p. 1425.
80 (ask): William Starr Myers, *The Republican Party: A History* (New York, 1931), p. 274.
80 (States): James Ford Rhodes, *History of the United States from the Compromise of 1850 to the End of the Roosevelt Administration,* Volume VIII (9 vols.; New York, 1928), p. 146.

81 (Gregory): George Frederick Howe, *Chester A. Arthur: A Quarter-Century of Machine Politics* (New York, 1934), p. 209.

82 (bill): John D. Hicks, *A Short History of American Democracy* (Boston, 1943), p. 522.

84-85 (do, bore, view): Elting E. Morison, ed., *The Letters of Theodore Roosevelt,* Volume II (Cambridge, 1951), p. 1136, 1157, 1485.

85 (future): Joseph Becklin Bishop, *Theodore Roosevelt and His Time: Shown in His Own Letters* Volume I (New York, 1920), p. 147.

88 (it): *See* Harold U. Faulkner, *From Versailles to the New Deal* (New Haven, 1950), p. 204.

88 (abilities): *The Autobiography of Calvin Coolidge* (New York, 1929), p. 71. *See also* William Allen White, *A Puritan in Babylon* (New York, 1938), pp. vii-viii, 443-444.

88 (duty): Coolidge, *op cit.,* p. 161.

90 (artillery, words): Harry S. Truman, *Years of Decision* (Garden City, 1955), p. 122.

91 (career): Jonathan Daniels, *The Man of Independence* (New York, 1950), p. 196.

91 (death): Truman, *op. cit.,* p. 5.

CHAPTER SIX (pages 94-120)

95 (personnel): *See* James Schouler, *History of the United States Under the Constitution,* Volume I (New York, 1908), p. 377.

96 (charges): The mechanics of the impeachment and removal process are emphasized here simply because they are so widely misunderstood.

98 (states): President Lincoln received the bill right at the end of the session of Congress. If Congress adjourns within ten days (Sundays excepted) of the President's receiving a bill and the President declines to sign it, then it is killed—by "pocket" veto. After Lincoln treated the Wade-Davis Bill in this way, Representative Henry Winter Davis and Senator Benjamin F. Wade, the bill's sponsors, issued a statement severely criticising him and accusing him of committing a "studied outrage on the legislative authority of the people."

100 (radicals): Johnson's social origin left him contemptuous of the slave-holding aristocracy of the South. In his earliest days as President he was apparently under the influence of Secretary

Stanton, who was inclined toward radical reconstruction. Later Secretary of State Seward wielded greater influence with Johnson. At the same time Lincoln was assassinated Seward was badly wounded at his home by a co-conspirator, Lewis Powell. He was unable to attend Cabinet meetings until past the middle of May, when Stanton's influence declined and Seward's increased. Seward favored moderation, along the lines Lincoln had contemplated.

100 (children): *Congressional Globe,* 39th Congress, 2nd Session, Part 2, p. 1317.

101 (impeached): *Ibid.,* Part 1, p. 320.

102 (grounds): Representative James F. Wilson of Iowa, chairman of the Judiciary Committee, reported that they were not prepared to submit a report but could report at any session after October 16. Five members of the Committee believed, he said, that there had been no high crimes and misdemeanors, but four were of the opposite view. *Congressional Globe,* 40th Congress, 1st Session, p. 565. *See also* 2nd Session, Part 1, p. 67.

103 (veto): *Supplement to the Congressional Globe, Trial of the President,* 40th Congress, 2nd Session, p. 52. (Hereafter called *Supplement*)

104 (him, unconstitutional):

Ibid., p. 51.

105 (meetings): J. G. Randall, *The Civil War and Reconstruction* (Boston, 1937), p. 766.

106 (misdemeanors): *Congressional Globe,* 40th Congress, 2nd Session, Part 2, p. 1329.

106 (order): *Ibid.,* pp. 1353-1354.

107 (way, impeachment): *Ibid.,* pp. 1386, 1400.

107 (states): *Ibid.,* p. 1402.

108 (Pennsylvania): To avoid expressing partisanship most party affiliations of Congressmen mentioned in this chapter have not been stated. They were: Thaddeus Stevens (R), James M. Ashley (R), John Covode (R), William S. Holman (D), George Washington Julian (R), John A. Bingham (R), George S. Boutwell (R), James F. Wilson (R), Benjamin F. Butler (R), Thomas Williams (R) and John A. Logan (R, but pre-war D).

108 (Vice President): A very good discussion of the issues of the trial will be found in William Archibald Dunning, *Essays on the Civil War and Reconstruction and Related Topics* (New York, 1898), pp. 272-299.

108 (Justice, God): *Congressional Globe,* 40th Congress, 2nd Session, Part 2, pp. 1644, 1671. Jeremiah S. Black had been selected one of the attor-

neys for the President, but just before the trial began Black's law firm asked Johnson for an official favor he could not see his way to grant. Black then withdrew from the case. *See* Robert Winston, *op. cit.*, p. 433. Black's place was taken by William S. Groesbeck.

109 (profit): *Supplement,* p. 30.

110 (interest): *Congressional Globe,* 40th Congress, 2nd Session, Part 2, p. 1671.

111 (preparation): *Supplement,* p. 7.

111-112 (before, people, unlawful): *Ibid.,* pp. 34, 40.

113 (elected, proper, done, issue): *Ibid.,* p. 134; argument of Mr. Curtis, pp. 36, 126.

113-114 (message, transaction, evidence, cause, presence): *Ibid.,* p. 225, 231, 233.

115 (grave): James Rhodes Ford, *op. cit.,* Volume VI, p. 258.

116 (him, 19): *Supplement,* pp. 411, 414.

117 (judge): *Congressional Globe,* 40th Congress, 2nd Session, Part 3, p. 2599. Ross was defeated for re-election to the Senate. He later affiliated with the Democratic Party and became a newspaper publisher. He was a delegate to the Democratic national convention of 1876 and an unsuccessful candidate for governor of Kansas in 1880. He was appointed governor of New Mexico Territory by President Cleveland in 1885 and served for four years. He practiced law in New Mexico and was secretary of the Bureau of Immigration from 1894 to 1896. He died in New Mexico in 1907. *See Biographical Directory of the American Congress 1774-1949,* House Document No. 607, 81st Congress, 2nd Session, p. 1759.

118 (view): Meyers *vs.* The United States, 272 U.S. 52 (1926).

118 (first): *Supplement,* p. 40.

Chapter Seven (pages 121-144)

121 (role): Dr. Everett S. Brown of the University of Michigan and Ruth C. Silva of Pennsylvania State College in response to Representative Celler's questionnaire gave rather convincing evidence that the framers of the Constitution intended that the Vice President should succeed only to the powers and duties of the Presidency and not to the office itself if the President dies. For a careful treatment of the subject see Ruth C. Silva, *Presidential Succession* (Ann Arbor, 1951).

122-123 (duties, archivist): *Congressional Record,* 65th

Congress, 3rd Session, Volume LVII, Part 1, December 3, 1918, pp. 23-26. Senator Sherman was a Republican and a bitter foe of Democratic President Wilson. The Senator's personal animosity was clearly indicated by this statement in support of the resolution: "The savory fragrance of incense offered by alien satellites may mount with intoxicating power to a head already strangely obsessed with the phantasy that he has become the state." Senator Williams was a Democrat and an ardent supporter of President Wilson.

123 (arose): George Frederick Howe, *op. cit.,* p. 152.

124 (persisted): *Idem.*

125 (her): Edith Bolling Wilson, *My Memoir* (Indianapolis, 1939), p. 289. Josephus Daniels, *The Wilson Era: Years of War and After, 1917-1923* (Chapel Hill, N. C., 1946), pp. 513-514.

125 (duties): Irwin Hood (Ike) Hoover, *Forty-two Years in the White House* (Boston, 1934), pp. 104-105. Hoover was chief usher at the White House during both Wilson administrations. He put in a total of forty-two years' service. He died in 1933, and his book was published posthu-

mously. Joseph Tumulty, *Woodrow Wilson As I Knew Him* (Garden City, 1921), p. 446.

126 (Wilson): Hoover, *op. cit.,* p. 105. Wilson, *op. cit.,* p. 299. Daniels, *op. cit.,* p. 517.

126 (shift): David F. Houston, *Eight Years with Wilson's Cabinet,* Volume II (Garden City, 1926), pp. 60-62. *See also* Thomas A. Bailey, *Woodrow Wilson and the Great Betrayal* (New York, 1945), p. 143.

127 (absence): Martin Packman, *The Vice Presidency,* Editorial Research Reports, Volume I, No. 13, April 4, 1956, p. 241n.

128 (to): James Madison, *Journal of the Constitutional Convention,* p. 614.

129 (presented): *Presidential Inability*: House Committee Print, Committee on the Judiciary, House of Representatives, 84th Congress, 2nd Session (72232) January 31, 1956 (Washington, 1956).

133 (divided): *Presidential Inability*: Hearings Before Special Subcommittee to Study Presidential Inability, Committee on the Judiciary, House of Representatives, 84th Congress, 2nd Session (76972), April 11 and 12, 1956 (Washington, 1956).

CHAPTER EIGHT (pages 145-162)

147 (alive): *Hearings* Before the Subcommittee on Reorgani-

zation of the Committee on Government Operations, U.S. Senate, 84th Congress, 2nd Session, on Proposal to Create Position of Administrative Vice President, January 16, 24, and 25, 1956 (71726), p. 15. (Hereafter called *Hearings*).

152 (nominations): *Ibid.,* p. 76 (Attachment B).

152 (civilian): *Ibid.,* p. 76 (Attachment C).

152 (agencies): *Ibid.,* pp. 68-69, 75 (Attachment A).

154 (proclamations): *Ibid.,* pp. 69-70.

158 (today): *See* Harold Laski, *The American Presidency* (New York, 1940), p. 158.

160 (1930): *Hearings,* p. 76 (Attachment C).

161 (three): Leonard D. White, *Introduction to the Study of Public Administration* (New York, 1955), p. 48.

161 (time): *Hearings,* p. 48.

CHAPTER NINE (pages 163-184)

164 (power, Vice President): *Annals of Congress,* 8th Congress, Volume 13, pp. 673-674.

164 (say): Woodrow Wilson, *Congressional Government* (Boston, 1892), pp. 240-241. *See also* Lucius Wilmerding, Jr., "The Vice Presidency," *Political Science Quarterly,* Volume LXVIII, March 1953, p. 41.

165 (governor): Morison, ed., *op. cit.,* Volume III, pp. 4, 570.

166 (acknowledgment): Detroit *News,* May 1, 1956.

166 (remark): *Time Magazine,* Volume LXIII, January 18, 1954, pp. 25-29.

168 (it): Coolidge, *op cit.,* p. 162.

169 (him): *Annals of Congress,* 8th Congress, Volume XIII, p. 674.

169 (Vice President, preside): *Hearings,* pp. 13-14, 18.

171 (presiding): *Ibid.,* p. 13.

171 (him): Quoted in Freder-

ick A. Ogg and P. Orman Ray, *Introduction to American Government* (New York, 1951), p. 331.

172 (bill, bill): Lindsay Rogers, *The American Senate* (New York, 1926), p. 170. By a clerical error, Rogers mentions Senator Tillman as being from North Carolina, when actually he was from South Carolina.

173 (milk): Senator Long's speech will be found in *Congressional Record,* Volume LXXIX, Part 8, 74th Congress, 1st Session, June 12, 1935, pp. 9091-9175.

174 (speech): *Congressional Record,* Volume LXVII, Part 1, 69th Congress, Special Session, March 4-18, 1925, pp. 3-4.

175 (legislation): *Congressional Record,* Volume XCV, Part 2, 81st Congress, 1st Session, p. 2174.

176 (session): *Ibid.,* pp. 2509-

2510, for text of Wherry substitute. For vote see p. 2724.

176 (Vice President): *See* "Table of Vacancies in the Presidency and the Vice Presidency" in Silva, *op. cit.,* p. 177.

180 (President, proposal, direction): Hearings, pp. 7-20. Senator Smith's observations are on pp. 12-14; Senator McClellan's are on pp. 18-19. Senator McClellan was not a member of the subcommittee but was chairman of the parent Government Operations Committee.

181 (direction): *Ibid.,* p. 55.

181 (department): *Ibid.,* p. 34.

183 (be): Truman, *op. cit.,* pp. 54-55.

184 (East): For an interesting account of increasing responsibilities of the Vice President see Irving G. Williams, *The American Vice Presidency: New Look* (Garden City, 1954).

CHAPTER TEN (pages 185-210)

188 (horse): *See* Irving G. Williams, *op, cit.,* p. 39. Williams refers to Garner's assertion that the Vice President's casting vote is really only the power to vote affirmatively and calls the vote "half a power."

189 (prestige): *Hearings,* p. 12.

190-191 (one, problem): *Ibid.,* pp. 13, 18.

192 (official): *Ibid.,* p. 14.

193 (wit): New York *Times,* May 13, 1956.

196 (concerned): Mr. Clifford's statement appears in *Hearings,* pp. 53-65.

197 (structure): With respect to strictly executive subordinates of the President, appointed with Senate consent, the President's power to remove is not subject to limitation by act of Congress (Myers *vs.* United States). With respect to independent commissions, such as the Federal Trade Commission, which are established to carry out specific Congressional enactments and which exercise extensive quasi-legislative or -judicial powers, the President's power may be limited by statute (Rathbun [Humphrey's Executor] *vs.* United States, 295 U.S. 602, 1935).

198 (appointed): *Hearings,* p. 19.

202 (them): Estes Kefauver and Jack Levin, *A Twentieth Century Congress* (New York, 1947), p. 72.

203 (matter): *Proposal to Create an Administrative Vice President,* Report of the Committee on Government Operations, made by its Subcommittee on Reorganization, U. S. Senate, 84th Congress, 2nd Session, (Report No. 1960), p. 8.

SOURCES CITED

Adams, Charles Francis, *The Life and Works of John Adams,* Vol. VIII, Boston, 1853.

Adams, Henry, *The Administration of Thomas Jefferson (History of the United States of America,* Vol. IV). New York, 1930.

Adams, John Quincy, *The Diary of John Quincy Adams.* Allan Nevins, ed., New York, 1929.

Administrative Vice President: Hearings before Subcommittee on Reorganization, Committee on Government Operations, U. S. Senate, 84th Congress, 2d Session, on Proposal to Create Position of Administrative Vice President (71726), January 16, 24, and 25, 1956. Washington, 1956.

Administrative Vice President: Proposal to Create an Administrative Vice President, Report of the Committee on Government Operations, made by its Subcommittee on Reorganization, U. S. Senate, 84th Congress, 2d Session, Report No. 1960. Washington, 1956.

Annals of Congress, Washington.

Bailey, Thomas A., *Woodrow Wilson and the Great Betrayal.* New York, 1945.

Bassett, John Spencer, *A Short History of the United States.* New York, 1930.

Bassett, John Spencer, *The Life of Andrew Jackson.* Vol. II, Garden City, 1911.

Beard, Charles A., *The Economic Origins of Jeffersonian Democracy.* New York, 1927.

Biographical Directory of the American Congress, 1774-1949. House Document No. 607, 81st Congress, 2d Session, Washington, 1950.

Bishop, Joseph Bucklin, *Theodore Roosevelt and His Time: Shown in His Own Letters.* Vol. I, New York, 1920.

Boak, Arthur E. R., *A History of Rome to 565 A.D.* New York, 1923.

Bowen, Catherine Drinker, *John Adams and the American Revolution.* Boston, 1950.

Bryce, James, *The American Commonwealth.* Vol. I, New York, 1889.

Channing, Edward, *Federalists and Republicans (A History of the United States,* Vol. IV). New York, 1935.

Chinard, Gilbert, *Honest John Adams.* Boston, 1933.

Christian Science Monitor.

Congressional Globe. Washington.

Congressional Record. Washington.

Coolidge, Calvin, *The Autobiography of Calvin Coolidge.* New York, 1929.

241

Corwin, Edward S., *The President: Office and Powers, 1787-1948*. 3rd ed., New York, 1948.

Daniels, Jonathan, *The Man of Independence*. New York, 1950.

Daniels, Josephus, *The Wilson Era: Years of War and After 1917-1923*. Chapel Hill, N. C., 1946.

Detroit News.

Dunning, William A., *Essays on the Civil War and Reconstruction and Related Topics*. New York, 1898.

Farrand, Max, *The Records of the Federal Convention*. 4 vols., rev. ed., New Haven, Conn., 1937.

Farrand, Max, *The Fathers of the Constitution*. New Haven, Conn., 1921.

Faulkner, Harold U., *From Versailles to the New Deal*. New Haven, Conn., 1921.

Ford, Henry Jones, *Washington and His Colleagues: A Chronicle of the Rise and Fall of Federalism*. New Haven, Conn., 1921.

Garrison, George Pearce, *Westward Expansion, 1841-1850*. New York, 1906.

Geer, Russell M., *Classical Civilization: Rome*. N. Y., 1940.

Greenridge, A. H. J., *Roman Public Life*. London, 1930.

Hamilton, Madison and Jay, *The Federalist*. John C. Hamilton, ed., Philadelphia, 1875.

Hatch, Louis C. and Shoup, Earl L., *A History of the Vice Presidency of the United States*. New York, 1934.

Hicks, John D., *A Short History of American Democracy*. Boston, 1943.

Hoover, Irwin Hood (Ike), *Forty-Two Years in the White House*. Boston, 1934.

Houston, David F., *Eight Years with Wilson's Cabinet*. Vol. II, Garden City, 1926.

Howe, George F., *Chester A. Arthur: A Quarter-Century of Machine Politics*. New York, 1934.

(Jackson, Andrew) *The Correspondence of Andrew Jackson*. John Spencer Bassett, ed., Vol. IV (1829-1832), Washington, 1929.

(Jefferson, Thomas) *The Writings of Thomas Jefferson*. Collected and edited by Paul Leicester Ford, Vol. IX, New York, 1898.

Kefauver, Estes and Levin, Jack, *A Twentieth Century Congress*. New York, 1947.

Laski, Harold, *The American Presidency, An Interpretation*. New York, 1940.

Levin, Peter R., *Seven by Chance*. New York, 1948.

Lorant, Stefan, *The Presidency: A Pictorial History of Presidential Elections from Washington to Truman*. New York, 1951.

Maclay, William, *The Journal of William Maclay*. New York, 1927.

McMaster, John B., *A History of the People of the United States from the Revolution to the Civil War.* Vols. I and II, New York, 1931.

Madison, James, *Journal of the Constitutional Convention.* E. H. Scott, ed., Chicago, 1893.

Marshall, Thomas R., *Recollections of Thomas R. Marshall, Vice President and Hoosier Philosopher.* Indianapolis, 1925.

Morse, John T., Jr., *John Adams.* Boston, 1884.

Muzzey, David S., *Through the Civil War (The United States of America,* Vol. I). Boston, 1933.

Myers, William Starr, *The Republican Party: A History.* Rev. ed. with additions, New York, 1931.

Nevins, Allan, *Fruits of Manifest Destiny, 1847-1852 (Ordeal of the Union,* Vol. I). New York, 1947.

New York Times.

Ogg, Frederick A., *The Reign of Andrew Jackson.* New Haven, Conn., 1919.

Ogg, Frederick A. and Ray, P. Orman, *Introduction to American Government.* 10th ed., New York, 1951.

Packman, Martin, *The Vice Presidency.* Editorial Research Reports, Vol. I (1956), No. 13, April 14, 1956.

Parton, James, *Life of Andrew Jackson.* Vol. I, Boston, 1876.

Presidential Inability: Hearings before Special Subcommittee to Study Presidential Inability, Committee on the Judiciary, House of Representatives, 84th Congress, 2d Session (76972), April 11 and 12, 1956, Washington, 1956.

Presidential Inability: (Questionnaire) House Committee Print, January 31, 1956, Committee on the Judiciary, House of Representatives, 84th Congress, 2d Session (72232), Washington, 1956.

Randall, James G., *The Civil War and Reconstruction.* New York, 1937.

Rhodes, James Ford, *A History of the United States from the Compromise of 1850 to the End of the Roosevelt Administration.* Vols. VI and VIII, new ed., New York, 1928.

Richardson, James D., *Messages of the Presidents.* Vol. I, Washington, 1896.

Rogers, Lindsay, *The American Senate.* New York, 1926.

(Roosevelt, Theodore) *The Letters of Theodore Roosevelt.* Selected and edited by Elting E. Morison, Vols. II and III, Cambridge, Mass., 1951.

Rossiter, Clinton L., "The Reform of the Vice Presidency," *Political Science Quarterly,* Sept. 1948, Vol. LXIII, pp. 383-403.

Schouler, James, *History of the United States under the Consti-*

tution. Vol. I (1783-1801), New York, 1908.

Silva, Ruth C., *Presidential Succession.* Ann Arbor, Mich., 1951.

Stanwood, Edward, *A History of Presidential Elections.* 4th ed., rev., Boston, 1896.

Stanwood, Edward, *A History of the Presidency, 1788-1897.* New ed., Vol. I, Boston, 1926.

Sumner, William G., *Andrew Jackson As a Public Man.* Boston, 1883.

Time Magazine.

Truman, Harry S., *Year of Decisions* and *Years of Trial and Hope* (*Memoirs*, Vols. I and II). Garden City, 1955, 1956.

Tumulty, Joseph, *Woodrow Wilson As I Knew Him.* Literary Digest Edition, Garden City, New York, 1921.

United States Reports (reports of cases decided by U. S. Supreme Court). Washington.

White, Leonard D., *Introduction to the Study of Public Adminis-* *tration.* 4th ed., New York, 1955.

White, William Allen, *A Puritan in Babylon.* New York, 1938.

Williams, Irving G., *The American Vice Presidency: New Look.* Garden City, 1954.

Wilmerding, Lucius, Jr., "The Vice Presidency," *Political Science Quarterly,* Vol. LXVIII, March 1953.

Wilson, Edith Bolling, *My Memoir.* Indianapolis, 1939.

Wilson, Woodrow, *Congressional Government.* Boston, 1892.

Wiltse, Charles M., *John C. Calhoun: Nullifier, 1829-1839.* Indianapolis, 1949.

Winston, Robert W., *Andrew Johnson, Plebean and Patriot.* New York, 1928.

Woodburn, James Albert, *Political Parties and Party Problems in the United States.* New York, 1924.

Young, Klyde and Middleton, Lamar, *Heirs Apparent: The Vice Presidents of the United States.* New York, 1948.